School Lunch Politics

POLITICS AND SOCIETY IN TWENTIETH-CENTURY AMERICA

Series Editors

WILLIAM CHAFE, GARY GERSTLE, LINDA GORDON, AND JULIAN ZELIZER

A list of titles in this series appears at the back of the book

School Lunch Politics

THE SURPRISING HISTORY OF AMERICA'S FAVORITE WELFARE PROGRAM

Susan Levine

PRINCETON UNIVERSITY PRESS

PRINCETON AND OXFORD

KH

Library of Congress Cataloging-in-Publication Data

Levine, Susan, 1947–
School lunch politics : the surprising history of Americas favorite welfare program / Susan Levine.
    p   cm.   — (Politics and society in twentieth-century America)
Includes bibliographical reference and index.

ISBN: 978-0-691-05088-1 (hbk. : alk. paper)
1. National school lunch program. 2. School children—Food—United States. 3. Children—Nutrition—United States. I. Title.
LB3479.U6L48 2008
371.7′16—dc22   2007028807

British Library Cataloging-in-Publication Data is available

This book has been composed in Sabon

Printed on acid-free paper. ∞

press.princeton.edu

Printed in the United States of America

10 9 8 7 6 5 4 3 2 1

9/3/09

Contents

Illustrations and Tables

Acknowledgments

This book first took shape when my children refused to eat school lunches. It became more focused when my mother-in-law suggested that I combine my two favorite activities and write something about the history of food. Since then, this project has seen my family through almost a decade of professional and personal change. My children are now grown and have embarked on careers and families of their own. A few years ago, Leon and I uprooted from our North Carolina home of over twenty years to take on the challenges of a major urban public university and Midwestern winters. It gives me great pleasure to be able to thank all the people who helped with these transitions and especially those who provided the intellectual and personal support that allowed me to complete this book.

Research for this project began in 1998 during a year at the Charles Warren Center for Studies in American History at Harvard University. My colleagues in the center's weekly seminar helped me see what shape a history of school lunches could take. Two colleagues in particular guided me into new territory. I'd like to thank Dan Horowitz for his generous intellect and Carolyn Goldstein for introducing me to home economics. It was also during that year that I met Princeton University Press editor Brigitta van Rheinberg, who convinced me to turn the school lunch story into a book. I warned her that the project would not proceed quickly, but she was unfazed. In 2001 a fellowship at the University of Illinois at Chicago's Institute for the Humanities allowed me to finish the research and begin writing the book. My colleagues at the institute gave chapter 1 its first critical reading. I would especially like to thank Katrin Schultheiss and John D'Emilo for our regular lunch discussions that year.

I have been fortunate to be able to draw on the critical eye of a number of readers along the way. Eric Arnesen, Susan Porter Benson, Sonya Michel, Judy Smith, and Brigitta van Rheinberg read an early draft of the manuscript. They were all incredibly generous (although not uncritical) with their comments, and I hope they see the result of their efforts. I am very sad that Sue Benson was not able to see the book to its end. She was an important colleague and a good friend and I miss her wit and wisdom. Peter Coclanis pointed me toward some useful sources in agricultural history. Janet Popendieck read chapter 4 and offered some important correctives. Linda Gordon and an anonymous reader from Princeton University Press read the final manuscript. They provided ideal readers' comments and I thank them for that. Several friends and colleagues helped with small but critical details. Diana McDuffee found an original copy of *Their Daily Bread*. Rebecca Foley and Emily LaBarbera Twarog helped me with the illustrations. Paula Dempsy provided the cover image and a conversation with Bruce Ornstein and Nancy MacLean clarified a last point. Last but by no means least, Leon Fink, was, as always, my sharpest critic and my most enthusiastic cheerleader.

This book is dedicated to the first of the next generation of school lunch participants, Nina Julie Fernandez Fink.

School Lunch Politics

The Politics of Lunch

If you search the Internet for "school lunch" these days, two types of sites will come up. The vast majority of references lead to cheery government articles about "team nutrition," brightly decorated menus from school lunchrooms, and manuals about managing cafeteria budgets. Sprinkled here and there among the search results, however, will be another type of article entirely. Celebrity chefs have lately entered school lunchrooms. They have come to prove that school lunches can be healthy. Their aim is to rescue children from greasy food and teach students to prefer zucchini over French fries. The task is daunting. The chefs are forced to use U.S. Department of Agriculture surplus commodities that hardly make for health-food menus. The chefs must also follow federal nutrition guidelines and meal subsidies, which generally allow for a maximum of about $2.40 per lunch for free meals. But these chefs soldier on, we are told, valiantly bucking the system in order to transform school lunches. Somewhere, buried in the articles, we inevitably find that private foundations are underwriting these experiments. In some cases, the food is subsidized, in others the chefs' salaries are covered—usually at rates considerably higher than those of ordinary school lunch employees.[1]

This book, in its own way, explains why celebrity chefs and private foundations alone cannot save the National School Lunch Program. Readers will become acquainted with the history of one of America's most remarkable and popular social programs. But they will also learn how the politics of school lunch created structural barriers that limited which children received nutritious meals and that shaped lunchroom menus. The history of school lunch politics encompasses a combination of ideals and frustrations, reflecting, at base, America's deep ambivalence about social welfare and racial equality. It also reflects the tension in American politics about whether public policy should address individual behavior—in this case, whether food policy should focus on convincing people to eat right—or whether policy should address public structures and institutions—for example, fully funding free lunch programs or establishing a universal child nutrition program.[2] The task faced by celebrity chefs in select school lunchrooms is daunting not simply because fast food is seductive and children are conservative eaters. Un-self-consciously, the chefs are entering an institution only partly governed by concerns for children's nutrition. Historically, concerns about national agricultural policies and poverty policy have regularly competed with dietary issues in the creation of school lunch programs. School lunch is, surely, rooted in the science of nutrition and ideas about healthy diets, but those ideas have never been sufficient on their own to shape public policy (or to change people's eating behavior, for that matter). School lunch, like other aspects of public policy, has been shaped by the larger forces of politics and power in American history.

Since its founding in 1946, the National School Lunch Program has been the target of critics from the right as well as from the left. It is clear that even after more than half a century of operation, the National School Lunch Program is deeply flawed. School meals are often unattractive, unappetizing, and not entirely nutritious. The menu has always depended more heavily on surplus commodities than on children's nutrition needs. Until the 1970s, the program reached only a small percentage of American children and served very few free lunches. All the while, however, the National School Lunch Program stood as one of the nation's most popular social welfare programs. Politicians as savvy as Ronald Reagan discovered that the American public is intensely committed to the idea of a school lunch program, particularly one that offers free meals to poor children. In fact, the National School Lunch Program, to this day, is the only comprehensive food program aimed at school-aged children.[3] Almost thirty million children in 98,000 schools eat school lunches each day. What is more, in most American cities, the National School Lunch Program is the single most important source of nutrition for children from low-income families. Almost 60 percent of all school children nationwide get free school lunches each day: 80 percent of Chicago's public school children qualify for free school lunches; 79 percent of the children in Atlanta's public schools receive free meals; New York City schools regularly feed almost 72 percent of their children for free; and in the state of Texas, over 70 percent of the children eat free or reduced price school lunches.[4] The National School Lunch Program, for all its nutritional flaws, provides a crucial public welfare support for our nation's youth. Without school lunches, many children in this country would go hungry; many more would be undernourished. Indeed, the National School Lunch Program has outlasted almost every other twentieth-century federal welfare initiative and holds a uniquely prominent place in the popular imagination. It suggests the central role food policy plays in shaping American health, welfare, and equality. A history of the National School Lunch Program is thus a crucial mirror into the variety of interests that continually vie for power and authority in American public life.[5]

School lunch politics have been marked by a shifting and not always predictable set of alliances over the course of the twentieth century. At first glance, the program's trajectory appears to be the typical story of American liberalism, thwarted by southern Democrats who held social welfare hostage to racial segregation and states' rights. Indeed, initiated by liberal reformers in the early part of the century, school lunch programs became institutionalized only when southern Democrats agreed to support federal appropriations in exchange for agricultural subsidies and under the condition that there would be limited federal oversight and unlimited local control. The result was a system that perpetuated the nation's deep racial, regional, and class inequalities. But the fact that school lunches involve both children and food, two subjects fraught with powerful cultural and symbolic significance, renders the story more complicated and the players' motives less transparent. It was conservative southern Democrats who, at the end of the New Deal, proposed a permanently funded federal school lunch program. Indeed, the 1946 bill creating a National School Lunch Program was named after Georgia senator Richard Russell, a staunch segregationist and opponent of civil rights. While Russell's first priority was to protect a program he believed would benefit American agriculture, he was also motivated by a lasting concern about poverty in his region and a deep post-war anxiety about national defense, which linked healthy children to the future of American prosperity and strength. Despite his defense of states' rights, Russell nonetheless crafted one of the most enduring and popular federal welfare programs of the twentieth century. Children's welfare confounded predictable political lines again during the late 1960s and early 1970s, when powerful images of hungry children propelled Republican president Richard Nixon to announce that he would, within a year's time, provide every poor child a free school lunch. Nixon vastly increased funds for free meals and, ultimately, turned the National School Lunch Program into the nation's premier poverty program. Once the school lunch program became a poverty program, however, the political alliances again proved surprising. To protect the program's ability to serve poor children in the face of an effective decrease in funds (the new federal monies only paid for free food, not for equipment, labor, or operating expenses), liberal senators like George McGovern, along with anti-poverty activists, found themselves—over the protests of nutritionists who had long opposed commercializing children's meals—advocating privatization. Hoping that fast-food corporations and giant food service companies would be able to bring down the cost of lunchroom operations, these reformers saw privatization as a way to allow lunchrooms to continue to serve both free and paying children. Thus, by the time Ronald Reagan suggested that ketchup be considered a vegetable on the school lunch tray, private commercial interests already had two feet in the door of the school cafeteria.

School lunch politics suggest that children's meals have always served up more than nutrition. Indeed, the National School Lunch Program, from the start, linked children's nutrition to the priorities of agricultural and commercial food interests, both of which carried more weight in the halls of Congress than did advocates for children's health. Most particularly, school lunches have been tied to the agenda of one of the federal government's most powerful agencies, the Department of Agriculture, and, more recently, to the corporate food and food-service industries as well. Nutrition in each of these arenas takes a back seat to markets and prices. During its early years, the National School Lunch Program provided substantial welfare for commercial farmers as an outlet for surplus commodities, but actually fed a relatively small number of schoolchildren and provided few free meals to those who were poor. Since the 1960s school lunches have been a vital part of the American welfare system, characterized by means testing, insufficient appropriations, weak enforcement, and often blatant racial discrimination.

But even as a welfare program, children's nutrition took a back seat to other interests. Most notably, in order to enable school lunchrooms to serve more free meals, the Department of Agriculture eased the restrictions banning commercial operations from school cafeterias. As poor children entered school lunchrooms in large numbers, so did processed meals and fast-food companies. Political compromises, first with agricultural interests and then with the food industry, have no doubt ensured the existence and expansion of a National School Lunch Program and today ensure the availability of free meals for poor children. What those compromises do not ensure is that those meals will provide a healthy cushion for children's growth and development. Ultimately, the answers to the questions of which foods children should eat, which children deserve a free lunch, and who should pay for school meals have bedeviled even the most well intended of policy makers.

If school lunch politics hinge on priorities other than children's health, school lunchrooms nonetheless reveal fundamental American attitudes about food and nutrition. As anthropologists have long observed, hierarchies of power and culture are embedded within the decisions about which foods are deemed suitable to eat, which foods constitute a meal, and which people are appropriate eating companions.[6] Nowhere, perhaps, is the link between food and culture more relevant than in school meals where scientific ideas about nutrition continually vie with individual food choices and the enormous variety in American ethnic food traditions. The very idea of crafting a National School Lunch Program with nutrition requirements and standard menus suggests an optimistic faith in science, education, and reason. But when it comes to nutrition, scientific advice continually changes and Americans tend to ignore expert proscriptions about what to eat. When the National School Lunch program began, for example, nutritionists recommended that children needed a high-calorie diet based on whole milk, cream-based sauces, rich puddings, and butter on every slice of bread. Rooted in the belief that poor, malnourished children were "underweight" and basically needed more calories in order to grow and thrive, the prescription for a high-calorie diet made sense. Today, experts warn about an epidemic of obesity among poor children and excoriate school menus for their high calorie and high fat content. But the current obesity debate reveals more than new nutrition insight. Neither underweight children in the past nor obese children today became that way solely as a result of individual eating habits, lack of nutrition education, or bad food choices. Rather, nutrition is tied directly to social and economic circumstance—for example, family income and access to fresh foods—as much as to individual behavior. How nutrition science is translated into children's health, therefore, has always rested on a larger context than food habits and individual choice.

This book traces the politics of school lunch from its origins in early twentieth-century science and reform to the marriage of children's lunches and agricultural surpluses during the 1930s and the establishment of a permanent federally funded National School Lunch Program in 1946 to the transformation of school meals into a major poverty program during the 1970s and 1980s. One set of major players includes nutrition reformers—education, health, and key welfare professionals, mainly women—who struggled mightily to translate nutrition science into public policy. Another set of players includes farm-bloc legislators and Department of Agriculture officials who created the institutional infrastructure for a national school lunch program. These groups, together with political leaders responding to the demands and interests of their constituents as well as to the popular appeal of children's health, shaped national food and nutrition policies. While the National School Lunch Program, like the American welfare system in general, is administered at the state level, the creation and fundamental outlines of the program—the development of national nutrition standards, eligibility requirements for free and reduced price meals, and the basic supply of donated foods available for lunch menus—emanate from Washington. This book thus views the nature of the school lunch and who pays for it as national policy concerns.

Chapter 1 argues that school lunch programs in the United States originated as part of the modernizing efforts of early twentieth-century social reformers. Using the new science of nutrition, professional women—home economists, teachers, and social workers—attempted to rationalize American eating habits and, in the process, bring new immigrants (and rural migrants) into a mainstream Anglo-American culture. Home economics, a new profession that attracted women who were excluded from scientific and academic careers, used the science of nutrition first to convince low-paid workers that they could "eat better for less," then to assimilate immigrants into American culture, and, finally, to rationalize American diets more generally. School lunchrooms appeared to be the perfect setting in which to feed poor children but, more importantly, to teach both immigrant and middle-class children the principles of nutrition and healthy eating. In this way, nutrition became part of a basic civics training for future citizens. While most school lunch programs before the 1930s were volunteer efforts on the part of teachers or mother's clubs, they drew on the expertise of professional home economists for balanced menus and scientifically formulated recipes. By the 1920s, home economists found an institutional home in the USDA's Bureau of Home Economics, thus linking school meals to agricultural research and, ultimately, to a national network of professionals committed to school lunchrooms both ideologically and occupationally.

Chapter 2 traces the transformation of school lunch programs from local volunteer efforts into state-sponsored operations. During the Great Depression, existing lunchrooms were overwhelmed by the numbers of children coming to school hungry. Teachers and community groups tried to expand school meal offerings by raising donations but ultimately began to look to municipal, county, and state governments for resources. At the same time, a group of agricultural economists in the USDA began to formulate policies to address the severe depression in farm prices. Committed to market-based strategies that ultimately favored commercial farm interests, these policy makers proposed that the federal government monitor supplies by purchasing surplus commodities. School lunchrooms appeared as the perfect outlet for federal commodity donations. With one stroke, the Department of Agriculture could claim to help both farmers and children. By the eve of World War II, schools in every state depended on surplus commodities for their lunchrooms.

As federal involvement in school lunches became increasingly institutionalized, nutritionists and child welfare advocates began to press for standards in nutrition and service. Chapter 3 traces the increasing federal oversight of school lunch programs through the development of operating contracts and meal guidelines. Nutrition standards for the nation's youth became increasingly significant as the United States prepared to enter World War II. Recalling the large number of young men declared unfit for service in World War I, both military and civilian policy makers began a campaign for "nutrition in the national defense." The Roosevelt administration enlisted the aid of prominent social scientists, such as Margaret Mead, and internationally known nutritionists, such as Lydia Roberts, to develop strategies that would prepare the civilian population for expected wartime food shortages. These women proposed a universal school lunch

program and "Recommended Daily Allowances" (RDAs) that would provide healthy diets for all children. While the idea of a universal child nutrition program never gained much traction, the RDAs formed the basis for
all future government-subsidized school meals. As significant as national
nutrition guidelines was the development of standard contracts governing
the operation of school lunchrooms. Schools receiving federal assistance
had to maintain sanitary conditions for food storage, handling, and service. The federal contracts also, for the first time, contained an anti-discrimination clause and required schools to provide lunches for free to
children whose families could not afford to pay. While the only enforcement mechanism was to withhold food supplies—and no public official
was interested in being accused of depriving children of food—the contracts represented a significant step in the institutionalization of the federal school lunch program.

Chapters 4 and 5 focus on the congressional debate surrounding the
establishment of a permanently funded National School Lunch Program
in 1946. These chapters argue that the compromises that were necessary
in order to mount sufficient congressional support for the bill had serious
consequences regarding which children received federally subsidized
meals and which schools participated in the program. Like much of the
American welfare system, the National School Lunch Program was characterized by weak federal oversight and a high degree of local control.
After a brief attempt by child welfare advocates to place school lunches
under the auspices of the commissioner of Education, the Department of
Agriculture succeeded in holding on to the program. Thus, for the first
fifteen years of its existence, the National School Lunch Program served
primarily as an outlet for surplus commodities and only secondarily as a
nutrition program for children. The congressional debate over the school
lunch program raised issues of racial and regional equity, including the
first attempt by New York representative Adam Clayton Powell to introduce non-discrimination language in federal legislation, but the Democratic party still relied heavily on its conservative southern wing for legislative success. While southern Democrats happily supported the idea of
creating a National School Lunch Program, they vehemently opposed
any direct federal role in how that program would be administered. Most
particularly, they resisted any effort to establish federal oversight, nutrition standards, or eligibility requirements. The results were predictable
when during its first fifteen years, few poor children received free meals
and even fewer African American children participated in the program.
The lack of federal oversight was particularly problematic when it came
to the bill's requirement that states match the federal contribution. With
no directives out of Washington, most states counted children's fees as
their matching contribution. While Department of Agriculture officials

gave lip-service to children's nutrition—developing healthy menus and testing recipes for surplus commodities—during the 1950s the National School Lunch Program reached only about one-third of America's schoolchildren. What is more, the program utterly failed to provide free meals for poor children who arguably were in most need of federal nutrition assistance.

Despite the National School Lunch Program's shortcomings, it gained widespread popular support during the 1950s. While few Americans probably knew how the program actually operated, legislators, policy makers, and the public at large touted America's school lunch program as a symbol of prosperity, equality, and democracy in the Cold War world. Only in the early 1960s, as the nation "discovered" poverty, did the limitations of the National School Lunch Program become embarrassingly clear. Chapters 6 and 7 trace the political movement to transform the National School Lunch Program from a popular, if misunderstood, agricultural subsidy into a poverty program. Galvanized by civil rights activism, and in the context of Lyndon Johnson's War on Poverty, a group of mainstream national women's organizations focused attention on the shortcomings of the National School Lunch Program. The women's report became crucial evidence in both Senate and House debates on race and poverty at the end of the 1960s and ultimately forced the Nixon administration to expand access to free lunches for poor children. Demands for a "right to lunch" insisted on access to free lunches for all poor children and national eligibility standards for free and reduced price meals.

Chapter 8 discusses both the expected and the unintended consequences of turning school lunches into a poverty program. Neither the program's congressional advocates nor liberal anti-poverty groups were willing to demand sufficient federal funding to allow school districts to serve large numbers of poor children free meals. Nor were the program's advocates—whether in Washington or in the states—willing to demand substantial local contributions. As a result, federal funds earmarked for free meals actually threatened to bankrupt school lunchrooms across the country. State subsidies rarely were sufficient to pay for the expansions necessary to meet the new federal free lunch mandate. The only course of action for local school lunch administrators appeared to be to raise the fees on full-price meals. As a result, paying children began to drop out of the program and school cafeterias became identified with poor children. There was, in effect, a great failure on the part of liberal anti-poverty activists and conservative legislators alike to craft a public child nutrition program that could effectively protect children's nutrition. By the end of the 1970s, many school lunch advocates saw privatization as the only way to keep lunchrooms afloat. While some nutritionists held out against the commercialization of children's meals, they had few suggestions for lunchroom operators who saw their deficits rising. The now-familiar fast food in school cafeterias appeared to be the only solution for school districts unable to sustain their mandated free-lunch program on public funds. Still, the National School Lunch Program continued to garner a tremendous amount of public support—far more than other programs for the poor. Indeed, when President Reagan tried to cut school lunch budgets by suggesting that ketchup could be counted as a vegetable, the public outcry revealed a depth of loyalty to the program that no one anticipated.

School lunch politics suggests that fixing lunch is more complicated than convincing children to eat right. Today's critiques of school meals have a long history in which children's welfare advocates have vied with the nation's food and agricultural interests for control over school menus. Still, the politics of school meals makes it clear that detaching the National School Lunch Program from those other interests would leave a lot of children hungry. The celebrity chefs now working in school lunchrooms are finding, as generations of nutritionists and food reformers before them did, that there is more to a national school lunch program than a nutritious menu. To truly fix lunch, they will need to build a political coalition committed to an agenda that links child nutrition to agriculture, food policy, and social welfare. Such a coalition, however, will need to fix lunch for all children, not just those lucky enough to attend schools with private benefactors. Fixing lunch will require a public commitment to health, welfare, and opportunity for all children.

CHAPTER 1

A Diet for Americans

School lunches owe their origin to the science of nutrition and the efforts of early twentieth-century social reformers to improve American diets and thereby mold American culture as well. Chemists, home economists, and child welfare advocates together engaged in a lengthy struggle to convince Americans that rational, scientific eating habits not only would improve individual health but would raise living standards and strengthen democratic institutions as well. It may have been a leap to go from the kitchen table to the ballot box, but scientists and social reformers alike believed the connection was direct and essential. Efforts to modernize diets, however, went beyond the usual Progressive Era attempts to Americanize immigrants, contain class or racial discontent, or shape a welfare state. Dietary reform addressed native-born white Americans who could afford to eat steak as much as it addressed workers on tight budgets or immigrants who preferred olive oil and sausage to white sauce and aspic. Indeed, the science of nutrition transformed eating into an act that went beyond pleasure and the satisfaction of hunger pains. Eating and cooking, particularly with regard to children, became, in the era of science, activities with implications far beyond the kitchen.

From the end of the nineteenth century until the Great Depression of the 1930s, nutrition scientists, home economists, and social reformers engaged in a long battle to transform American eating habits. They were only partially successful. Their efforts, however, provide a window onto some of the central issues confronting the nation's political and social development in those years. Food reform before the New Deal suggests, first, the central role science played in shaping American attitudes about class, race, and ethnicity. Food reform also speaks to ideas about the causes and cures for poverty and inequality, particularly in a democratic society. Food reform finally, reveals the gendered dimension within American reform in the early twentieth century. Food reform and nutrition science provided women an important avenue through which they could contribute to scientific knowledge and also influence public policy.

Food reformers, however, do not fit into neat categories. While dietary prescriptions appear to be, for example, the epitome of social control and cultural imposition, nutritious diets could, in fact, significantly improve the health of children as well as adults. Hunger and malnutrition threatened poor families most directly, but, as nutrition scientists discovered, even people who were not hungry could suffer from nutritional deficiencies. Herein lay a central tension marking food reform and efforts to establish school lunch programs. Efforts to popularize nutrition science were aimed not only at poor people, immigrants, and other groups outside the "mainstream" of white, middle class America. Indeed, food reformers continually battled to modernize the eating habits of the middle-class just as they struggled to Americanize immigrant or African American food preferences. Thus, the central policy question attached to nutrition, particularly when it came to children's meals, was whether to target all children or to concentrate on only those most obviously suffering from hunger and malnutrition.

One of the central arenas in which food reformers sought to influence American eating habits was children's meals, most notably, school lunches. Originally the purview of charity workers and mother's clubs, school lunches in the nineteenth century had little to do with nutrition science. They were, basically, benevolent activities designed to provide free meals to the poor. With the discovery of nutrition science during the late nineteenth century, however, school lunches entered the realm of public policy. Although food reformers were largely unsuccessful either in convincing native-born Americans to "eat right" or in convincing immigrants to forsake their traditional fare, they were much more successful in building a network of lasting institutions in school lunchrooms and a powerful base of operation within the United States Department of Agriculture. As the federal agency most concerned with the nation's food supply, the USDA provided a natural home for nutrition research. Indeed, discoveries about the relation of food to human health originated in research about livestock and agricultural products. While the federal government did not become directly involved in school lunch programs until the 1930s, USDA nutritionists and home economists early on began to translate nutrition research into popular recipes and menus. Food reformers, whether within the USDA or in other arenas, however, never resolved the fundamental policy tension that underlay their work: should nutrition education and food programs target people who were economically needy, that is, people who literally did not have enough to eat, or should they target the nutritionally needy, people who might have plenty to eat but who did not understand a balanced diet? School lunch programs neatly combined the two goals.

During the early twentieth century, nutrition science defined a set of ideas that described what Americans needed to eat in order to maintain their personal health and the health of the nation as well. Institutionalized in schools throughout the country by the 1920s, the lunchroom became an arena in which children (and, by extension, their parents) could learn the principles of nutrition and the importance of science in daily life. School lunch programs solved two central problems raised by science and its emphasis on food as a nutrition delivery system. On the one hand, hot lunches promised to protect America's youth from the scourge of malnutrition. Healthy children, like public education more generally, signaled America's democratic strength. At the same time, school lunches promised to Americanize immigrant families by teaching children the values of science and health. As Jane Addams, the era's most well-known social reformer, said, "an Italian girl who has had lessons in cooking . . . will help her mother to connect the entire family with American food and household habits." Food and household habits had always been two pillars of cultural identity. In the lunchroom they became pillars of civic culture as well.

The Search for a Scientific Diet

Nutrition, perhaps more than other scientific endeavors, blurred the line between science and culture. Developed in nineteenth-century European chemistry laboratories, the science of food was aimed first at improving livestock and agricultural productivity. Only toward the end of the century did scientists begin to apply their discoveries about animal feeding to human health. Unlike animal feed, however, human diet was always and intimately tied to deeply held cultural habits and beliefs. Scientific discoveries regarding the connections between food and health almost inevitably bumped up against a realm of human behavior that was governed more by emotion than reason. People rarely, then or now, eat what they "should" rather than what they want. Nutrition science thus inevitably, if inadvertently, inserted itself into social policy, particularly when it came to the relations among poverty, hunger, and food choices. Hunger and malnutrition, traditionally the central physical manifestations of poverty, appeared ideally suited to scientific remedy. If the poor could learn to eat better for less, one of modern society's most intractable social problems might be conquered. Rich or poor, nutrition science held out the promise of improved health for all.

Between 1880 and 1930 science informed a generation of social reformers and policy makers who sought to shape American society—and American diets. Dubbed the Progressive Era by historians, this period was marked by an energetic and optimistic effort to bring efficiency, expertise, and rational organization to industry, agriculture, public policy, and the domestic sphere as well. Scientific motherhood, for example, suggested that healthy and successful child-rearing depended as much or more on the knowledge and advice of experts—physicians, teachers, and home economists—as on the accumulated wisdom of mothers and grandmothers. Elevating mundane domestic chores like cooking and cleaning, science also promised to enhance housework and make women's sphere more efficient and productive.[1] In more general terms, science promised to improve public health, eliminate disease, and lengthen life expectancy as well as improve industrial efficiency and promote social order. It was a tall order that spoke to a belief in human progress and social improvement. At the same time, of course, science could as easily reinforce social inequalities as laud democratic progress. The prevailing theories of racial hierarchy and eugenics claimed scientific bases, as did theories like Dr. Edward Clark's about the "natural" differences between women and men. As a number of scholars have suggested, however, a scientific consciousness permeated popular beliefs at least by the time of the first world war.[2]

In the United States, as in Europe, the years between 1890 and World War I were marked by unprecedented social and economic transformations. Industrialization, urbanization, and immigration signaled at once the tremendous potential of human endeavor and lingering legacies of inequality, including pervasive racial discrimination and a fundamental reluctance to recognize women as full-fledged citizens. On both sides of the Atlantic, industrialization produced enormous wealth for some and unmitigated poverty for others. In modern urban centers, poverty was increasingly visible and the gulf between rich and poor provided space for festering resentment along with opportunities for reform and social renewal. In the United States, social distances were exacerbated by immigrants from Southern and Eastern Europe who arrived in unprecedented numbers to work in American industry. Bringing with them languages, cultures, and foodways unfamiliar to native-born white citizens, the newcomers appeared to be both intriguing and threatening. In the American South, racial segregation was solidified and legitimated in Jim Crow laws and the threat of violence by the Ku Klux Klan. Finally, a series of major industrial strikes during the 1880s and 1890s sparked the formation of a national labor movement and legitimated the demands of industrial workers for living wages and an "American standard of living." In this mix of social tensions, the science of nutrition held out the promise of a base-line opportunity for all Americans. Indeed, a healthy, egalitarian democracy needed to provide nourishment for both the minds and the bodies of its citizens.

Key to Progressive Era reform was a generation of women who appeared on the public scene ready to assert not only their own rights to citizenship but their abilities, indeed, expertise, in social problems. Daughters of the middle class, both white and black, Progressive Era women reformers organized a vast array of organizations and institutions aimed at solving the social problems of the day. Represented most notably by Jane Addams and her settlement house cohort, women reformers across the country addressed housing, health, labor, and education. Labeled by some historians as "maternalists," women reformers of the Progressive Era represented, as in any social movement, a range of beliefs and strategic goals. Their demands included paved streets and garbage collection in urban immigrant neighborhoods, window screens and sanitation for rural farm families, health services and day-care for children, and social insurance for widows. While women reformers concentrated particular attention on children's welfare, they also promoted industrial health and safety, consumer protection, and municipal improvements as well. Ultimately, Progressive Era reformers, both men and women, laid the foundations for twentieth-century welfare states. In the United States, women reformers, in many ways, became the architects of public welfare and social policies that were codified into law only during the 1930s.[3]

Dietetic solutions to social problems had a long history. More than most laboratory scientists, nutritionists understood that their work might hold important implications for everyday life and ordinary people. Indeed, regulation of diet and body dated back to the eighteenth century or earlier. During the nineteenth century, however, bodily discipline and orderly life-styles became intimately linked to discussions about industrial efficiency and the nature of middle-class family life. As one historian put it, "diet discourse" developed into a secular science that had both a moral and a rational component.[4] The dual nature of nutrition as a moral and a scientific discipline characterized its practical applications from early on. Thus the science of nutrition was taken up by a wide range of professionals, from home economists and social workers to businessmen and politicians. Dietary theories held particular significance, however, for those working with women and children. Housewives, of course, held the key to family health with every meal they served. Their market decisions, kitchen habits, and household management skills determined the family's standard of living as much as did the husband's wage. At the same time, children, particularly those in the captive audience of school classrooms, might be particularly open to new ideas that they would then take home to their parents.[5]

In the United States, nutrition science influenced social policy largely through the efforts of three individuals. Wilbur O. Atwater, a laboratory scientist, Edward Atkinson, a businessman, and Ellen Richards, founder of the home economics profession, together established the scientific basis for popular ideas about food and nutrition and laid the groundwork for institutional food service. Atwater pioneered in the discovery of vitamins and the idea that it was the nutrient, not the particular food, that was important for healthy development. But even more significant was Atwater's commitment to building an institutional base for nutrition science and, ultimately, food policy, within the USDA. Edward Atkinson directly applied nutrition science to the question of poverty and standard of living. Wading directly into the era's fears that industrialization was resulting in increased inequality, he insisted that workers needed only to understand and apply the principles of nutrition science in order to live well on factory wages. Atkinson's most lasting contribution to dietary reform, however, came through his financial backing for Ellen Richards and her efforts to establish a new profession devoted to bringing scientific methods to the domestic sphere. As one of the founders of home economics, Richards was perhaps the most influential of the three. Her work with diet and nutrition laid the groundwork for institutional food service and, ultimately, for a national school lunch program.

Wilbur O. Atwater translated the chemistry of food into practical, everyday terms. As a chemist at Wesleyan University in Connecticut and later as the first director of the USDA's Office of Experiment Stations, Atwater spent his career searching for ways to improve agriculture and enhance the work of American farmers. Chemical fertilizers, improved seed strains, and selective livestock breeding all required research and resources that went far beyond the means of most American farmers of the era. In his espousal of what one historian has termed the "transcendent virtue of productivity," emphasizing the era's belief in efficiency and productivity, Atwater, perhaps inadvertently, laid the basis for the large-scale, mechanized, highly capitalized operations that came to characterize American agriculture in the twentieth century.[6] In his work, he hoped to realize the human potential of agricultural improvement for the consumer as well as for the farmer. As Director of Experiment Stations Atwater oversaw the beginning of a major expansion in public funding for agricultural research, including food and nutrition.[7] His work thus prefigured what would later become an intimate connection between the Department of Agriculture and American food policy.

Human nutrition was an infant science at the turn of the twentieth century. Like most chemists of his time, Atwater believed that the human body essentially worked like an internal combustion engine. This popular mechanical metaphor suggested that nutrition was simply a matter of putting enough of the right fuel into the human—or animal—engine. During the 1880s chemists identified three distinct types of food/fuel—proteins, fats, and carbohydrates. The amount of energy each food/fuel generated was measured in something called calories.[8] Atwater set the stage for future food and agriculture policy by connecting nutrition as fuel not only to animal husbandry and horticulture, but also to human productivity. The key to individual moral and intellectual progress, like The key to agricultural or industrial productivity, Atwater believed, lay in the application of scientific research to daily life, whether on the farm or in the kitchen.[9]

One of Atwater's major research projects put him on the cutting edge of international nutrition research. At the end of the nineteenth century chemists in Europe began to isolate some other substances in food besides proteins, carbohydrates, and fats that seemed essential to healthy development. These substances, dubbed "vitamins," were as necessary for growth and survival as were the traditional food/fuels. Indeed, vitamins seemed to be directly linked to the ability of the human engine to function. In his Experiment Station laboratory, Atwater became one of the first American scientists to identify what later became known as vitamin A. This discovery revolutionized nutrition science. During the first two decades of the twentieth century, vitamins B and C were also isolated. The vitamin theory, known as the "new nutrition," quickly captured both professional and public attention.[10]

Atwater's most lasting contribution to nutrition science was his theory of substitutions. He demonstrated that foods such as eggs and beans supplied the same amount of energy as meat, and fats such as lard had the same nutritional value as butter. Atwater's theory of food substitutions revolutionized the social meaning of nutrition by suggesting that cheap foods could be perfectly healthful. He went so far as to suggest that housewives should not think about buying milk or meat for their families, but rather should look at food as "nutritive substances." Under this theory, women could enhance their families' living standards simply by learning to use inexpensive cuts of meat, lard, and beans. To assist women (and the public in general) in understanding these principles, Atwater published elaborate tables showing the nutrition equivalents among foods and giving the daily amounts of fat, protein, and carbohydrates that people needed to thrive and grow. These tables and equivalents formed what one historian has called the "building blocks for scientific cookery" and remained in use well into the twentieth century.[11]

Nutrition science moved perhaps too easily from laboratory to social policy. From the start, scientists and reformers articulated two different and not always compatible goals in their work. On the one hand, science promised to modernize and improve American diets generally. It took a while, however, to shift ideas about food away from concerns with hunger per se and into the more encompassing realm of nutrition education and modern diets. Indeed, at first, food reformers focused largely on the health and eating habits of poor people, immigrants, and industrial workers. The earliest studies of human nutrition explored the health of slaves, soldiers, and factory operatives. Pre–Civil War plantation owners in the

American South, for example, used ideas about food as fuel to calculate how much to feed slaves in order to make them work most efficiently. Similarly, in England during the "cotton famine" period of industrial unemployment, physicians studied food consumption and nutrition among the thousands of mill workers who found themselves unemployed and hungry. The aim was to figure out the relation of wages to living standards in terms of nutrient requirements.

At its base, nutrition science suggested a relatively simple solution to the period's endemic poverty. Teach the poor that cheap food was as nutritious as expensive fare and living standards would automatically rise. Intentionally or not, nutrition science fed the notion that social inequality was due to cultural habit rather than economic condition. Ultimately, nutrition science became a significant factor in the raging political debates about wages and living standards.[12] Where British trade unionists and socialists, for example, claimed that low wages were at the root of hunger and poverty, conservative politicians used nutrition science to argue that workers simply were not managing their money properly. British psychologist A. V. Hill famously declared, "I should not condemn men for studying human diet, but the motive should be the discovery of scientific facts, not the demonstration that the British working class is underfed."[13]

In the United States, one of the most outspoken proponents of nutrition science was an industrialist whose explicit aim was to prove that workers could live well on low wages. Edward Atkinson, capitalist, manufacturer, and free-trade advocate, turned to nutrition science after the Civil War. When the workers in his cotton mill went on strike for higher wages, Atwater determined to prove that they could live decently on the wage he paid. He was convinced that workers regularly squandered their money on unnecessarily expensive foods, and he embarked on a campaign to convince his (and all) workers that they could easily eat better food for less money than their wives were used to spending. Not incidentally, this also meant that he could reduce the pay in his factory without feeling overly guilty about the impact on the workers' living standards. Indeed, when Atkinson cut his workers' pay he also "extended considerable effort in instructing them how to purchase and prepare food economically." The thankful workers, he later claimed, "told me they had been better off on the wages of four days . . . than they had previously been on the wages of a week."[14] Atkinson's nutritional solution to low wages earned him the scorn of labor leaders such as Eugene V. Debs, who dubbed him "Shinbone" and declared that "American workingmen are resolved not to be further degraded, scientifically or otherwise."[15]

Undeterred by his critics, Atkinson began touring the country in his mission to bring nutrition science to American workers. His message was that workers could learn to eat better for less. In 1896 he published a book, *The Science of Nutrition*, in which he estimated that the average manual laborer "need not spend over 24 cents a day for food."[16] At the time, the average industrial wage for white men was around $1.50 per day.[17] Atkinson's plan was particularly attractive, of course, to employers like himself who sought to lower their labor costs. His work gained popular attention, most notably among other industrialists. According to Atwater's biographer, Andrew Carnegie put a copy of the book in every public library in the nation.[18]

The social implications of nutrition science, particularly when it came to income and class, could not have been more clear. If workers (or their wives) would simply change their eating (and cooking) habits, their incomes would go farther and their standards of living would not be reduced even in the face of wage cuts. Atkinson spent much of his time and fortune trying to transform the diets of American workers. During the 1890s he promoted his own invention, the "Aladdin Slow Cooker," as a practical means by which housewives could bring nutrition science into their homes. A forerunner of the modern "crock pot," the Aladdin Cooker promised to "make a tough old turkey" tender overnight. Atkinson's advertisements boasted that women could feed their families on less than twenty-five cents a day.[19] Although the Aladdin Cooker failed to catch on with working-class housewives, it found a more enthusiastic reception among middle-class reformers. According to Atkinson's biographer, the device found its way into settlement houses (including Jane Addams's Hull House in Chicago) and was put into use at Booker T. Washington's Tuskeegee Institute.[20] The Aladdin Cooker was also adopted by home economics pioneer Ellen Richards. The appeal of the slow cooker, of course, was that it could make cheap food more palatable. In scientific terms, both Richards and Atkinson adopted Wilbur Atwater's theory of nutritional substitution.

Ellen Richards and her fellow home economists became the key conduits between nutrition laboratories and the American public during the early twentieth century. Like other middle-class women of their generation, home economists sought work and professional recognition in what had traditionally been all-male arenas. The first group of women to attend college in large numbers, this generation found, on graduation, that they were singularly unwelcome in scientific laboratories, law offices, and academic disciplines. Undeterred, women founded their own institutions and professional associations, in the process exerting an extraordinary influence on social reform and public policy. In was in this era, for example, that women academics, shut out of many universities, formed the American Association of University Women, the first organization to support women in higher education and to insist on equality in curriculum and graduate requirements.[21] Jane Addams similarly forged the new field of

Figure 1.1. Ellen Swallow Richards founded home economics after facing gender barriers in academic chemistry. Richards is pictured here with the MIT Chemistry Department faculty. Courtesy MIT Museum.

social work and established Chicago's Hull House, the nation's premier social settlement institution, attracting both men and women to careers in academic as well as applied social investigation. Social work, like home economics, ultimately became labeled a "female profession," signaling the inherent tension faced by women who, blocked from full participation in the male professions, used their talents to study areas men seemed to ignore: family, community, and the household.[22]

Ellen Richards wanted to be a laboratory chemist but instead became one of the most visible and vocal popularizers of nutrition reform and scientific eating. As an undergraduate at Vassar College during the 1870s, she studied chemistry with the nation's foremost female scientist, Maria Mitchell. Despite Mitchell's enthusiastic recommendations, Richards, to her life-long disappointment, found no graduate chemistry program either in the United States or in Germany that would accept women. Mitchell finally convinced MIT to accept Richards as a "special student," but the university refused to allow her to work in any of their established laboratories.[23] Instead, with the support of her husband (an MIT professor and mining engineer) and financial backing from Edward Atkinson (whom she had met while working on a study of water quality for Boston), Richards opened her own "women's laboratory."[24] It was there that Richards developed what became known as the domestic sciences, including studies of human nutrition and food preparation.[25]

Like Edward Atkinson, Richards and the early home economists believed American's living standards would significantly improve if only people understood the principles of nutrition. Excited about the new discoveries in food science, including Wilbur Atwater's substitution theory, home economists turned their attention first to the eating habits of workers and immigrants. While they were convinced that everyone might benefit from a knowledge of nutrition, the problem of poverty presented the most immediate and dramatic challenge. Early home economics research specifically sought to demonstrate that nutritious diets did not need to be expensive. As Richards put it bluntly, "if once the public can disabuse its mind of any idea of close connection between 'food value' and cost—namely that a cheap food is a poor food, that a dear food is a good food—then a beginning in scientific dietaries can be made."[26] Home economists became enthusiastic proponents of the "low-budget meal" and menus directed at housewives with a limited food budget. In 1877, for example, in the midst of serious economic depression and the nation's first major railroad strike, Juliet Corson, founder of one of the first American cooking schools, published *Fifteen Cent Dinners for Workingmen's Families*.[27] In this pamphlet Corson suggested that a worker's family of six could easily have three nutritious meals a day for less than $3 per week if they ate cheese pudding and stewed tripe.[28] Like Edward Atkinson, Corson believed that a change in diet would improve workers' living standards even in the face of low wages. By showing housewives "how to make the best of what they have," she said, "I am proving myself a better friend to them than those who try to make them still more discontented with the lot that is already almost too hard to bear."[29] A decade later Mary Hinman Abel, an aspiring chemist who, like Richards, ended up in home economics, made her name by publishing "five food principles" for low-budget meals.[30] Abel's advice applied Atwater's substitutions to practical recipes designed for working-class housewives. Insisting that while workers' families might not be able to afford "many good tasting things," they could nonetheless eat healthy meals by following her recipes for bread soup and by serving dinners of "flour soup, fried bread, cheese, and toast" for supper. Abel's work found a national audience when she received first prize in the American Public Health Association's essay contest, and Richards invited her to Boston to help start a model public kitchen.[31]

Richards tirelessly devoted her professional career to introducing the public to the principles of scientific nutrition. Her singular contribution was the development of institutional kitchens, the first large-scale food service operations. Institutional cooking brought modern, industrial principles to what had been a private, highly individualized domain. In the institutional kitchen, science most directly informed the era's belief in standardization, efficiency, and rational management. Richards's first experiment in institutional feeding was the New England Kitchen (NEK), which opened in a working-class Boston neighborhood in 1890. With the financial backing of Edward Atkinson (the NEK became a key demonstration site for the Aladdin Cooker) and recipes based on Wilbur Atwater's nutrition science, Ellen Richards operated what might be called the nation's first "take out" restaurant. Located in a Boston storefront, the NEK offered model workingmen's lunches as well as tins of food to take home for dinner. With each meal the patron received a card listing the calorie and nutrient content on one side and Atwater's daily nutrition recommendations on the other. Every dish was scientifically developed and carefully measured so that it was easily standardized and could be reproduced at home. Unfortunately, the scientific diet of Indian pudding, oatmeal cakes, pea soup, and cornmeal mush turned out to have little popular appeal. One customer reportedly told Richards, "I'll eat what I want to eat." Another, objecting to the decidedly Anglo-Saxon tone of the menus, warned Richards not to "try to make a New Englander out of me."[32] After three years the NEK was forced to close due to a lack of customers. Although in operation only for a short time, the NEK nevertheless became a model for institutional meal service and standardized menus.

Despite the failure of the NEK, Richards's experiment established significant principles in institutional feeding and nutrition education. Her standardized recipes and menu cards became models for large-scale food service operations. Richards proudly declared her beef broth, for example, to be as "as unvarying in its constituents as the medicine compounded to meet a physician's prescription."[33] Thus the recipe could be replicated at home on a small scale or in a school, hospital, or factory for large numbers of people. In either case, the nutrition content and the taste would be consistent. In 1898, again backed by funds from Edward Atkinson, Richards opened another model kitchen at the Chicago World's Fair. Here she distributed menu cards that included the weight and nutrition components of each dish. The World's Fair venue, known as the Rumford Kitchen, fed thousands of fairgoers and opened nutrition science to a whole new audience: the middle-class consumer.[34] Standardization combined with education to produce the first modern institutional food service model. Home economists added to their agenda studies of food processing and preservation, food service management, and, increasingly, lunchroom administration.[35]

Richards's World's Fair project signaled an important shift in home economics and nutrition research. While the early studies took as their task improving the health and diet of the nation's poorest groups, the World's Fair kitchen attracted workers and middle-class people.[36] Here was an opportunity to influence people who might be able to afford plenty to eat but who might not understand the principles of nutrition. Indeed, Richards expressed the central tension in food reform when she suggested that anyone, "working man, student, or millionaire," could suffer from poor nutrition. The challenge, she wrote, was not "how to get enough food, but how to choose from the bewildering variety offered that which will best develop the power of the human being." Nutrition, in her view, promised not only an efficient, healthy life, but intellectual and moral development as well. Poor diets, she insisted—and the inability to avoid the temptation of "bad" foods—"weakens the moral fiber and lessens mental as well as physical efficiency."[37] Richards thus committed herself to modernizing the American diet and bringing the gospel of science to a middle-class audience. Whether rich or poor, she concluded, everyone needed nutrition education.

Shortly after the end of the 1898 World's Fair, Richards hit upon the perfect system for bringing nutrition science to a wide public: the school lunchroom. Here she could teach children the value of nutrition, and, what is more, the children would take those lessons home and influence mothers as well. Richards could reach children who came to school hungry, but also those who were well fed but potentially nutrient deficient. She opened her first lunchroom almost by accident. While conducting a study of the sanitary conditions in Boston public schools, she discovered that the high school janitors were selling food to the students. The janitors, of course, were in business for profit and did not care about the nutrition content of the food. Richards convinced the Boston School Committee to let her open a scientific lunch program. Her effort got off to a rocky start when the janitors refused to help, and local restaurants posted signs announcing, "Here you can get what you want to eat, and not what the School Committee says you must."[38] Richards's scientific message, however, won the allegiance of the School Committee, and within a year five thousand students were eating lunch at school every day.

Richards's experiment proved a triumph for nutrition science. Indeed, despite their zeal, home economists and nutritionists had been relatively unsuccessful in changing popular eating habits. While scientific advances surely held the potential to improve everyone's health, most people regularly eschewed expert advice. As a result, experts themselves often adopted a judgmental tone that only alienated their audiences even more. Home economists, largely native-born, white, middle-class, educated women, easily adopted a moralistic, if not proselytizing tone in their food advice. As one historian has observed, "like the schoolteachers, social workers, librarians, and settlement house workers, the women home economists could act as missionaries trying to save society and its victims through better nutrition and home life."[39] Poor food habits were regularly labeled "sins," and women who served inadequate meals were often dismissed as poor or neglectful mothers. Home economist Lucy Gillett, for example, considered coffee and tea "the worst food sins of children."[40] > Indeed, the new nutrition discoveries, particularly vitamins, lent themselves to a missionary purpose. Home economists as educators particularly took as their duty the effort to convert the American public to a belief in nutrition and to convince ordinary people to behave (i.e., eat) according to the new gospel. Richards herself set the tone when she observed that "the parent who neglects this part of his child's upbringing is culpable and his sin will surely be visited upon the third and fourth generations."[41] Richards and her followers, however, did not limit their missionary activities to immigrants or the poor. Echoing the eugenicists' theory that Anglo-Saxon Americans were in danger of committing "race suicide," Richards warned that the "well-to-do" classes "are being eliminated by their diet." It was the rich, even more than the poor, she believed, who were "most in need of missionary work" when it came to nutrition.[42] To this day, Richards's professional and intellectual descendants equate proper eating with virtue. The reward for scientific eating would go beyond healthy individuals by invigorating American democracy itself.[43] And what better way to promote the virtues of a nutritious diet than to begin with the young, in the school lunchroom?

A DIET FOR AMERICANS

By the 1920s, a science and a culture of nutrition permeated discussions about food in the United States. World War I had revealed a shocking level of malnutrition in America. By most estimates, almost one-third of all young men called up for military service had been rejected either because they were underweight or because they suffered from some nutrition-related condition, such as rickets or poor teeth.[44] Traumatized by the specter of a weak defense and malnourished citizenry, army officials, public health physicians, and home economists spent the next decade preaching the science of nutrition and trying to get the American public to adopt scientific eating. Schools, hospitals, and even some factories began to run meal programs on a scale never imagined by Ellen Richards. Nutrition was becoming public policy.

In the post–World War I climate of relative prosperity (at least in certain sectors of the economy and certain sections of the country), nutritionists

as well as the rapidly expanding food industry promoted a more general-
ized concern with well-being, health, and nutrition—and malnutrition as
well. Pioneering a new consumer age, food advertisements touted the vitamin content of foods and provided testimonials to their product's contribution to individual vigor and energy. Well-baby clinics and pure milk
movements sprang up throughout the country. As one home economist
in the Bureau of Home Economics observed, "it is high time that every
mother should know as much about feeding her family as the thousands
of successful farmers now know about feeding livestock."[45] The discovery
of the nutrition age was that anyone—rich or poor—could suffer from
malnutrition. Where discussions about food had for centuries connected
hunger and poverty, the modern nutrition message combined compensa-
tory nutrition for the poor with a general mission to improve the health
of all Americans. Nutrition science had, in essence, dramatically altered
the relationship between food and poverty. As New York home economist
Lucy Gillett observed, one could find "underweight and malnourished
children in all types of families, in the families of those who have plenty
of money as well as in families of limited means."[46] Poor people might
suffer from insufficient quantities of food, but it was the quality of what
they ate that really mattered. At the same time, even people with plenty
to eat might face malnutrition if they did not make informed food choices.

The search for an American diet during the 1920s thus focused on two
goals. First, food reformers, usually women who were native-born and
middle-class, hoped to translate nutrition science into practical, everyday
menus that all housewives could prepare. This meant teaching immigrant
women to eat "American" food, but it also meant teaching middle-class
housewives about vitamins, proteins, and calories. At the same time, food
reformers, along with teachers, doctors, and social workers, faced the
continuing problem of poverty—people who had limited food choices
and, by definition, poor diets. In either case, however, reformers believed
that the key lay in teaching children how to eat right. Although food
reformers struggled to teach women to prepare what they considered to
be balanced, healthy meals, housewives were notoriously stubborn in
their food habits and reluctant to adopt new foods or new recipes. Reformers thus turned to the children. Instilling the values of nutrition and
good food habits at an early age, reformers were certain, would reap re-
wards far into the future.[47] Not only would the children develop into
healthy adults, but they would take nutrition lessons home to their mothers, who would learn to serve healthy meals to the entire family. As a
captive audience, schoolchildren appeared to be the perfect candidates for
nutrition education and the school lunch the perfect vehicle through
which to introduce new foods.[48]

Yet what exactly was the purpose of school lunch programs? Nutrition scientists, home economists, child welfare advocates, and school administrators rarely had a clear answer to this question. In some schools mothers, teachers, or civic groups simply provided free meals to poor children. In other schools, home economics teachers used the lunchroom to train girls in domestic skills. These home economics classes would often sell lunch to other students, albeit at relatively low prices. Many schools used lunchrooms as revenue-generating operations, hiring managers and selling meals to children who could pay. While home economists insisted that lunchroom operations should always be paired with nutrition education, in most cases the education consisted of a poster or an occasional assembly. During the 1920s, however, home economists and child welfare advocates began to envision school lunches as part of a comprehensive public health and nutrition program. While the desire to feed poor children continued to underlay school meal plans, an expanded notion of universal child health gradually began to inform nutrition education and school cafeterias. Throughout the 1920s, food reformers engaged in an ongoing battle with school administrators and welfare workers over the purpose of lunch and what should be served.

The question of what to serve for lunch was no simple matter. Indeed, battles over what constituted "proper" food went far beyond ideas about the science of nutrition. Although food reformers aimed to modernize American diets generally, their message carried different meanings for different ethnic and racial groups. Recent historians have interpreted the early twentieth-century reform impulse, particularly in its Americanization efforts, as an exercise in social control if not cultural imperialism. Historians regularly point to lessons in Americanization through housework to suggest that reformers held only scorn for their clients' cultures and traditions. Gwendolyn Mink, for example, observes that the "centerpiece of cultural reform was the cooking class."[49] Laura Shapiro argues that the ubiquitous white sauce found in American recipes symbolized the desire to transform ethnic differences into a homogeneous "perfection salad." George Sanchez describes the efforts of home economists to convince Mexican-American women to forsake chilis and tomatoes as elements in "a system of social control intended to construct a well-behaved citizenry."[50] Harvey Levenstein suggests that "the acrid smells of garlic and onions wafting through the immigrant quarter seemed to provide unpleasant evidence that their inhabitants found American ways unappealing; that they continued to find foreign (and dangerous) ideas as palatable as their foreign food."[51] Indeed, one need not look far to find examples of "food imperialism" in the writings of home economists. Descriptions of workers who "reek of food and strong breath" were the common stuff of scientific as well as popular reporting.[52] There were plenty of descriptions like Dorothy Dickins's in the September 1926 *Journal of Home Economics* complaining that "the ordinary country Negro woman is a poor cook, and only years of careful training from some white woman can justify her reputation for good cooking."[53] Columbia Teachers College nutritionist Mary Swartz Rose regularly peppered her reports with ethnic stereotypes and racial characterizations, noting, for example, that it "is no easy task to feed little Jews, and Italians . . . when they have never had regular meals nor acquired a taste for the right kind of food."[54]

While it is true that Progressive Era and 1920s nutrition reformers, like most public activists of their generation, often paid insufficient attention to the preferences of the nation's new immigrant working class or to the cultures of rural people, whether black or white, their diet lessons cannot be dismissed simply as one more effort to Americanize immigrants and subsume all ethnic differences under a ubiquitous white sauce.[55] Nutrition science held the very real promise of improved health, stronger bodies, and longer lives. Indeed, one might argue that the work of reform through food was more complex and not as singularly biased as the either historians or the contemporary rhetoric might suggest. When it came to eating habits, nutrition reformers seemed to understand both the cultural significance of food and the limits of their own power to change people's preferences. Their efforts to modernize diets had a larger purpose than assimilating immigrants. They believed they had in their hands the potential at once to eliminate malnutrition, the most visible symbol of poverty and inequality, and to improve the health of all Americans in the process. A closer look at the research on malnutrition as well as on immigrant diets suggests a complex interplay of science and culture.

In the search for a scientific or American diet, home economists understood as well as any sociologists of the day the deep cultural significance of food. As one research team observed, "dietary habits are remarkably fixed habits."[56] Food reformers, however, were firm believers in science, and this was the lesson their dietary advice was designed to promote. Home economist Grace Farrel, for example, believed that while it would be "impossible to graft all the American habits" onto immigrants, her profession could "give them a vision of the better, easier, and more modern way of life."[57] Two women, in particular, offer examples of the complex outlook governing food reform during the 1920s. Lucy Gillett, a home economist who worked for the New York Association for Improving the Condition of the Poor during the 1920s and served as chair of the Social Services Section of the American Dietetic Association, conducted a major study of immigrant food habits during the early 1920s. Sophonisba Breckinridge, a pioneer social worker at the University of Chicago and a major figure in the early twentieth-century woman's movement, conducted numerous studies of immigrant lives. One of her most important works, *New Homes for Old*, was published in 1921 as part of the Americanization Studies series sponsored by the Carnegie Corporation.[58] Both women expressed a belief in scientific diet that verged on cultural arrogance and an appreciation of ethnic diversity in American democracy and a sensitivity to the particular limitations on immigrant women in the markets and kitchens of their new homeland. Breckinridge acknowledged, for example, that "the problem of how far the immigrant groups should be encouraged to modify their diet can be determined only after a careful study of their dietary practices."[59] It was unclear, she said, to what extent "racial customs" should enter into any "Americanization scheme."[60] Gillett counseled her students that, "by showing respect for and acknowledging the good that is in all diets[,] there is sure to be an interchange of food habits which will be one of the ways of amalgamating the people living in one country."[61] Indeed, Gillett concluded, "So far as I know we have very little evidence that the better class of Italians need attention *more* than the better class of Americans."[62]

Nutrition reformers allowed that some ethnic foods could be part of a proper American diet. Nutrition science, particularly Atwater's theory of substitutions, afforded reformers some measure of respect for immigrant diets.[63] In particular, they understood Edward Atwater's substitution theory to mean that there was more than one way to get enough of the essential vitamins, proteins, fats, and carbohydrates needed for healthy living. Lucy Gillett, for example, advised social workers and home economics teachers to learn the names of various vegetables in the languages of their students.[64] The only reason to change immigrant food habits, Gillett argued, was to "make them consistent with health, and perhaps of greater convenience to the people."[65] Gillett and Breckinridge were particularly critical of young social workers or home economists who blindly criticized immigrant food habits. "The foreign born woman," Gillett wrote, "does not see why she should change the customs of centuries to suit the whim of a youthful person who does not know what her perfectly good food habits are."[66] Breckinridge similarly took young reformers to task for not understanding the cultures of their clients. In a widely quoted report from Massachusetts, for example, a young social worker blamed the peeling wallpaper in tenement housing on the ubiquitous steam rising from pots of cabbage that immigrant housewives kept on their stoves. The social worker tried to convince the women to fry their food instead of boiling it. Breckinridge dismissed this advice as "misguided" and cautioned against trying to "give advice on diet without . . . knowing much about it."[67]

Much nutrition knowledge may have been lost in translation. While traditional diets may have contained many elements of nutrition, immigrant housewives—often via their children—had to learn new names for familiar foods and to substitute unfamiliar items for staples not available in American cities. The immigrant housewives interviewed by Breckinridge, for example, admitted that they did not know how to ask for the foods they needed. The result, Breckinridge said, was that they ended up "eliminating various essential elements and completely upsetting the balance of the traditional diet."[68] Even when women were willing to try new foods, however, they often did not know how to prepare them. A Detroit welfare worker, for example, complained that her clients "boiled whole grapefruit for hours and still found it tough," while others cooked the leaves of the cauliflower and "threw away the flower."[69] American diet lessons were often limited by the structure of the grocery industry as well. Breckinridge found, for example, that stores in Chicago's Lithuanian neighborhoods rarely stocked fresh vegetables. Restricted diets, she wrote, were due less to women's unwillingness to try new foods than to the fact that "the markets afford so little variety."[70] (It was for this reason that Breckinridge became an early advocate of standardized, chain grocery stores.)[71]

While home economists had long preached the gospel of eating better for less, those familiar with working-class and immigrant kitchens knew that immigrant housewives lacked more than a knowledge of vitamins. As Lucy Gillett observed, "we must make the conditions possible for good nutrition."[72] There is, Sophonisba Breckinridge acknowledged, "the question of the means with which to buy."[73] According to most estimates, the average semi- or unskilled male worker during the early 1920s earned less than $2,000 per year, often considerably less.[74] Breckinridge's own 1921 cost of living figures found that, on average, immigrant families spent more on food as a proportion of their incomes than did native-born families. In her study, immigrant families earned an average of $900 to $1200 per year and spent between 35 and 40 percent of that on food.[75] The estimate that working-class families spent about one-third of their incomes on food was confirmed continually through the 1960s.

An American diet hinged on more than just the right food. Modern eating required a modern kitchen as well. The lessons of scientific eating might be difficult to apply whether in urban tenement kitchens or in tenant farm shacks. During the 1920s home economists developed classes for women in household management. They also targeted girls in school.[76] Finally, many American kitchens lacked modern appliances and electricity well into the mid-twentieth century.[77] Poor women often owned only a few cooking utensils and might not always have enough money to pay for gas to fuel a stove. Agricultural Extension workers in the American South, for example, found that large numbers of tenant farm houses had no stoves, so the women cooked over open hearths.[78] Urban immigrant women had to learn how to use appliances (if they could afford them) and cooking utensils that were different from the ones they had grown up with. One research team commented that immigrant women were not familiar with egg beaters, tin cook ware, or double boilers. Lucy Gillett admitted that it was difficult to teach scientific cooking to women whose "entire outfit consists of two saucepans, perhaps only one, a knife, a spoon, and a tea cup." She worried about whether the young girls in her nutrition classes who came from tenement homes would know how to apply what they learn.[79]

A modern diet for Americans promised nutrition and health regardless of income or ethnicity. Yet as food reformers were acutely aware, many Americans, whether out of ignorance or poverty, did not enjoy the benefits of healthful diets. During the 1920s, at the very moment that the nutrition message was becoming part of popular culture, malnutrition loomed as an ominous threat to the nation's progress.[80] For this reason, food reformers, along with teachers, doctors, and social workers, waged an intense battle during the 1920s with malnutrition. "The improper and unscientific feeding of children," observed Columbia University home economist Mary Swartz Rose, "is one of the most common causes of disease, disability, incapacity for work, both mental and physical, loss of energy, susceptibility to contract and inability to withstand disease."[81] Malnutrition studies documented deficiencies that, while traditionally linked to poverty, appeared now to be subject to scientific—as opposed to social—remedies. And if poverty no longer sufficed as an explanation for malnutrition, then, indeed, nutrition education and school lunches would be essential elements in modern life.

NUTRITION AND MALNUTRITION

Defining and measuring malnutrition, however, proved to be an inexact science. Like food advice in general, discussions of malnutrition revealed deeply held cultural notions about health and body type.[82] Traditionally, skinny bodies, pale skin, and sunken eyes were taken to be signs of malnutrition. Physician James Kerr, for example, in his 1916 book on school hygiene, told his readers, "There is no danger of giving too much food."[83] Subjective observations of body types did not, however, suffice in the scientific age. By the 1920s, physicians and nutritionists had developed elaborate height-weight tables and calorie charts to guide assessments of malnutrition and children's healthy development. Drawing on Wilbur Atwater's tables, measures such as the Dunfermline Scale and later the Baldwin Wood tables used height-to-weight ratios to set standards for normal development.[84] Mary Swartz Rose, who advocated for the establishment of national height and weight standards, proposed that children should be labeled malnourished if "they show disturbance of the normal weight curve."[85] Most doctors and nutritionists agreed that that "if the child weighs 10 per cent less than the average . . . he probably has something the matter with him."[86] Inevitably, a norm based on "American-born children of fortunate circumstances" labeled many others as malnourished and in need of professional intervention.[87]

The seemingly objective height and weight tables provided powerful tools for measuring children's health, but they were equally powerful in establishing racial and gendered body norms. These norms reflected ideal body types that individuals rarely achieved. Most problematic was the fact that the height-weight ratios and calorie recommendations were based on studies of adult males, often soldiers or laborers, and, equally as often, of Anglo-Saxon origin.[88] Needless to say, the children of immigrants, as well as African American children, frequently came up short. Thus, not surprisingly, a 1921 study of boys in public and private schools found the public school boys significantly smaller in stature. On the basis of this comparison, the study concluded that malnutrition constituted a serious problem in the nation's public schools.[89] At the time, of course, the racial, ethnic, and gendered limitations of these norms were quickly dismissed. Lucy Gillett, for example, attributed the small size of Italian immigrant children to the "high-strung atmosphere" of their households, not to mention their preference for macaroni, olive oil, and "Roman cheese," which, she complained, left them open to "a deficiency of both iron and vitamines [sic]."[90] While Mary Swartz Rose acknowledged that a standard based largely on people of "English, German, and Scandinavian stock" might not be entirely appropriate for Italian children, she believed that science did not yet know "the growth capacities of some of these short-statured peoples." Short stature was not, she insisted, a "racial characteristic," but rather was developed by an "unfavorable condition of diet or environment or habit." Rose was convinced that a healthy diet would bring all children up to the norm.

Underweight school children were subjected to intense programs of behavior modification and nutrition education. Beginning during World War I and continuing through midcentury, women's clubs, community groups, health departments, and teachers sponsored campaigns to identify underweight children. Special examinations and regular weigh-ins became common in schools throughout the country.[91] Part of an extensive movement centered in the Children's Bureau and led by women reformers and mothers' groups, the weigh-ins reflected a growing concern with children's welfare and maternal health. Culminating in the passage of the Sheppard-Towner Act providing health education for pregnant women and mothers, this movement encompassed well-baby clinics, vaccination campaigns, and nutrition education.[92] The weigh-ins were accompanied

Figure 1.2. Schools regularly weighed and measured children to identify those who were malnourished. Children are pictured here calculating gains in weight. National League for Nursing Archives, 1894–1952, National Library of Medicine.

by extensive propaganda urging children to eat properly. The focus of most school nutrition campaigns was to encourage children to gain weight. In one program, those children who gained properly were placed at one end of the class, and "those who do not gain at the other end." "The children who gain are praised for their achievement; the one who gains the most receives a gold star."[93] Another program celebrated little Anna Carado's "graduation" when she gained the proper amount of weight by rewarding her with yellow balloons that said "good health" and a familiar tune saying, "Anna Carado keep it up, Anna you're a dandy, Don't forget the milk and fruit, and leave alone the candy."[94] Children's school meals and nutrition classes, it seemed, provided the perfect laboratories in which nutritionists could explore the best means to convince people to change their eating habits. As one researcher put it, "if children are to acquire good food habits, they must be taught to like the foods that are essential for growth."[95]

Not surprisingly, the campaign to weigh all schoolchildren uncovered a staggering number who were "underweight." Armed with objective measures of malnutrition, home economists, physicians, and teachers began to see cases everywhere. Indeed, coinciding with the discovery of nutrition, malnutrition "scares" appeared with regular frequency in both the professional and the popular press.[96] The *Journal of Home Economics*, as well as *Parents Magazine*, regularly published malnutrition studies. A 1917 of New York City children estimated that 21 percent were undernourished, while a study the next year estimated that as many as one-quarter of all children in the nation were malnourished. In 1921 another study suggested that 10 percent of all urban children were more than 10 percent underweight, half had rickets, and 90 percent had decayed teeth.[97] Yet another study found that over half of Michigan's public school students and 60 percent of those in parochial schools were underweight.[98] These shocking figures provided ready evidence that the nation's children needed nutrition education, not to mention nutritious meals.

By the 1920s, a consensus was forming among professionals, teachers, and parents alike that lunch programs could address the most serious nutrition problems facing American children.[99] Like the benefits of public schooling itself, lunch programs promised a certain leveling of class and ethnic differences and socialization into mainstream American culture. As early as 1901 home economist pioneer Caroline Hunt observed that school lunches not only "satisfied the bodily needs" but developed "the cultural side" of children as well. The question of school lunches she noted, should "properly be regarded as an educational one."[100] Studies of school lunch programs unanimously found improvements in children's health and enhanced performance in school. In 1922, for example, a study concluded that children would "do much better in school work in the afternoon" if they ate a hot lunch.[101] Montana State College home economist Lottie Milam found that the hot school lunch "has brought about greater interest in school work improvement in the general physical condition of pupils, less need of discipline, increased interest in home work, improved attendance especially on cold days, less hurried eating, habits of cleanliness and neatness, good table manners, and proper eating habits."[102] In New York, home economists noticed "a marked improvement in physical condition and orderly ways" of children who had received milk in the morning and soup at noon.[103] Mary Swartz Rose estimated that the grades of well-nourished children averaged 3 to 4 percent higher than those of their more poorly nourished peers. In Detroit, Rose documented that underweight boys earned 1.5 percent lower grades than did those whose weight was "normal." Indeed, she observed that boys "who were ahead of their age in weight performed 2.6 percent above average."[104] In Winslow, Arizona, the school lunch manager claimed "significant weight gain among Mexican children." The school board there was so impressed with the results of the hot lunch program "that it voted to continue the work at any cost."[105]

School Lunch as Public Policy

Until Richards's experiment in Boston, school meals in the United States, as in Europe, had mainly been arenas of private charity. During the late nineteenth century, voluntary organizations regularly operated free lunch programs for poor children in American cities. In Philadelphia, for example, the Home and School League sent home economists into high schools to teach girls how to prepare meals and to feed children who could not afford to bring their own lunches. The Women's School Alliance of Milwaukee similarly offered lunches to poor children using donations from churches, individuals, and private clubs. Cleveland high school principals arranged for lunch baskets to be delivered to their schools "to avoid dangers of food sold by corner groceries, push carts, and street vendors."[106] In many towns and cities, women's organizations like the mother's clubs and the General Federation of Women's Clubs sponsored milk programs or lunch wagons.[107] While some of these school meal programs paid no heed to nutrition but rather had as their purpose simply feeding hungry children, others took up scientific motherhood and promoted nutrition education along with nutritious meals.[108] Richards's efforts, for the first time, codified nutrition education for school children. Her efforts also marked the entry of the state into the arena of children's nutrition.

During the early twentieth century, both European and American reformers began to envision state-sponsored welfare systems that would mitigate the inequalities resulting from industrial development. While in the United States, the state governments had always been deeply involved in both education and social welfare, until the early twentieth century, the federal government rarely intruded itself into the daily lives of citizens. During the second decade of the twentieth century, however, largely drawing on trans-Atlantic social welfare initiatives, American reformers began to push the federal government to become more active through a range of social and economic regulatory legislation including income tax, workmen's compensation, and industrial protective legislation. In Europe, school lunches had long been part of traditional state-sponsored programs for the poor. Beginning in the late eighteenth century, for example, local governments in Germany and France provided food as well as textbooks and clothing to needy children. Other nations adopted similar measures, and by the end of the nineteenth century, most European states fed children either in schools or in poor-houses. After the 1898 Boer War, British policy makers became alarmed at the poor health of military recruits. As a result, the 1905 Provision of Meals Act in England became a model of state-sponsored child welfare. This act authorized local educational authorities to use public funds for school lunches. Under the

Provision of Meals Act, an estimated 100,000 children received hot noontime meals. Lunchroom equipment became a regular part of equipment expenditures, and "restaurants" became permanent features of English schools. Other European countries enacted similar provisions shifting school lunches from the realm of charity to state-supported public welfare.[109]

In the United States, children's school meals, like other social welfare programs, developed as a combination of private and public initiatives. While until the 1930s, the labor, food, and equipment in most American school lunchrooms was supplied by local charities or volunteer groups, most of the expertise in nutrition and meal planning was nurtured by government-sponsored research and training. Indeed, dating from Wilbur Atwater's tenure as Director of Experiment Stations, the USDA became not only one of the biggest federal agencies, but also home to large numbers of professional women working in nutrition research and home economics. Atwater had long insisted that the state had an interest not only in agricultural productivity but in human productivity as well. His efforts to expand the Department of Agriculture's work in nutrition were eagerly taken up by women who found in government service a professional home denied them in academic circles and private industry. Indeed, during the Progressive Era, women developed what one historian has called a "female dominion" in government agencies like the Children's Bureau and the Women's Bureau, both parts of the Department of Labor. Here women with professional skills and training created an institutional base through which they could shape public policy, particularly directed at the welfare of women and children. In a similar vein, women became prominent in research and policy in the Office of Home Economics, created in 1915 as a result of the Smith-Lever Act establishing the Agricultural Extension Service.[110] In 1924, the Office became the Bureau of Home Economics.[111]

While the Women's and Children's Bureaus attracted women trained in social policy, the Bureau of Home Economics drew women interested as much in scientific research as in welfare per se. Like Ellen Richards, however, women rarely found opportunities to pursue research in chemistry or biology. Instead, women drawn to these disciplines often ended up in home economics. Indeed, home economists as a profession owed much to government support. While a few private universities, notably, Columbia Teachers' College and Stanford, opened home economics departments during the early twentieth century, the profession's base lay in the public land grant colleges. The expansion of the Department of Agriculture proved particularly significant for women who were interested in scientific research but who continued to be excluded from academic careers. By the eve of World War I the Department of Agriculture stood as the nation's largest employer of women scientists—almost all in the Office of Home Economics.[112]

Beginning in the World War I period, the Department of Agriculture dramatically expanded its research and educational programs. One historian has characterized the USDA as "the most dynamic portion of the national state in the early twentieth century." The department became, by World War I, "a reservoir of expertise and administrative capability that put it in a position to harvest the fruits of the farmers' discontents, as well as to respond to new middle-class concerns."[113] Ideas about expertise, efficiency, and scientific knowledge permeated agricultural policies just as they influenced the industrial and social arenas. While American agriculture was still numerically dominated by small family farms and tenant or sharecrop arrangements, large-scale farm production held the promise of increased productivity for the growing urban, consumer market. The push to increase farm output led, for example, to research on things like more productive seed strains, hardier livestock, and the development of chemical fertilizers.[114] At the same time, of course, rural Americans remained among the poorest of the nation's citizens. Thus, while agricultural research concentrated on improving productivity, home economists and agricultural extension agents concentrated on teaching scientific methods—including nutrition—to farmers and their wives. The 1914 Smith-Lever Act and the 1917 Smith-Hughes Act funding vocational education proved particularly important for home economists. Their discipline now had federal support as one of the major areas of vocational education for women.[115] According to one historian, the "significant linkage of agriculture, science and government" contributed to a dramatic increase in the number of USDA employees. Between 1909 and 1917 the Department of Agriculture grew from 11,279 employees to 20,269, becoming the third largest branch of the federal government after the Departments of War and the Interior.[116] Indeed, the number of extension agents increased from 2,500 at the beginning of 1917 to 6,215 by the end of the war.[117] The USDA employed large numbers of women Agricultural Extension agents and teachers in the related land-grant colleges and as researchers and administrators working out of Washington, D.C.

World War I saw an expansion of government interest in food and nutrition. Food conservation programs galvanized home-front support for the war effort as campaigns for "wheatless" and "meatless" days brought nutrition science into ordinary kitchens and turned everyday eating into patriotic duty. Herbert Hoover's War Food Administration (WFA) publicized vitamins and calories and catapulted home economists into the public light as the architects of popular nutrition education programs. Hoover brought private industry food processors and distributors, as well as researchers and academics, into "close collaboration" with government agents in his leadership of the WFA.[118] In 1917, for example, Hoover appointed Columbia Teachers College professor Mary Swartz Rose as Deputy Director of Food Conservation. Rose, one of the most prominent home economists and nutrition researchers of her time, developed wartime menus stressing the "three pillars of home economics": conservation, efficiency, and food substitution.[119] Rose also worked closely with Hoover to oversee domestic food production and to coordinate post-war food relief efforts abroad. She was instrumental in introducing scientific recipes and balanced menus to military planners and pioneered in the development of what became known as army rations.[120]

Herbert Hoover's experience in World War I significantly influenced the development of food policy in the United States after the war. Coming from a Quaker background, Hoover was educated at Stanford University, site of one of the few academic programs in nutrition science. He majored in geology and spent much of his early working life as a mine inspector and technologist Australia and China. When World War I began, Hoover was living in London and was tapped by the United States Embassy to coordinate aid for Americans who were stranded there. This work directly led him to the Committee of Relief for Belgium, a group trying to get food to the starving people behind the German lines. As part of the relief effort, Hoover's group set up lunch programs for school children. The Belgium relief work drew considerable public attention and was his first foray into food aid; it would prove formative for both Hoover and the United States. When America entered the war, President Wilson appointed Hoover to be the nation's first U.S. Food Administrator. In that capacity Hoover oversaw food consumption and distribution efforts and pioneered in national conservation campaigns. As Secretary of Commerce in the Harding administration after the war, Hoover continued his work in agriculture and food policy.[121]

Wartime experience in large-scale military feeding operations provided the model for domestic food service industries as well. By the 1920s, hospitals, schools and even some factories were running cafeteria operations on a scale never imagined by Ellen Richards. The war opened the way to an expansion of the food processing industry in the United States and introduced new products like canned foods and breakfast cereal to wider markets than ever before. It was perhaps the war, more than any food advice offered by home economists, that began to alter the American diet. Just as women were trying new products and recipes at home, soldiers were introduced to new foods in the Army mess halls. As the food historian Harvey Levenstein observed, military service (and the rise in wages after the war) significantly altered working-class eating habits as, for example, army cooks served "spaghetti, food of our ally."[122]

By the 1920s a culture of nutrition had permeated public awareness, particularly regarding children's development. During the 1920s school systems throughout the country began to offer hot lunches. The programs varied considerably in structure and purpose and in nutritional content. While most school lunch programs during the 1920s depended on contributions of both money and labor from mothers' "hot lunch clubs" or parent-teacher fund-raisers, some school districts began to appropriate public funds to lunchroom operations. Some programs offered free meals to poor children, others charged for food. In many schools, girls' home economics classes prepared the meals, thus training the girls while at the same time providing nutrition education for other children. Most state Agricultural Extension Service Offices ran school lunch programs and developed nutrition education materials for home economics teachers.[123]

Home economists, like social workers and other professional women, struggled to build professional identities and establish the legitimacy of their field. The women who ran school lunch programs worked hard to instill their domain with professional standards and the latest scientific methods. Indeed, by the mid-1920s professionals claimed control over the majority of the nation's lunchrooms. According to a study by Bureau of Home Economics researcher Mabel Kitridge, half of all school lunch programs were operated by professional managers and another quarter were run by home economics teachers. In Kansas City, Missouri, for example, home economics classes prepared and served the lunches. In Buffalo, New York, the home economics teacher held night classes to train women to be "practical lunch-room managers." These semi-professional managers were supervised by dietitians paid by the city's board of education.[124] Home economists institutionalized their own professional status by instituting home economics curricula, which included nutrition education as well as practical cooking experience for junior high and high school girls.

During the 1920s, home economists actively publicized their nutrition message. Using the latest advertising techniques, including radio commercials, they distributed recipes, preached the virtue of vitamins, and published family meal plans. Even with these "new methods of psychological persuasion," the imprimatur of scientific expertise and the seal of government approval through the Bureau of Home Economics, nutrition advice met resistance. Study after study suggested that Americans were falling below adequate nutrition standards.[125] Indeed, the very repetition of dietary advice indicates the extent to which people resisted any change in their food habits.

In the case of children's meals, home economists often found themselves at odds with other women in the community, notably teachers and mothers. Nutrition professionals were notoriously skeptical about lunchrooms that were run by volunteers not trained in the science of food content and preparation. "The average teacher," noted the *Journal of Home Economics*, "does not know enough about food preparation" to serve adequate meals. The professionals trusted mothers even less than teachers to understand the principles of nutrition. Mothers, they feared, would turn lunch preparation into "cooking contests" and ignore "food values." Worse, untrained women would give children "bad foods" like coffee, candy, "frankforts," potato chips, pickles, or olives.[126] Volunteer lunches, one *Journal of Home Economics* reporter concluded, "did not fulfill the real purpose of a school lunch, which is to provide the proper kind of food for children."[127]

Providing the proper kind of food for children promised to enhance the health of the entire nation. By the end of the 1920s, a wide range of children's welfare advocates adopted the gospel of nutrition. In 1926, for example, Mabel Kitridge, concluding a study of school lunch programs, declared that "a spirit of service and real democracy is developed."[128] Recognizing that meals represented more than the opportunity to ingest nutrients, home economics translated lunch into an opportunity for civic and moral lessons as well. A hot lunch, the *Journal of Home Economics* assured its readers, would allow "both students and teachers [to] enjoy a quiet social lunch hour during which many lessons in food selection and good habits may be incidentally taught."[129] Mary Swartz Rose emphasized the two pillars of school lunch programs: "first, the knowledge of how to build a good body through daily food, and second of how to care for the machine built and maintained at so great a cost to the end that it may have the greatest usefulness for the human spirit it carries."[130] From the start, experts as well as the public were convinced that school lunch programs offered tremendous benefits not only to individual children but to the nation at large. Despite an emerging agreement about the value of nutrition, however, food reformers continued to struggle with the public over what exactly should be served at lunch—and who should pay for children's meals.

CHAPTER 2

Welfare for Farmers and Children

At the end of the 1920s nutrition reformers and home economists were poised to shape a national food and nutrition policy that would address hunger and poverty and at the same time promote modern, healthy diets for all Americans. The economic depression of the 1930s and the New Deal's vastly expanded federal role in relief, recovery, and social welfare opened opportunities for nutrition reformers, farmers, and social welfare advocates to promote their varied agendas. During the next decade and a half, to a remarkable degree, the food reformers succeeded in their efforts to popularize ideas about vitamins, calories, and nutrients. By the end of World War II, the American public regularly looked for vitamins in their foods, and housewives—at least those who read popular magazines and newspaper food columns—understood the mechanics of a balanced meal. What is more, in 1946, Congress created a National School Lunch Program that, at least in theory, offered free meals to poor children and subsidized healthy lunches to all American children. Yet while the science of nutrition provided a theory—not to mention a menu—for healthy eating, a national food and nutrition policy required political savvy and an entirely new set of allies.

In fact, the National School Lunch Program created in 1946 bore only slight resemblance to the goals of nutrition scientists and home economists. The program was, in its goals, structure, and administration, more a subsidy for agriculture than a nutrition program for children. Indeed, the political will to forge a national school lunch program came not from the New Deal social welfare coalition but rather from the Department of Agriculture and a group of southern Democratic legislators who generally opposed federal social programs. While women in the Bureau of Home Economics as well as nutritionists and children's welfare advocates insisted that government-subsidized meals adhere to scientific nutrition standards, the gendered structure of Department of Agriculture policy making meant that their influence on the program would be relatively limited. Within the Department of Agriculture, home economists took a back seat to agricultural economists when it came to developing relationships with legislators and formulating policy. In the end, nutrition science provided a convenient and appealing justification for a school lunch program that was designed primarily as an outlet for surplus food. Nutrition

reformers—the women who had pioneered home economics food research—got what they wanted, a national school lunch program. But the
school lunch program crafted in the political arena did not look like the
scientific meal program imagined by Ellen Richards and her followers. In
the arena of congressional politics, nutrition reformers were forced to
compromise on the content of school lunches and to entirely give up any
sustained public support for nutrition education in the schools. What is
more, the women home economists who pioneered in child nutrition also
ceded control over the federal administrative apparatus of the school
lunch program to agricultural economists, usually men, who formed a
key part of the large Department of Agriculture bureaucracy devoted to
surplus commodity disposal and distribution. In return, however, the nutrition reformers encoded into law the potential for a universal child nutrition program along with the principle of free lunches for children unable
to pay for subsidized school meals.

During the 1930s, President Roosevelt's New Deal catapulted the federal government into the business of social welfare in unprecedented
ways. The twin crises of industrial unemployment and plummeting farm
prices made food a central element in local as well as federal relief and
recovery efforts. Fears of spreading malnutrition among the urban poor,
particularly young children, raised calls for direct food relief and reinforced the importance of nutrition education. As the depression deepened,
however, another relief front began to open up. With agricultural prices
at record low levels, farmers too began to demand relief from the government. In a happy convergence in an otherwise unhappy era, agricultural
policy makers found a way to protect farm prices and send food to American children at the same time.[1] Indeed, the school lunch program that
emerged during the depression was shaped by a market-based model of
surplus commodity disposal even more than on theories of nutrition or
plans for children's welfare. Still, for nutrition reformers, the opportunities were clear. As the government began to buy surplus food and send it
to schools, the women and men who had long advocated for nutrition
science found new legitimacy and an institutional base from which to
promote public welfare through scientific eating.

School Lunches for Hungry Children

Hunger and malnutrition reappeared during the economic depression of
the 1930s as major threats to the nation's well-being. While no one knew
the actual extent of malnutrition—whether among adults or among children—reports from almost every state suggested that hunger was on
the rise.[2] Bread lines in the nation's cities and images of homeless farm

families whose land mortgages had been foreclosed by the banks starkly suggested the extent of the Depression's reach. Teachers were worried about hungry children in their classrooms, and doctors documented the resurgence of nutrition-related diseases including anemia, dental cavities, and rickets. In October 1932, for example, a group of New York physicians warned of a serious problem in the city's schools. Fearing the winter would be "one of the gravest facing the community," the doctors estimated that at least 20 percent of school-aged children were malnourished. Dr. Charles Boldurn, director of New York City's Bureau of Health, warned that the effects of poor nutrition on children would soon result in "reduced resistance to infectious diseases."[3] Researchers in Texas similarly estimated that 20 percent of the state's children were anemic. A South Carolina study discovered dangerously low hemoglobin levels among poor children, and in Louisiana, 13 percent of the state's white children and a quarter of the black children were found to be malnourished. Outside the South, conditions were no better. One study estimated that 85 percent of Vermont's children suffered from rickets and poor teeth.[4] In Chicago 72 percent of schoolchildren, according to one study, "failed to meet a standard lower than that recommended by the National Research Council." Detroit reported 20 percent malnutrition rates among schoolchildren, and a study in Ohio estimated that 31 percent of the state's children were underweight.[5] The litany of poor health continued as the Depression deepened.[6] In 1936, Columbia Teachers College nutritionists reported that American children weighed significantly less than they had five years earlier.[7]

School lunches appeared as a logical form of relief for the Depression's generation of hungry children. Physicians and home economists alike had long documented the debilitating effects of hunger, both physical and mental, on children. Children who came to school without proper meals, nutritionists warned, would be unable to take advantage of their education, nor would they fully develop into strong and responsible citizens. "A good meal at school," nutritionists and child welfare advocates agreed, "could do much to help correct these conditions."[8] Teachers and parents testified to the marked improvement in children's health and school performance resulting from a good hot lunch. Rose Widtsoe, head of the University of Utah's home economics department, articulated a common view when she lauded her own state's school lunch effort. "The teachers," Widtsoe said, "cannot find words to express the change in pupils since they are being properly fed. Their application has improved; their deportment, their general health, and their interest in everything has increased." Social workers similarly observed a "sudden desire of children to attend school," and attributed this to the fact that this might be their only opportunity for a "proper and well-cooked" meal.[9]

Sparked by the magnitude of local unemployment and hunger, ad hoc school lunchrooms sprang up throughout the country. Parent Teacher Associations (PTAs) organized free meal programs for poor children, and teachers brought in food for their students. In 1932, for example, New York City teachers raised over $260,000 for a free lunch program. George H. Chatfield, Director of School Attendance for the Board of Education, set up eighty lunch centers and fed 45,000 children during the next year. Serving cheese and lettuce or chopped egg sandwiches along with creamed onion soup, canned peaches, and chopped apples, the teachers' lunch program offered nutrition to children of the city's unemployed. Soon the lunch program also became a source of emergency employment as state funds were used to hire lunchroom workers. Chicago's Board of Education similarly established a lunch program in 1934. Using donated food and volunteer labor, the city operated lunchrooms in fifty-five high schools and 126 elementary schools, about half of all the schools in Chicago.[10] Other cities followed suit, as did rural communities. In Kentucky, for example, a volunteer school lunch program aimed to offer "every child in school" a nutritious and appetizing meal. Kentucky officials, however, did not abandon earlier nutritionists' goals linking food habits to socialization and Americanization. Their lunch program aimed to develop "good food habits . . . good table manners . . . [and] habits of cleanliness."[11]

While states had long supported public education and regularly appropriated money for buildings, teachers' salaries, and textbooks, lunch had always been considered a family responsibility. Before the 1930s, school boards and municipal governments occasionally appropriated local taxes for cafeteria operations or to hire home economics teachers, but most lunch programs depended on donated food and women's volunteer labor. This all began to change when increasing numbers of children began coming to school hungry. Local charities and volunteer efforts were generally overwhelmed by the numbers of unemployed, homeless, and hungry families. Neither school administrators nor volunteer housewives could cope with the numbers of children now seeking hot meals at school. By the mid-1930s the states began to enact laws allowing local boards of education to use tax money to pay for children's milk and school meals. In 1934, for example, the New York legislature agreed to use $100,000 of its relief funds for free lunches.[12] California approved a special district tax for free lunches, Washington put state money into a special milk program for poor children, and the Louisiana legislature appropriated a million dollars for school lunches.[13] These local appropriations were strictly temporary, though, and could not meet the increasing demand to feed hungry children.

Figure 2.1. School lunch programs offered etiquette and hygiene along with hot meals. Penasco, New Mexico, pupils "must wash their hands before eating hot lunch in school." Photo by John Collier. Farm Security Administration, Library of Congress.

State appropriations for education and welfare were nothing new. What was new during the 1930s was the expanding role of federal relief agencies. New Deal programs, for the first time, brought Washington-based funds and federal officials into the nation's schools. By the end of the 1930s, "a clearly organized social welfare bureaucracy" existed within the federal government.[14] The New Deal also deepened the federal government's role in agriculture and farm policy. One scholar has described the period of the New Deal as the development of an "agricultural welfare state."[15] The 1933 Agricultural Adjustment Act along with the 1935 Social Security Act were the core of New Deal welfare. Indeed, according to some theorists, New Deal agricultural policy proved more lasting and successful than industrial recovery or social relief, largely because of the strength of agricultural interests both in Congress and within the USDA. The core New Deal welfare programs, however, reflected fundamental inequalities in American society. Social Security, for example, excluded whole categories of work—notably, domestic service and agriculture work, occupations that employed large numbers of women and African Americans. The administration of New Deal relief also rested on local officials who reproduced regional and racial attitudes that excluded blacks in particular, and other minorities as well.[16]

The expansion of federal welfare functions during the Depression encompassed children's nutrition as well as public health and food aid. Indeed, nutritionists' long-standing concern with the diets of poor people and their work on menus for low-income families provided a scientific rationale for food relief in the deepening economic crisis. As the USDA's M. L. Wilson put it, "There is a widespread acceptance of the idea that low-income people should be well fed as a health measure—at public expense if necessary."[17] Beginning in the early 1930s, a number of federal agencies began to distribute food to needy families and also to school lunch programs. In 1932 one of the New Deal's central relief agencies, the Reconstruction Finance Corporation began to lend money to communities that wanted to start school meal programs. These funds went to states and school districts to pay for cafeteria space or equipment. Within a few years, almost every state had signed on to receive those funds.[18] In 1935, the Works Progress Administration (WPA) also got into the school lunch business. While normally favoring (white) men in its emergency work programs, the WPA instituted a sizable school lunch operation that employed women as bakers, cooks, and clerks in school cafeterias. Ultimately, the WPA employed over 5,000 women in its lunchroom projects.[19] The WPA also ran gardening and canning projects that produced food for school lunches.[20] The agency employed men in state food warehouses as well as in shipping and storing donated food for children's meals.[21] Other federal agencies also contributed to school lunch projects. The National Youth Administration, for example, employed about 16,000 young people in school lunchrooms. Federal regulations prohibited the youth from handling food, but they were allowed to clean and maintain the facilities and take care of the lunchroom equipment.[22]

Communities throughout the country happily accepted federal funds to supplement local efforts to feed poor children. In Jefferson City, Missouri, for example, black and white children in the public schools as well as children in the city's Catholic schools ate lunch in WPA-sponsored cafeterias. Federal relief funds paid for labor, while the state relief commission supplemented food costs and the local Community Chest provided funds for milk. In addition, the local newspaper sponsored a fund-raising campaign that netted about $1,500 for food in 1935.[23] In Colorado, where surveys had revealed that 50 percent of the children were malnourished, the WPA fed hot lunches to over 20,000 students and employed 400 "needy women" as well. Washington, D.C.'s WPA program served 8,000 children. There, 150 women prepared sandwiches, fruit, and milk packages in a central kitchen. The packages were then delivered to schools throughout the city. Children from the "foreign district" of Springfield,

Figure 2.2. Schools took advantage of surplus food for children's meals. School lunch program, Federal Works Project, location unknown, 1939. Kansas State Historical Society.

Massachusetts, enjoyed hot meals at school, and in Mississippi both black and white schools operated lunchrooms.[24] By the early 1940s, WPA "school lunch units" operated in 35,000 schools throughout the country and served an estimated two million children.[25] Using menus and recipes along with guides for food storage and preparation developed by women at the Bureau of Home Economics, relief-based lunchrooms became, in effect, test kitchens for a national school lunch program.

Eating the Surplus

A key element in the new school lunch programs was the availability of federally donated food. At the start of the New Deal, a battle waged within the Roosevelt administration and the Department of Agriculture over how best to address the nation's agricultural problems. On the one hand, a group of liberal policy makers sought deep social transformation of the agricultural sector, including a redistribution of land that would allow tenant farmers to own the land they worked. By the mid-1930s, this vision was soundly eclipsed by a group of policy makers led by

M. L. Wilson and Chester Davis, who believed that farmers' problems could best be solved by maintaining price levels and market strength.[26] For Wilson and his cohort of agricultural economists, a modern, healthy farm sector required government assistance in the form of commodity supports and the technical assistance necessary to ensure increased productivity (e.g., mechanization, fertilizer, and new seed strains). This approach favored landowners over tenant farmers and sharecroppers and pointed toward large-scale operations that would, in the years after World War II, come to characterize the rise of industrial agri-business and the decline of the family farm. Most notably during the 1930s, however, these policy makers promoted the formation of a Surplus Marketing Administration (SMA), which ensured commodity price levels by allowing the government to purchase surplus products.[27] While at first the SMA embarrassed itself and the Roosevelt administration by destroying crops while hungry people waited in bread lines for food, the agency ultimately hit upon a brilliant strategy: send the surplus food to school lunchrooms.[28]

The surplus marketing strategy dramatically changed American food relief policy. Under Section 32 of the Agricultural Adjustment Act, Congress authorized the Department of Agriculture to purchase surplus farm commodities and donate these goods to schools and welfare offices in every state. This effectively transformed free commodity distribution into agricultural price support rather than food aid, and for the first time, national welfare policy became intimately linked to agriculture. Under Section 32 the Secretary of Agriculture now had considerable authority to both intervene in commodity markets and influence children's nutrition, as schools became a key element in an emerging market-based strategy of recovery for the agriculture sector.[29] Agricultural economist Milo Perkins and his colleague, H. R. Tolley, two architects of the surplus marketing strategy, declared the plan would "lick" the twin problems of hunger in the cities and low prices on the farm. School lunches, they believed, would "be of benefit to both farmers and to consumers."[30]

The surplus marketing strategy tied national food and welfare policy together in unprecedented ways. State welfare offices distributed federally donated commodities directly to families as part of local relief efforts. Surplus food also formed the basis for a short-lived Food Stamp Program under which families on welfare could purchase food stamps and use them to buy surplus food at lower than market prices.[31] The most important and lasting part of the surplus disposal program was the distribution of food to school lunch programs. Noting that the "wisest" strategy was to find outlets for surplus food "as soon as possible," SMA administrator Marvin Jones eagerly recruited schools into the new program. Farmers and children would both benefit, Jones said because "everyone liked to see children well fed."[32]

TABLE 2.1.
Children Participating in the Surplus Marketing Administration School Lunch Program, Public and Parochial Schools, by Region, 1941

Region*	Children participating	School enrollment	Percentage participating
West	585, 665	2,547,538	23.0
Midwest	881, 497	7,231,682	12.2
East	891,881	7,973,709	11.2
South	2,356,208	9,381,634	24.1
Total**	4,663,113	26,821,128	17.4

Source: H. M. Southworth and M. I. Klayman, The School Lunch Program and Agricultural Surplus Disposal, United States Department of Agriculture, Miscellaneous Publication No. 467, October 1941 (Washington, D.C.: United States Government Printing Office, 1941), 28.

* West: Arizona, California, Colorado, Idaho, Montana, Nevada, New Mexico, Oregon, Utah, Washington, Wyoming. Midwest: Illinois, Indiana, Iowa, Kansas, Michigan, Minnesota, Missouri, Nebraska, North Dakota, Ohio, South Dakota, Wisconsin. East: Connecticut, Delaware, District of Columbia, Maine, Maryland, Massachusetts, New Hampshire, New Jersey, New York, Pennsylvania, Rhode Island, Vermont, West Virginia. South: Alabama, Arkansas, Florida, Georgia, Kentucky, Louisiana, Mississippi, North Carolina, Oklahoma, South Carolina, Tennessee, Texas, Virginia

** Continental U.S. (In Puerto Rico, 16% of children participated; in the Virgin Islands, 52.7% participated.)

The availability of federally donated food sparked an immediate expansion in the number of schools offering lunchtime meals. Education administrators throughout the country signed on to receive surplus commodities for their lunchrooms. In the first year alone, an estimated 60,000 schools in twenty states received donated food.[33] In 1936 the Department of Agriculture boasted that it was feeding almost 350,000 children each day. The number of schools participating in the federal program increased each year, and by 1942, the Department of Agriculture estimated that 78,851 schools and over five million children were involved in the program (see Table 2.1). These figures represented about one-third of the total number of elementary and secondary schools in the country and about one-quarter of all schoolchildren.[34]

The USDA economists believed that the ability to send surplus commodities to schools exerted a positive effect "throughout the market." Overall, they claimed, there was a rise in prices and an increase in the quantity of food available to consumers. In 1942 the SMA distributed 4.5 million pounds of food valued at over $21 million.[35] The program, agriculture officials concluded, "added increase in farmers' incomes over and above the value of the net quantity removed from the market." What was more, school lunches, at least in theory, created new demand for farm goods by "introducing foods to children that they might never have tasted." Department of Agriculture officials declared that "no other method of surplus disposal brings farmers so large an increase in income per dollar of government subsidy as does the school lunch program."[36] Even critical assessments that questioned the program's actual impact on farm prices admitted its significance as a social measure. The school lunch program, noted agriculture historian Don Paarlberg, "gave the lobbyist, the congressman, and the secretary of agriculture a chance to improve relations with farm constituents." The program's combination of "myth, self-interest, and goodwill was the process by which Johnny got his hamburger, his applesauce, his prunes, and his peanut butter."[37]

The problem was, of course, that Johnny as often got surplus apricots or olives as hamburger and applesauce for lunch. Tying school menus to agricultural surplus significantly shaped school menus and the nutritional content of children's diets. Department of Agriculture officials appealed to Wilbur Atwater's food substitution theory, to justify an admittedly unbalanced and inconsistent supply of surplus commodities. As one historian put it, "The USDA was trying to create the very problem that commodity distribution was originally supposed to ease—consumers' ability to afford a nutritionally adequate diet."[38] Bureau of Home Economics school lunch recipes, for example, advised cafeteria operators that eggs could replace meat "as a protein in the lunch" at least a few days a month. School administrators knew, however, that abstract nutrition theory would not work in the lunchroom.[39] Stories of "dumping" food in school cafeterias took on the status of urban legends. Sidney B. Hall, a professor of school administration at George Washington University, complained that USDA supervisors sent "loads of onions or grapefruit or whatnot to communities, when, as a matter of fact, the people there did not need those commodities."[40] Similarly, New York City Board of Education member George Chatfield reported that the USDA shipped huge quantities of apples to his city schools. "Do you know where they went?" Chatfield asked. "They came so frequently in the lunch program that they went in the toilets. The kids didn't eat them."[41] Montgomery County, Maryland, cafeteria supervisor Gertrude Bowie reported that the children in her district used the surplus grapefruit "to play catch with" because they were unfamiliar with the fruit and refused to eat it. Other schools reported receiving so many eggs that they had to serve hard-boiled eggs for days at a time. The result of such a menu, complained one cafeteria manager, "may be that the children will revolt at the very sight of eggs."[42]

While schools were happy to receive free food, under the surplus commodity program lunchroom administrators never knew from month to month, or from one year to the next, which foods would be available. Just ten commodities, for example, made up 90 percent of the food sent to schools. While milk and dairy products were generally available, as one report put it, "what foods are provided at any time and how much of them depend on the current purchase programs of the Surplus Marketing Administration, and these programs are planned primarily to meet farmers' needs," not the needs of children's nutrition.[43] This made it difficult to plan meals and even more difficult to plan budgets, because cafeteria administrators had no way to know how much extra money they would need to supplement the donated commodities. Schools that participated in the program were required to accept whatever foods were distributed and thus had to craft meals often out of foods most children refused to eat. Indeed, the Bureau of Home Economics, in recognition of this dilemma, produced scores of recipes and menus based on items like almonds and apricots, in an effort to help cafeteria managers use the surplus foods. Even so, a 1940 study of nutrition in school lunches found the meals "might well have been more ample in some nutrients."[44] Uncertain supplies and a reliance on surplus commodities from the start seriously undercut the claim that school lunch programs could provide children with nutritious meals.

The Institutionalization of School Lunch

While the benefit of school meals either to children's nutrition or to farm prices may have been questionable, federal food and federal dollars had a powerful impact on schools and communities. By the end of the 1930s, local communities and schools had become very attached to—indeed, dependent on—federal resources, whether from the Department of Agriculture or from relief agencies. Federally funded nutritionists, paid through the maternal and child provisions of the Social Security Act, appeared in almost every state. State nutritionists, administered by the Children's Bureau, acted as liaisons with local education and welfare agencies and supervised school lunch programs. By the end of the decade, almost every state plus the District of Columbia and Puerto Rico supplemented federal funds and included school nutritionists in their regular budget appropriations. School lunches, according to one report, had come to be widely viewed as "a corollary of compulsory education."[45]

Nurtured by government resources, an extensive network of federal, state, and local officials depended on school lunch programs for their professional identities and careers. Secretary of Agriculture Henry A. Wallace oversaw a growing school lunch bureaucracy located in the Bureau of Agricultural Research, the SMA, and the Bureau of Home Economics. Indeed, a new profession known as school food service was quietly emerging, nurtured largely by the expanding role of school lunch programs within the Department of Agriculture. While women had traditionally dominated school lunch programs, school food service attracted increasing numbers of men interested in agricultural economics and business administration. Thus, while the SMA oversaw commodity supplies and prices, women in the Bureau of Home Economics developed recipes, menu plans, and administrative guidelines for school cafeterias.[46]

The school lunch network stretched beyond Washington. By 1940, every state used federal funds to employ nutritionists and administrators to oversee local school lunch programs. State school lunch administrators worked with civic groups, usually PTAs, teachers, or community welfare organizations, to run the meal programs. According to one estimate, as many as 64,000 federal employees worked outside Washington in school lunch–related positions.[47] Beyond the federal and state level, of course, every community and school system that participated in the program developed its own staff and volunteer structure. By the time the United States entered World War II, a nationwide network of professionals identified with school food service and were financially dependent on public resources for their livelihood and the livelihood of their lunchrooms. Local school boards, state education administrators, county commissioners, and town managers as well as parents, welfare workers, and farmers began to see the school lunch program as a natural part of the public school system. At the same time, Department of Agriculture officials increasingly saw school lunch programs as a vital part of their own policy strategy—and their professional careers. As war preparations invigorated the idea of universal health and modern diets, nutritionists came into prominence as professionals who could guide the nation's health. Secretary of Agriculture Claude R. Wilkard told the American Dietetic Association in 1943, "You nutritionists and dietitians are at last coming into your own." The war, he said, "drives home the fact that it pays to have people properly fed."[48]

In early 1940, the Department of Agriculture organized its network of school lunch advocates into a Coordinating Committee on School Lunches. Headed by New York City School Board chairman, George R. Chatfield, the committee sought not only to maintain federal school lunch subsidies but to expand the public role in children's nutrition. Declaring that school lunches "are an increasingly important factor in our national life," this committee saw nutrition as a critical part of children's welfare and pushed for an extension of the New Deal safety net to cover children's health and nutrition. The federal government, the group's mission statement announced, "has a stake in the future of all the children."[49] The Coordinating Committee on School Lunches became a public-private collaboration of groups ranging from nutritionists and child welfare advocates to food industry representatives and farm lobbyists. Including representatives from government agencies and schools as well the PTA, the Red Cross, and the United States Public Health Service, this group became the center of policy discussions about nutrition, children's health, and federal food policy.[50] "Because the country is at war," the committee announced, "school lunches are now more important than ever. Many children can no longer depend on the home to supply a nourishing noon meal. Many mothers who formerly made a full-time job of taking care of their families are now spending their days in war industries, leaving no one to serve a meal to the children who come home from school at noon."[51] The farm lobby, too, advocated for school lunches as an essential element in the national defense. National Farmers Union spokesman M. F. Dickinson said that "the right of every American school child to at least one square meal a day regardless of the economic status of his parents surely requires no defense in logic or justice at this time when our Nation is fighting for the survival of democracy."[52]

Popular support for school lunches emboldened Congress to maintain funding for children's meals even as agricultural surpluses began to disappear. During the summer of 1942, as Congress considered its wartime budget, there was some threat that school lunch funds would be cut. Georgia senator Richard Russell, whose interests were solidly with the USDA, immediately told President Roosevelt that the school lunch program "is more important than ever before." Russell reminded the president that "many women are now employed in defense work and do not have time to prepare meals at home." He chided the President, saying that "at a time when England is enlarging her school lunch program I do not see how we in this country could justify curtailment here." The president promised Russell he would support "the school lunch plan" and told him, "I share wholeheartedly your sympathy with the needs for our school children."[53]

A sign of how effective the school lunch coalition would be came in 1943 when Congress disbanded the New Deal's central relief efforts, including the WPA. As relief funds dried up, schools faced the elimination of federal support they had come to depend on for their lunchrooms. While schools could still receive surplus food, money would no longer be available to pay for cooking, transportation, or administration. This meant that school districts that had eagerly signed on for federal support during the late 1930s would have to raise state and local funds to keep their meal programs afloat. The fact was, however, that local school districts, whether in the rural South or in northern cities, found lunchroom funds difficult to come by. Most school lunch programs regularly supplemented public and private contributions by charging children a minimal fee for meals. The withdrawal of federal resources meant that local districts would have to take up the slack, and many were unwilling to do so. Some had grown used to federal contributions; others were too poor to raise much more local funds.

The Coordinating Committee on School Lunches immediately launched a nationwide effort to "save the school lunch program." Chatfield galvanized an all-star lineup of professionals, liberals, civic and religions organizations, and Department of Agriculture representatives, particularly from the Bureau of Home Economics, to build public support for a national school lunch program and to lobby Congress to continue funding children's meals.[54] Drawing on themes of wartime unity and national defense, the well-known journalist Dorothy Thompson went on air telling American housewives to urge their schools to sign on to the federal lunch program. This, she argued, would be a far better post-war plan "than a soldier monument to honor the young men who won't come back."[55] If the federal lunch subsidy disappeared, Thompson warned, the public costs in malnutrition and poor health would be very high.[56] Declaring that school lunches "are an increasingly important factor in our national life," Chatfield's committee advocated for a federal child nutrition program. The federal government, the group's mission statement announced, "has a stake in the future of all the children."[57] In a well-organized and highly orchestrated campaign, the Coordinating Committee urged school administrators, local officials, nutritionists, teachers, and parents from every state to cable their congressional representatives. One congressman commented that he had never seen a measure that had such support "from people from one end of this country to the other, regardless of race, creed, or color." Another said, "In my twenty years in Congress, I have never seen such an intensive campaign."[58] Senators and congressmen reported receiving thousands of letters from teachers, city officials, civic clubs, social workers, ministers, and schoolchildren themselves.[59]

The school lunch coalition proved remarkably effective. Unwilling to appear unsympathetic to children's health, particularly as the nation was mobilizing for war, Congress quickly voted to continue appropriations for school lunches. Indeed, by an overwhelming margin, Congress actually increased the appropriation, voting $50 million per year for three years. There was considerable tension, however, about the administration of these funds, because in 1943 President Roosevelt shifted responsibility for most food programs into the new War Food Administration (WFA).[60]

While the Department of Agriculture continued to purchase surplus commodities and distribute them to schools, the WFA took over direct administration of school lunchrooms under a new "Community School Lunch
Program." For the duration of the war the WFA would oversee a dramatic
expansion of school lunch programs throughout the country. At the end
of the war, however, the USDA would reclaim authority over children's
meals.[61] By that time, the Community School Lunch Program would be
operating in an estimated 60,000 schools and providing subsidized meals
for eight million children. Another million children would be participating in the Agriculture Department's "penny milk" program.[62]

When the United States entered World War II, food policy was shaped by a
coalition of interests centered in the Department of Agriculture, including
home economists and agricultural economists as well as farm lobbyists
and food industry representatives but extending outward to child welfare
advocates, school teachers and administrators, physicians, parents, wom-
en's organizations, and civic groups. School lunch programs, while administered out of the Department of Agriculture, were still claimed by
home economists and nutritionists as their special purview. Like New
Deal reformers generally, food reformers believed the war would open
important opportunities to extend public welfare programs and expand
public awareness about scientific diets, nutrition, and health. While food
reformers may have had reservations about the extent to which school
lunch programs were being shaped by agriculture policy and surplus food
supplies, they nonetheless welcomed both the expansion of federal resources and the opportunity to legitimize healthy eating.

CHAPTER 3

Nutrition Standards and Standard Diets

As the United States mobilized for war, nutrition reformers and school lunch advocates seized new opportunities to promote their agendas. Whether on the battlefield or on the homefront, however, decisions about food policy were informed by the twin interests of nutrition and agriculture. The country was, M. L. Wilson observed, "at the beginning of an epoch where it becomes the duty of society, as a matter of public health and welfare, to see to it that all its members get a diet that squares with scientific standards."[1] That duty rapidly transformed into a matter of national defense. Federal food policy during World War II addressed military requirements as well as home-front supplies. As the government became more heavily involved in food production and distribution, school lunch programs expanded around the country. A key element in state oversight was the development of standardized administrative procedures as well as national nutrition standards and dietary recommendations. While these standards promised equity in the distribution of federal resources, in practice, federal officials exerted only weak oversight over local program administration. Few in Washington had the political will to seriously challenge the deep-set racial and regional inequities that divided American society.

World War II presented food reformers with an unprecedented opportunity to influence American eating habits and introduce nutrition science to new audiences. Like professionals in other fields, nutritionists eagerly enlisted in domestic defense campaigns and civilian advisory committees. Two problems initially confronted wartime food experts. First, they needed to consolidate recent nutrition research and translate it into terms that would assist the army in formulating mass feeding plans for soldiers both at home and abroad. Second, they had to translate nutrition science into popular terms and foster new eating habits in the civilian population. Wartime planners saw institutions like the school lunch program as an opportunity to expand the public education and welfare functions of government not only during the war but into the post-war era as well.[2]

SCHOOL LUNCH STANDARDS

A decade of economic depression exacerbated the widespread fear that there would not be enough healthy men to defend the country. Memory of large numbers of World War I draftees found unfit for service stood as a vivid reminder of the importance of diet and nutrition for national defense. United States Surgeon General Thomas Parran warned Congress that "there is a very close correlation between the (draft) rejectees" and "the boys with the poorest diets."[3] New York City School Board head George Chatfield drew the connection starkly. "The loss of men for the Army," he said, is directly attributable to "lack of proper nutrition in early childhood."[4] Undernourished children, Chatfield noted, made for poor workers as well as poor soldiers. Those were the men, he warned, who became "the absentee from school and later, the absentee from essential war production, the drifter, the early incapacitated worker."[5] War production and home-front security depended on a healthy citizenry, ready to defend the country both at home and abroad. As Minnesota congressman August Andresen put it, feeding all children a balanced diet would "give them better character and better bodies and have the boys become better soldiers and sailors."[6] In this effort, school lunch programs played a critical role in developing a healthy generation of children— particularly boys—who would be able to defend the nation. In 1943, as a signal of the significance of children's nutrition for national health, not to mention in order to better coordinate national food supplies, the War Food Administration took over management of the federal school lunch programs. "If it is wise policy to see that each child is educated and trained for citizenship," declared Secretary of Agriculture Claude Wilkard, "it is also good policy to see that he can obtain the sort of diet that will make him strong and vigorous."[7]

The looming war crisis, as President Franklin Roosevelt observed, "made it evident that food and nutrition would be at least as important as metals and munitions" in the national preparations. In late 1941, to mobilize popular support for war measures, especially the inevitable restrictions on food and consumer goods, Roosevelt convened a White House National Nutrition Conference for Defense. Bringing together nutrition researchers as well as community and labor activists, state and local officials, school superintendents, farmers, and food processors, the conference provided a vehicle through which nutrition reformers and farm advocates could pool their efforts in developing a national food policy. The "newer knowledge of nutrition," the conference report insisted, should be used not only for the nation's armed forces but also for "the civilian population as a whole," particularly for women and children.[8] Surgeon General Thomas Parran warned that the poor nutrition of citizens "means a slowing down of industrial production, a danger to military strength, and a lowering of the morale of millions."[9] The conference recommended "vigorous and continuous" nutrition research as well as "translation" of nutrition recommendations "into terms of everyday foods and appetizing meals." In addition, the conference stressed using school lunches, along with food stamps and milk distribution, to "bring nourishing, adequate meals to those who could not otherwise afford them." At the same time, the report pointed out, this would "help distribute food surpluses at a fair return to the farmer."[10] The conference marshaled all of its expertise and authority to the development of a national wartime food policy based both on the science of nutrition and on continued government support for the agricultural sector.

Chief among the conference concerns, of course, was the health of army recruits. Food and nutrition in this context were essential elements not only to physical health but to the nation's "virility" and its ability to defend itself. When the Selective Service Commission began drafting young men for service, just as in World War I, alarming numbers of boys were found to be physically unfit. Lewis B. Hershey, head of the Draft Board, estimated that "probably one-third" of the men rejected for service suffered from "disabilities directly or indirectly connected with nutrition." This fact, Hershey warned, "should be disturbing to us as a people." Surgeon General Parran warned that "the great preponderance of boys who were rejected for the draft were found to be boys who in earlier school life had poor nutrition."[11] It was clear that these officials believed malnutrition to be a serious threat to the nation's strength on the battlefront as well as on the home front. America cannot be strong, Hershey starkly declared, "when one-half of her sons are substandard physically. America needs whole men not half men."[12] Estimating that two out of every five men called up for the draft were unfit for service, Hershey declared nutrition to be a national concern. Indeed, malnutrition threatened not only the quality of the nation's defense forces but the vigor, if not the virility, of democracy at home. According to Parran, the problem began well before the boys appeared before their draft boards. Most of the recruits who were rejected, he said, "had poor nutrition" as schoolchildren.[13] Both Parran and Hershey warned post-war planners that weak soldiers could not defend the nation abroad and weak citizens could not protect democracy at home. The specter of national weakness worried Congress as well. Richard F. Harless, Democratic congressman from Arizona, for example, warned that if one segment of the population "is weak either physically or mentally, it affects the whole of this Nation."[14] Another Democrat, Virginia's John Flannagan, said, "If we develop a strong, virile, intellectual race, consideration will have to be given to the development and training of the mind and body alike." Democracy, he warned, "is not the creature of intellectual weaklings any more than it is the creature of physical weaklings. It sprang from the loins of men of strong minds and bodies. And if it is to be preserved it will be preserved by the same kind of men."[15] Nutrition had clearly become a key element in maintaining a strong army abroad and a healthy citizenry at home. The link between food and democracy that would characterize cold war foreign policy took shape well before the end of the war.

Fears about the strength of the nation's "manpower" led, of course, to concerns about changing gender roles at home. During World War II, as in other wars, women took on traditionally male jobs both in the public realm and in the private sphere. Ever larger numbers of women, for example, took jobs outside the home in war industries and in other paid employment. By one estimate, almost half of all women were in the labor force by the war's end. What is more, increasing numbers of mothers worked outside the home: the percentage of married women in the work force rose from 14 percent in 1940 to 23 percent four years later.[16] In this case, changing gender roles fit well with the emerging concern about nutrition in the national defense. With more mothers in the work force, the case for a national school lunch program appeared even more compelling. George Chatfield's Coordinating Committee warned that mothers working in war industries could not be expected to be home at noon to prepare lunches for their children. Indeed, working mothers, Chatfield observed, did not have time in the morning to pack "well-planned lunches" for children.[17] With so many women in the work force, the Office of Civilian Defense declared that school lunches had a "new significance."[18] Work outside the home, combined with food shortages and rationing, left mothers hard-pressed to provide balanced lunches for their children. Frank P. Whalen, assistant superintendent of the New York City Schools, claimed that rationing had "thrown mothers off their stride." Women, he said, "just don't know where to go, and they pick one thing and another, and they put together a very badly balanced diet."[19] Universal child nutrition was perhaps even more important in wartime than it had been during the Depression. In the economic crisis, feeding children who were poor took precedence. In wartime, the nation needed to ensure the health and vigor of all its children. Predicting that women's wage work would become a permanent feature in the post-war years, United Auto Workers Union spokeswoman Anna Berenson told a congressional hearing on school lunches that "few wartime problems on the home-front have caused so much conflict and confusion as that of proper care and nutrition for the children of working mothers." A national school lunch program, she believed, now had to be a matter of national health policy.[20]

Americans seemed happy to concede lunch to the public sector. Unlike European cultures in which the midday meal held major family and social significance, American work habits and social structures emphasized evening dinners over less formal lunches. The argument that the state bore a major responsibility to maintain the health of its citizens—particularly its children—was particularly compelling during wartime. By this time, of course, the federal government already had considerable resources invested in school lunch programs all over the country. School lunch advocates both in and outside Washington mounted a steady call for more permanent funding for children's meals. In early 1940, veteran nutrition reformers in the Bureau of Home Economics, including Lucy Gillett, Hazel Kyrk, and Hazel Stiebeling, began talking with Children's Bureau officials about expanding the school lunch program as part of the campaign for "nutrition in the national defense."[21] Their influence was most dramatically evident in 1943 when Congress authorized continuing funds for school lunches and consolidated the various federal programs (including those operating under the now defunct WPA) into a Community School Lunch Program.[22] One of the most notable features of the Community School Lunch Program was the establishment of federal contracts governing school cafeteria operations.

The school lunch contracts codified expert nutrition advice and expanded the federal bureaucracy invested in school lunch programs. Women in the Bureau of Home Economics and the Children's Bureau had been critical in shaping New Deal child welfare policy. When it came to nutrition policy, however, the women vied for authority with male policy makers in the Department of Agriculture as well as in the War Department. The women were successful, however, in establishing national standards for child nutrition and for the school lunch programs that were now operating throughout the country. School lunch contracts established standards governing food preparation and service as well as cafeteria administration and record-keeping. The contracts also stipulated that every child in the community was to receive a "lunch of optimum nutritional value," and every child from a low-income family or a family on welfare was to receive a free meal.[23] The Department of Agriculture hired an entire staff of officials, both in Washington and in the states, to verify the nutrition content of meals, maintain records on the cost of lunches, monitor the number of children served—both those who paid and those who ate for free—and generally document lunchroom operations throughout the country. The significance of the contracts, however, rested less on actual lunchroom operations (in most cases, the contract provisions were only minimally enforced) than on the fact that the federal government, for the first time, asserted national standards for a school-related program.

While the school lunch contracts stipulated standards for lunchroom operations and children's nutrition, there were serious limitations on the use of federal resources. Federal funds, for example, could be used only to purchase food and to pay for professional nutritionists. Schools had to raise local resources if they wanted to expand existing kitchen facilities or to build new lunchrooms. This was a particular problem in urban schools, most of which had been built without lunchrooms. Pre–World

War II city planners by and large assumed that the mothers would prepare lunch at home for their school-aged children. While this was clearly
not the case in many working-class neighborhoods, urban schools nonetheless lacked kitchen facilities. Schools were also prohibited from using
federal resources to pay salaries for lunchroom labor. At the same time,
however, school lunch contracts required schools to maintain professional rather than voluntary staffs. This meant, in effect, that only
schools in areas with sufficient local resources could sign on to the
community school lunch program. While this provision was intended
both to ensure proper management and, not incidentally, to create a demand for professional dietitians, it precluded schools from using their
traditional (largely free) labor force of neighborhood volunteers and
PTA mothers.

Federal school lunch contracts firmly established professional authority
over school meals. Participating schools had to hire trained dietitians or
nutritionists to oversee lunchroom operations, and they were prohibited
from contracting with private restaurants or commercial vendors to provide food or services. While the women (and men) crafting these measures
believed they were establishing national professional standards of operation, as is often the case with good intentions, these provisions had far-
reaching and unanticipated consequences. Most states, for example, simply hired one nutritionist or dietitian to administer all of their school
lunch programs. This, in effect, meant that most schools operated with
little direct supervision, as one person tried to supervise dozens of programs often spread out over wide geographic areas. Similarly, the provision prohibiting schools from contracting with private operators was intended to ensure that school lunches adhered to scientific nutrition
standards and that the meals served were of high quality. But this provision had the unintended consequence of limiting school lunch programs
to those schools, districts, and states that had the will and the resources
to raise local funds to supplement the federal resources. Thus the contracts that were intended to establish equity and standardization in children's lunches in effect ensured deep inequalities in the program.

The most far reaching element in the school lunch contracts was the
stipulation that schools receiving federal funds serve all children equally
and provide free meals to poor children.[24] Congressional legislators were
particularly insistent on this matter. At every opportunity over the next
two decades, senators and congressmen regularly quizzed school administrators and Department of Agriculture officials about local practices regarding the distribution of free lunches. Over and over, despite the realities of segregation and discrimination in communities across the nation,
school lunch administrators insisted that they treated all children equally.
No one, the administrators insisted, knew which child paid and which

received a free lunch. This was, of course, patently absurd. Every child in every school lunch line knew perfectly well which ones received free lunches. While Congress insisted on a rhetoric of equity and opportunity, it neglected to include any enforcement mechanisms in the contract provisions. True, federal officials could withhold resources from schools that did not meet the standards, but few public officials wanted to be accused of refusing to feed children. The War Food Administration's school lunch chief, William C. Ockey, admitted that he held little leverage over states or districts that did not operate according to standard. Most particularly, local officials could distribute the federal school lunch resources in any way they saw fit. School lunch programs therefore largely mirrored local inequalities. This was particularly significant for southern states, which operated racially segregated school systems. Virginia, for example, received over $400,000 in federal funds, but the money went to only a few schools in the state. Iowa, which received fewer dollars supplemented federal resources with state tax funds and so was able to feed more children than Virginia was. Similarly, Texas, which received nearly 1.5 million from the federal government, only provided about 200,000 lunches; New York, which received substantially less federal money, used local taxes and fed 372,000 children.[25] What is more, even those states contributing local funds did not provide substantial numbers of free meals. Indeed, most states relied on children's fees to match federal contributions and to cover the costs of operation. This meant that, from the start, paying children subsidized free meals for the poor. While almost six million children ate government-subsidized school lunches by the time the United States entered World War II, few of those lunches were served free and few of the children served were poor.

Nutrition in the National Defense

The new federal nutrition standards in school lunch contracts came directly out of the work of home economists and nutrition scientists. Working both within the Bureau of Home Economics and in academic departments, home economists and nutritionists had long been involved in trans-Atlantic discussions about food policy and human nutrition. Two women were particularly influential in shaping this conversation. Lydia Roberts, a pioneer in home economics, during the 1930s established an international reputation in child health and nutrition. She spent her youth as a schoolteacher but in 1915 left teaching to study home economics. In 1928, she published *Nutrition Work with Children*, which became the standard text in the field and was reprinted regularly through the 1950s.[26] In 1930 Roberts became chair of the Home Economics Department at the University of Chicago. From this post she led in both domestic and international food and nutrition policy. Roberts was particularly instrumental in establishing the idea of "protective foods," which included green leafy vegetables, eggs, milk, fish, and meat. These foods were known to contain essential nutrients, including vitamins, and formed the basis for what became popularized as "food groups" during World War II. Roberts's younger colleague, Hazel Stiebeling, an Ohio farm girl, studied home economics with Mary Swartz Rose at Columbia Teachers College. During the 1920s she conducted a series of research projects on women's nutrition and the role of vitamin D, finally earning a doctorate in chemistry from Columbia in 1928. Academic opportunities for women scientists were still limited but, like the generation before her, Stiebeling found a home in the new Bureau of Home Economics where she remained for the rest of her career. One of Stiebeling's major interests was the establishment of a national nutrition standard for American diets, which she felt would aid in planning both for agriculture and for welfare. According to most reports, Stiebeling was the first to suggest the idea of "Recommended Dietary Allowances" as a useful category for policy and planning.[27]

In 1935, Stiebeling and Roberts took their expertise abroad to participate in the development of international diet and nutrition standards. That year, the two women represented the United States on the League of Nations–sponsored international committee on dietary standards. Drawing on the latest vitamin and mineral discoveries, international nutrition standards became important tools for "rational" planning for food and agriculture policy both during and after the war. The League of Nations recommendations were based on World War I estimates that called for 3000 calories and 70 to 80 grams of protein to maintain the health of soldiers and workers (all, of course, assumed to be men). During the 1930s, vitamins were added to the recommendations and increased emphasis was placed on the consumption of protein and green vegetables.[28] Working with other women scientists, Stiebeling elaborated on the dietary allowances, adding thiamin (vitamin B_1) and riboflavin (vitamin B_2) and asserting the efficacy of their recommendations as the minimum nutritional requirements for "normal people."[29] The recommendations included vitamins A and D, and tables for calories, fat, proteins, calcium, and iron. By the end of the 1930s, under the guidance of the League of Nations, most European governments as well as Canada had established nutrition councils to promote the dietary standards.[30]

At the start of World War II, nutrition reformers became key figures in United States planning for food policy, both military and civilian. The Community School Lunch Program provided a unique forum for nutrition education. The newly instituted school lunch contracts presented

Figure 3.1. School lunch programs were institutionalized during World War II. "Every Child Needs a Good School Lunch" poster, NWDNS-44-PA-735. National Archives.

the women with their first opportunity to establish national nutrition standards for children. As the United States government enlisted experts in business, science, and the professions to help with the war effort, social scientists, welfare advocates, and nutrition reformers joined the cadre of professionals in Washington planning circles. In early 1940, the National Research Council created two high-profile civilian boards to implement a national food policy. Lydia Roberts chaired the Food and Nutrition Board (FNB), which was charged with developing national nutrition standards that would govern food policy, regarding primarily army meals but also children's lunches. The FNB also had to translate the latest scientific research into popular terms. The well-known anthropologist Margaret Mead chaired the complimentary Committee on Food Habits, which had the responsibility of translating nutrition guidelines into a more popular format.

While the FNB's central task was to develop nutrition standards for military diets, the board also developed guidelines for civilian meals and school lunches as well. Aiming to "enlist" the nation's housewives in the "all-out effort for preparedness," the FNB embarked on a public nutrition education campaign.[31] Hazel Stiebeling convened a group of social reformers including Faith Williams, a social worker from the Bureau of Labor Statistics, Martha May Eliot, a physician with the Children's Bureau, and Harriet Eliot, also with the Children's Bureau, to sift through the latest nutrition research and make recommendations. Soon the committee expanded to include nongovernmental groups with an interest in wartime mobilization, including the Red Cross, the American Home Economics Association, and the American Dietetics Association. Harriet Eliot applauded the group's ability to work together, saying, "All of us have a major defense job to do—the job of improving our standard of living and of keeping ourselves strong and physically fit."[32]

Roberts and the FNB had no easy task in front of them, as the research on human nutritional requirements, while prolific, was often conflicting. Roberts recalled that when her committee was initially charged with developing a set of RDAs, she feared that nutrition science had too many different methodologies and approaches and that the morass of competing priorities among food and nutrition researchers would make it impossible to come up with a unified recommendation. She nonetheless persevered, bringing together a prominent group of nutrition researchers in what she termed a "democratic" effort to identify the appropriate studies and methodology. The task proved even more difficult than Roberts feared because the food industry carefully monitored the committee's work, making sure that their products and commodities were not slighted. Stiebeling, for example, had to fend off congressional efforts to prevent federal funds from paying the salary of "any person advocating lessened consumption of any wholesome food." Of course, every agricultural industry representative believed his crop to be entirely wholesome, so when nutritionists counseled, for example, substituting beans or eggs for beef, the cattlemen objected.[33] Ultimately, despite industry efforts to shape the process, Roberts and her committee settled on a set of RDAs based on international standards that called for between 2,500 and 4,500 calories for men and 2,100 to 3,000 calories for women. The range depended on how active individuals were during the day. Thus, laborers or domestic servants required more calories per day than clerks or saleswomen. Children's RDAs increased with age, with teenaged girls requiring between 2,400 and 2,800 calories and boys a full thousand over that.[34]

As chair of the FNB, Roberts had to reconcile scientific research with political and economic agendas. She also had to contend with a scientific establishment that preferred not to recognize the research contributions of women. Roberts's committee was scheduled to announce a set of nutrition standards at the National Nutrition Conference for Defense convened by President Roosevelt in May 1941. As Roberts recalled, the committee had a great deal of trouble agreeing on a clear set of RDAs. The night before the conference began, Roberts gathered a small group of women together in her hotel room. "While the men, we felt sure, were out seeing the town," Roberts recalled, she, along with Helen Mitchell and Hazel Stiebeling, "thrashed out" a set of standards. These were presented to the conference the next day and, along with the newly created "food groups," quickly became the standard government dietary recommendations.[35] By all accounts, the establishment of the RDAs "represented the most authoritative pronouncement on human needs" since the League of Nations addressed the subject during the mid-1930s.[36]

Within a short time, the RDAs, accompanied by suggested menus and recipes, appeared in newspapers, women's magazines, radio programs, and posters in school lunchrooms. Particularly with the beginning of food rationing during the war, the RDAs became important elements in the national campaign of nutritional instruction. In 1941, the Bureau of Home Economics released a pamphlet calling on Americans to "do your part in the National Nutrition Program" by eating from each food group every day.[37] Lauding the publication's timely contribution to the defense effort, the *New York Times* told housewives they would find "the most thorough education in how to feed their families ever provided by any nation in the world."[38] The pamphlet counseled housewives to look at the content of food labels and familiarize themselves with vitamins, minerals, and the various food groups. Although the number of recommended food groups kept changing, the principle became firmly entrenched in the popular imagination. Where, for example, a 1941 poll indicated that most people did not know the difference between a calorie and a vitamin, by the end of the war, vitamins, RDAs, and the idea of "balanced meals" became part of a shared vocabulary.

Insisting that the RDAs could be satisfied by a wide variety of diets and products, the home economists hoped both to include ethnic and regional food preferences and not to offend any particular farm group. The food groups, as two historians put it, included "the full range of American food and agricultural products."[39] Because the foods in each group were essentially interchangeable as far as nutrition went, Stiebeling assured the public that every community could make its own choices. "Food habits differ from one part of the country to another;" she said, "so, we would not want to specify any more closely than we have in our diet plans."[40] The goal, she insisted, was "to introduce new foods into regional and racial diets."[41] Despite regional variation, however, Stiebeling recommended what became known as the "basic seven." In 1943 the USDA released Stiebeling's suggestions in what became one of the department's most widely circulated and often reprinted pamphlets. The "National Wartime Nutritional Guide" (after the war, simply the "National Food Guide") recommended seven food groups: green and yellow vegetables; oranges, tomatoes, grapefruit; potatoes; milk and milk products; meat, poultry, fish, eggs, and dried peas and beans; bread, flour, and cereals; and butter or margarine. Based largely on Wilbur Atwater's substitution tables, the USDA guidelines suggested alternative choices in each group—a particularly practical idea given the wartime shortages of many food items.[42]

The extent to which Americans actually embraced the value of "scientific nutrition" is unclear, of course, Indeed, if the protestations of nutritionists and home economists are any indication, "balanced meals" actually appeared on few American dinner plates. While the Bureau of Home Economics insisted that its dietary recommendations could be met even on limited incomes, many housewives probably found it difficult to prepare "balanced" meals. The BHE's "sample low-cost dietary" appearing in women's magazines and newspaper food columns throughout the country, for example, suggested that adults needed to consume a pint of milk, three ounces of meat, two servings of vegetables, two fruits, bread, butter, and sugar at every meal in order to meet the RDAs. Even when the menus were changed to reflect wartime shortages in sugar and flour, expensive and scarce items such as beef, milk, and butter held strong. The suggested meals not only revealed an unrealistic assessment of American family food budgets, but promoted a decidedly bland Anglo-Saxon menu as well. Popular food writer M.F.K. Fisher loudly protested the whole idea of "balanced meals." Calling the RDA charts "one of the stupidest things in an earnest but stupid school of culinary thought," she scoffed at the idea that meals should be "balanced" at all. She heaped even more scorn on the suggested monthly menu plans "marked into twenty-six or so squares with a suggested menu for each meal of the week." Asserting that it was difficult enough to prepare even one "supposedly tempting" dish a day, Fisher declared scientific meal planning to be "hard not only on the wills and wishes of the great American family, but it is pure hell on the pocketbook" as well.[43]

EATING DEMOCRACY

Food writers and housewives notwithstanding, the food policy recommendations of the FNB had a significant impact on the nation's school lunchrooms. Most notably, the RDAs were immediately included in the Community School Lunch contracts. All schools participating in the federal program had to certify that they served "balanced meals" that followed the USDA nutrition recommendations.[44] School lunch contracts provided three levels of subsidy for children's meals, depending on the extent to which they satisfied the child's RDAs over the course of a week. The highest level of subsidy went to the "Type A meal," which had to provide at least one-third to one-half of a child's RDAs and include at least one cup of milk. Schools could choose a lower level of subsidy by serving a "Type B" meal, including only one-quarter to one-third of the RDAs plus milk. Finally, the lowest level of subsidy went to schools serving the "Type C" lunch, which consisted simply of a glass of milk.[45] Estimating the vitamin, protein, fat, and carbohydrate needs of children over the course of a week, Bureau of Home Economics researchers devised menus and recipes for school lunch operators. Most notably, the lunches contained high levels of fat in order to bump up the calorie content of the meals. Nutritionists and children's welfare advocates operated under the assumption that children, in particular poor children, required a high-fat, high-calorie diet in order to thrive.[46]

Better nutrition required cultural change as well as scientific eating. This is where Margaret Mead's Committee on Food Habits (CFH) took the lead. Gathering together a high-powered group of social scientists, including anthropologist Ruth Benedict and sociologist Lloyd Warner, Margaret Mead led an extensive study of American food habits and the social meaning of food and mealtimes, particularly in times of crisis. The CFH translated the scientific findings of the FNB into terms that policy makers and public officials could use to plan for food distribution and emergencies during the war. Mead had worked extensively during the 1920s and '30s with leading American anthropologists, including Franz Boaz and Ruth Benedict, who had been developing theories about human cultures. Well known by 1940 for her work in the South Pacific, Mead believed that the study of "faraway" peoples would help Americans understand themselves better. During the World War II period, Mead became increasingly interested in the variety of cultures that made up American society itself. Mead drew on social science to develop a theory of rational choice in food habits. She also drew on educational theories, particularly ideas about the transmission of culture through the education of children. Mead remained an important voice in discussions about food and culture, reprising during the 1960s her role as a consultant to public policy.[47]

The CFH focused particular attention on large-scale feeding centers, such as school lunchrooms and industrial cafeterias. Social arenas like these, the committee believed, would be especially important in fostering common tastes and a unified democratic culture. A food-centered cultural agenda had wide-reaching implications not only for food preferences but for behavior as well. Institutional meal settings, if properly managed, could, for one thing, alleviate any lingering concerns that might attach to feeding children lunch away from home. While a large lunchroom, Mead warned, could easily devolve into chaos, one that was well ordered could recreate the environment of a "family meal, especially in the face of a "breakdown of family ties." The CFH recommended that food service managers provide amenities such as small tables, designated "family" groups for eating, and a quiet atmosphere. School lunchrooms could also teach important lessons in gender roles as well as nutrition. Some schools adopted Mead's family model by organizing their lunchrooms along the lines of a "well-regulated family group."[48] In Rye, New York, for example, a boy and girl at each table served as "host and hostess" and were responsible for "table courtesies," including lessons in nutrition, etiquette, and conversation. Food choice and gender roles also pointed toward middle-class behavior norms. At the historically black Peabody Women's College demonstration school cafeteria, for example, teachers designated hosts and hostesses for each lunchroom table. Here, race and class behavior were carefully nurtured as "conversation, table manners, English, art, and food selection" all formed part of the children's educational curriculum.[49]

Mead's goal was not simply to improve the nation's health and morale, but to do so in a democratic manner that would, as historian Amy Bentley observed, allow for "diversity and personal choice."[50] Taking a cue from the experiences of home economists of previous decades, the CFH went to great pains to transcend the diversity of American cultures and to play down the differences that marked ethnic Americans. Wartime diet recommendations, Mead insisted, must reflect good relations among different regional, national, religious, and racial groups. Hollywood films as well as government-sponsored newsreels and pamphlets reflected the CFH advice, regularly featuring a panoply of ethnic characters. Indeed, as Mead noted, "the systematic exploitation of such cultural differences is part of the enemy tactic in war."[51]

American food policy, Mead counseled, needed to appreciate ethnic difference and to build a unified national identity. To do both, however, was a challenge. Most people developed their food preferences in family kitchens and dining rooms. In wartime, however, institutional meal settings, whether in the army, in factories, or in schools, offered the opportunity to transform diverse ethnic food cultures into a national identity. School menus, for example, could go a long way toward overcoming ethnic diversity and encouraging national unity. Every child eating in school and every adult eating in a public cafeteria, Mead insisted, should be comfortable with the food offerings, but cafeteria planners should also take the opportunity to introduce children to nutritious food and new dishes. "Because of the great diversity of food differences in the United States," Mead observed, "it is more practicable to try to establish feeding patterns which *do not offend* any group." School lunchrooms and other cafeterias, she suggested, should offer only "food that is fairly innocuous and has low emotional value." This meant that menu planners should seek the path to consensus by eliminating as much distinctive flavoring as possible. Indeed, the only seasoning Mead recommended was salt. All others she said, would alienate one group or another. The best route, Mead's CFH counseled, was to prepare "low toned foods" such as plain soups; beef, chicken, or meat pies; and plain vegetables. In a dramatic reversal of culinary advice, the CFH recommended staying away from all creamed dishes and warned cooks to avoid buttered vegetables. Despite a new suspicion of white sauce, however, the old idea that spicy foods were unhealthy gained new legitimacy in menu recommendations that stressed broiled fish, potatoes, boiled spaghetti, and eggs.[52]

While food reformers generally advocated relatively standardized modern diets, Mead reminded them that choice and ethnicity were keys to American democratic culture. Menu choices, whether in the home or in institutional settings, could validate ethnic traditions and reinforce the pluralism that characterized the wartime idealized version of American national identity. "Most foreign born groups," Mead wrote, commonly rejected "American" food but should be given some choice on their lunch trays. "Choice in food is one sign of being an adult in America," she noted, and the lack of choice would "reduce the adult to the status of a child with the consequent development of dependency and lowering of morale." Menu choices also ensured that no group would be offended by the selections offered, whether in army mess halls or school lunchrooms. Indeed, Mead counseled cooks to use menu choices to introduce Americans to new foods, presumably modernized versions of traditional ethnic dishes. In particular, the CFH agenda for wartime food policy stressed introducing children to new foods, nutrition, and healthy eating.

Children, however, needed to learn to make the right choices. "Children will accept many foods which adults are less likely to accept," Mead noted; thus, hot school lunches became important sites of cultural as well as nutritional lessons. Mary C. Kelly, describing her experience with the Hartford, Connecticut, school lunch program, recalled, "I was surprised to discover that many of the students were wholly unfamiliar with fresh vegetables, fruits, salads, and puddings. . . . It seemed as if it were largely a question of becoming acquainted with certain foods."[53] John Washam, director of Chicago's school lunchrooms, observed, "We do not allow a child to exercise freedom of choice as to what he shall study and how he shall study it." Before school lunch programs began, Washam said, "the child had no guidance in the selection of food at all."[54] Nutritional guidance combined with a variety of healthy food choices had long been the goal of home economists and school lunch operators. During the war this goal was legitimized and operationalized in the Community School Lunch Program.

Ethnic appreciation went only so far, however. At base, public meal programs and a national food policy aimed to build a unified civic identity. Children, in other words, had to learn to "eat democracy." The *CIO News* (the official journal of the Congress of Industrial Organizations), for example, enthusiastically promoted the National School Lunch Program with the headline, "Kids Eat Democracy."[55] In particular, professionals and policy makers alike wanted school lunches during World War II, as in earlier eras, to Americanize immigrant children. Home economist Mary Kelly believed the lessons at lunch should also include "development of citizenship responsibilities" not only in food preferences, but also "in regard to neatness, appearance, and order in the dining rooms."[56] Bringing children together in school lunchrooms, Mead's committee insisted, would reinforce a commitment to American culture and strengthen children's identity as citizens.[57] Joseph Meegan, director of Chicago's Back of the Yards Neighborhood Council, regularly served lunch to the children of stock-yard workers. Through the council's efforts, both public and parochial schools in the neighborhood started their own lunch programs. Claiming great success in improving children's health, Meegan became an outspoken advocate for federal school lunches. The collective eating experience brought the neighborhood's myriad of ethnic groups together. "Polish, Lithuanian, Mexican—yes, and Catholic, Protestant, and Jewish" children, Meegan said, all ate different dishes at home. The Poles "ate Polish sausage and Kiebasa [*sic*], the Lithuanians ate . . . Kugli," but in the lunch program, Meegan boasted, where they all sat down together, "they actually ate democracy."[58]

Eating democracy required more than nutrition theory and cultural transformation. It also required an administrative structure and centralized standards for lunchroom operations. Mead's committee stressed the significance of creating well-regulated institutional settings from which to incorporate diverse people into the national polity. Indeed, the war presented public administrators with remarkable opportunities to put theories of efficiency, productivity, and central planning into practice. In addition, wartime idealism infused public works with an added dose of ideological mission. Most notably, as the nation fought abroad against totalitarianism and racial discrimination, public institutions—and politics—at home began to reflect new demands for equal access.

The Community School Lunch Program reflected wartime idealism and a new push for administrative regulation and standards. Lunch Program sponsors, usually school boards, were required to sign formal contracts with federal officials.[59] Programs could claim reimbursements for the purchase of "any agricultural commodity that can be used to meet the lunch requirements," and schools also had to accept a certain amount of surplus food.[60] While surplus food and federal relief funds had been flowing to school lunch programs for almost a decade, the Community Lunch contracts signaled a new level of federal involvement in children's nutrition as well as in school operations. The federal government now entered the school building—an arena that had heretofore been the exclusive purview of the states. While the contracts were written and administered by state officials—and differed from state to state—Congress required the Department of Agriculture to monitor state compliance and to report regularly on the state of the program.

Wartime standardization of school lunch menus and standards of service reflected both the optimism of policy makers during the 1940s and the competing claims on public programs. Scientists as well as social reformers believed the war—and the post-war period—signaled the opportunity for an expansion of social programs and rational social planning. Food and nutrition planners, in particular, viewed the institutionalization of school lunch programs as a major sign of progress in their campaign to convince Americans to adopt more healthy eating habits. Agricultural planners similarly saw school lunchrooms as key to expanding the market for farm products after the war. In authorizing school lunch funds, furthermore, Congress signaled at least rhetorical commitment both to children's health generally and to the welfare of poor children in particular. While the actual practice of school lunch program may have belied these lofty goals, the very existence of a federal program, at the very least, put the state in the business of overseeing children's health and welfare. The challenge came during the post-war years when Congress, the Department of Agriculture, and child nutrition advocates had to work out what a national school lunch program would really look like.

CHAPTER 4

A National School Lunch Program

The *Ladies Home Journal* of October 1944 told American housewives that a new "national disease" threatened America's children. "Johnny's bones aren't straight and Susie can't seem to grasp her [arithmetic] problems," the *Journal* ominously observed. Both Susie and Johnny suffered from malnutrition. Writing at the end of World War II, the *Journal* warned that malnutrition sapped the nation's civic strength and threatened domestic as well as military security. The editors suggested a simple solution. The government should provide all American children with a hot lunch every day at school. In other words, Congress should permanently fund the school lunch program that the Department of Agriculture had been operating on year-by-year appropriations since the mid-1930s. For over half a century, the *Journal* said, Congress and the Department of Agriculture sponsored programs to improve livestock and farm crops and to protect commodity prices. It was now time to do the same for the nation's children.[1]

Two years later, in June 1946, Congress created the National School Lunch Program "as a measure of national security, to safeguard the health and well-being of the Nation's children and to encourage the domestic consumption of nutritious agricultural commodities and other foods."[2] It was a historic act and a triumph for a generation of home economists, nutritionists, and child welfare advocates who had long struggled to improve American diets. It was also a triumph for the Department of Agriculture and a generation of farm policy makers who believed that government-supported price supports were essential to the growth and prosperity of the farm sector. When President Harry Truman signed the bill into law, he declared that "no nation is any healthier than its children or more prosperous than its farmers." The School Lunch Bill, he assured the American public, "contributed immeasurably to both."[3] Yet the health and welfare of farmers and of children were not so obviously linked, nor were children's welfare activists and farmers such natural allies. Indeed, the two groups continually vied for control over the American diet, most particularly, children's meal programs. Child welfare reformers used the apparent success of wartime school lunch programs to begin pushing hard for post-war universal child nutrition programs. At the same time, Agriculture Department officials mobilized their own political networks—particularly southern Democrats—to lobby for a long-term congressional commitment to a federal surplus commodity support system.

The 1946 National School Lunch Act was an uneasy compromise among an unusual set of allies. That the bill was passed at all had more to do with the influence of southern Democrats in Congress and the power of the agricultural lobby than with a public commitment to nutrition education or even to children's welfare. Nutrition reformers and child welfare advocates, of course, enthusiastically greeted the School Lunch Act as the culmination of their campaign to improve American diets. The 1946 bill, however, bore little resemblance to the type of child nutrition program reformers had envisioned. Instead, it reflected both the constraints of American regional and racial politics and the limits of the New Deal welfare system. The nature of the school lunch compromise revealed much about the fate of social policy and the nature of American food and agricultural policies after World War II. Ultimately, the administrative structure of the school lunch program limited its ability to deliver universal child nutrition or to feed poor children. Nonetheless, despite their aversion to liberal social programs, southern Democratic legislators oversaw the creation of one of the nation's most enduring and popular federal entitlement programs.

President Harry Truman's post-war political agenda, dubbed the "Fair Deal," promised to continue federal oversight of the social welfare and economic support programs initiated by New Deal Democrats. Between 1946 and 1950, for example, in addition to the School Lunch Act, Congress endorsed public housing, expanded Social Security coverage, and raised the minimum wage.[4] The 1946 National School Lunch Program optimistically promised prosperity for farmers and nutrition for children, an essential combination in maintaining strong citizens, a healthy democracy, and national security in the post-war world. Historian Alan Brinkley has characterized the post-war liberal agenda as one aimed at increasing consumer prosperity rather than reshaping "the economic and social environment."[5] Promising to protect the agricultural economy while at the same time encouraging the consumption of American farm products, a federally subsidized school lunch program fit such an agenda very well. Like Truman's Fair Deal, however, the school lunch program had serious limitations. The post-war liberal agenda foundered on the fraying coalition of conservative southerners and liberal reformers that had sustained New Deal social programs. While the southern part of the coalition stuck with the Democratic president when it came to national security, they were less willing to go along with post-war civil rights or labor-oriented initiatives. Domestic legislation, couched in idealistic rhetoric—increasingly so as the Cold War heated up—often fell short of effective delivery. Truman's housing initiative, for example, while promising affordable housing for all Americans, in fact built very few units.[6] The Democrats created the National Science Foundation and the Atomic Energy Act, but were unable to enact health insurance or convince Congress to pass any substantial aid to education. Ultimately, school lunch politics, like the postwar liberal agenda, could not reconcile national goals—equal opportunity and social welfare—with local inequalities and entrenched regional power.

AGRICULTURE OR EDUCATION?

Nutrition reformers emerged from World War II optimistic that the nation's post-war prosperity would finally ensure not only sufficient food but proper nutrition for all Americans. The growth of the Community School Lunch Program during the war convinced nutritionists as well as children's welfare advocates that the moment for universal children's lunch was at hand. Children's Bureau physician Martha May Eliot observed that "nutrition is the next great problem and the new task."[7] She believed that "a free lunch of optimum nutritional value for every school child" should be a central post-war goal.[8] Faith Williams, veteran child welfare advocate and head of the Bureau of Labor Statistics Cost of Living Division, confided to the Department of Agriculture's school lunch administrator, M. L. Wilson, "I personally have come to be of the opinion that free school lunches should be made available to all children in public schools."[9] Williams and Eliot were not alone in their conviction that postwar America should provide healthy lunches to all children. At the very least, Bureau of Home Economic nutritionists Lucy Gillett and Hazel Kyrk believed, the post-war Congress should make free lunches available to all low income or "needy" children. By the war's end, a national school lunch program was squarely on the legislative agenda for children's welfare reformers.[10]

School lunches were also on the post-war agricultural agenda. World War II expanded the role of government in food production and distribution and consolidated the power of policy makers within the Department of Agriculture, most notably, those who promoted a strategy of mechanization, productivity, and price supports. Despite the fact that the agricultural surplus had all but disappeared with the start of the war, farm-bloc representatives and agricultural planners were convinced that the commodity disposal program would be essential to the health of the post-war farm sector. Agricultural economists such as H. R. Tolley, Milo Perkins, and M. L. Wilson continued to believe that government oversight of com-

modity prices—buying the surplus and donating it to schools—would ensure farmers ready markets for surplus commodities and build demand
for new food products. The nation's basic agricultural supply problems,
they were convinced, had not disappeared but, rather, could "be expected
to recur in intensified form," unless "intelligent plans" were made to meet
the problem after the war.[11] A school lunch program, Tolley and Perkins
believed, would act as an insurance policy in the event post-war agricultural prices began to fall. As early as 1943, then, with the support of
major farm and food industry groups including the Dairymen's League,
the Grange, the American Farm Bureau Federation, and the Independent
Grocer's Association, Tolley and Perkins began to draft legislation that
would permanently authorize a national school lunch program as an outlet for surplus farm products.

It was not hard to gain the support of food and nutrition reformers or
of children's welfare advocates for a federal school meal plan. The New
Deal "women's dominion" of child welfare advocates and social reformers enthusiastically mobilized to support the creation of a national school
lunch program.[12] In their view, however, a permanent program needed to
be part of a broad-based social welfare agenda and should no longer be
controlled by the Department of Agriculture. The Women's Joint Congressional Committee, for example, speaking for mainstream women's
organizations, declared that the Department of Agriculture had begun "a
very fine piece of work," but that a permanent school lunch program
would be most effective "if it were under the more intimate supervision
of the Office of Education."[13] National Education Association spokesman
Dr. Howard Dawson agreed. A school lunch program, he said, is "more
than feeding children." Nutrition should be, he said, "fundamental in the
educational program and should be administered according to the proper
pattern."[14] Indeed, with the disappearance of the agricultural surplus, nutrition reform became the most persuasive justification for continuing the
program. Agnes Winn of the National Education Association told the
House Committee on Agriculture in 1945 that "the program can no
longer be defended as a means for lifting the economic level of rural life."
The main reason for continuing the program, in her view, was in terms
of "the educational and health objectives which are advanced as the food
habits of youth are intelligently changed and improved."[15] General Federation of Women's Clubs spokeswoman Mrs. Harvey W. Wiley put it
bluntly: "The main question is the health of our children." In the post-war
years, she continued, American children would need to better "absorb the
education provided for them to fit them for democratic living."[16]

At the end of the war, American policy makers could also look abroad
for models of child health and welfare plans that included school lunch
programs. In England, for example, historian James Vernon argues,

school meals, which had traditionally been part of state or private charitable programs, were taken over by the treasury to become universal in scope. Where in the United States, state-sponsored school lunches were rooted in agricultural policy, in Britain school meals formed an important element in the post-war welfare state. According to one account, expansion of school meals and milk "as quickly as possible" became part of British national food policy in 1940. Taking children's health and nutrition to be a national responsibility, the British War Cabinet increased the number of school meals served and provided milk for every child. Where prewar school lunches were "of a poor quality, at the end of the war, "both the quantity and quality of service" improved. Described as "a revolution in the attitude of parents, teachers, and children," British school lunches no longer were regarded as charity but, rather, "became a social service, fused into school life."[17] This, indeed, was the model American reformers were after.

While the American social welfare community and school officials believed school lunches should, by right, be educational in nature, the political clout necessary to gain congressional support for a national program resided solidly in the Department of Agriculture. The USDA continued to be one of the most powerful agencies in the federal bureaucracy. At the start of World War II, for example, the Department of Agriculture absorbed fully 10 percent of the total federal budget. Between 1930 and 1946 the number of USDA employees jumped from 25,741 to 75,199, and the department budget increased over eight-fold.[18] By 1944, the Department of Agriculture had an enormous investment in school lunch programs in terms of food supply, menu planning, and administrative bureaucracy. Under the leadership of USDA officials, farm state representatives, particularly those from the South, had come to view school lunches as an important element in the surplus commodity program. Southern representatives also saw school lunches as part of the department's extension service serving rural families and bringing what they considered to be modern farm techniques to the region. Senate Agriculture Committee chairman Richard Russell, for one, made it clear that his support for a school lunch program hinged on its remaining in the USDA. The program, he said, came into being "in that paradoxical age when we had so much food to eat that people were starving and farmers were producing so much that they were going into bankruptcy because they could not dispose of their products."[19] The main reason he continued to "so strongly" support the program, he announced, "is that I think the continuation of the school-lunch program depends on [the agricultural] feature."[20] If school lunches were "not connected with the disposition of surpluses," Russell declared, he would vote to disband the program.[21]

The Liberal Compromise

Despite their general inclination to oppose federal welfare schemes, southern Democrats eagerly endorsed school lunch legislation. Indeed, Georgia senator Richard Russell and his Louisiana colleague Allen Ellender rightly claimed to be "founders" of the National School Lunch Program. Both men occupied influential positions on the Senate Agriculture Committee from the 1940s through the late 1960s, and both believed that federal commodity support policies would help small (white) farmers and relieve the region's persistent rural poverty. In a certain sense, Russell and Ellender both sympathized with poor rural families, whether black or white. But that sympathy did not imply any deviation from the southern code of racial segregation and states' rights. The two senators represented the most conservative wing of the Democratic party's New Deal coalition, reluctantly supporting President Roosevelt's state welfare programs, including Social Security, only so long as the Democratic party refrained from seriously pushing for racial equality. This had been most manifest in the limitations encoded into the Social Security law that left agricultural and domestic workers uncovered and that rested administration of the program in the hands of state and local officials.

Richard Russell's support for a national school lunch program dramatically illustrates the Democratic party's compromise between liberal welfare ideals and its conservative southern wing. Russell served in the Senate from 1933 until his death in 1971 and is perhaps best known as mentor to Lyndon Johnson and later as "the single most powerful figure in the Senate."[22] In 1944, when he introduced a National School Lunch bill, Russell was still the state's junior senator but had clearly staked out his role as a leader of the southern farm bloc. Russell's political base was among Georgia's small-scale, white farmers, although he claimed considerable support among Georgia's rural blacks as well. At the same time, he was openly paternalistic and unabashedly racist in his attitudes toward his black constituents. Even a sympathetic biographer noted, "White supremacy and racial segregation were to him cardinal principles for good and workable human relationships."[23] Despite his open opposition to anything smacking of civil rights or racial integration, Russell understood that his state's grinding rural poverty—white and black—would ultimately stymie any hope for economic development. He liked to think of himself, at least according to one historian, as a "representative of a maligned agrarian way of life."[24] To pull his region out of poverty, Russell believed, would require federal as well as private resources. To that end, he vigorously worked to bring federal money into Georgia in the form of military bases, for example. A national school lunch program, he believed, similarly would contribute more "to the cause of public education ... than any other policy adopted since the creation of free public schools."[25] At the same time, of course, Russell equally vigorously opposed any measure that hinted at dismantling segregation and was one of the most vocal opponents of any form of civil rights legislation. In 1946, for example, while sponsoring the establishment of a national school lunch program, he loudly condemned the creation of a Fair Employment Practices Committee, which would have monitored equal employment for blacks in any newly established federal facilities in the South.

Louisiana senator Allen Ellender's support for a national school lunch program similarly revealed the compromises central to the Democratic party's post-war liberal agenda. Like Richard Russell, Ellender viewed school lunch legislation primarily as a subsidy for southern (white) farmers but also as a way to help poor children both black and white. First elected to the Senate in 1937, Ellender had served in the House since 1924, including a stint as Speaker from 1932 to 1936. Ellender may have been slightly more moderate in his views than some of his southern colleagues—he refused, for example to join the Dixiecrat revolt in the late 1940s, but he voted with Dixiecrats to oppose labor and civil rights legislation. Ellender remained in the Senate until his death in 1972, championing the school lunch program but strenuously opposing any measure that would expand federal authority over the structure, finance, or administration of local lunchrooms. Ellender, according to one biographer, "assumed blacks to be inferior to whites" and believed that civil rights legislation "discriminated against the South."[26] For him, as for southern Democrats in general, race represented an absolute divide he would not cross, viewing almost any federal administrative authority as an attack on segregation. Ellender, for example, supported federal aid to schools "provided the administration of these funds is under the jurisdiction of the various states," and not under the control of officials from Washington.[27] While Russell and Ellender, along with a significant number of other southerners, happily endorsed federal assistance for farmers and children, they fiercely resisted any hit of interference in "local custom" regarding the organization of schools—and other social spaces—in their region.

Southern Democrats were not alone in linking school lunch policy to farm policy and agricultural development. Northern New Deal liberals saw an opportunity at the war's end to expand federal social programs, but they also believed in the Department of Agriculture's policies of commodity support and market expansion. California's Democratic Representative Jerry Voorhis, for example, was particularly articulate in connecting school lunch legislation to the modernization of agriculture as well as to children's welfare. He believed that an aggressive agricultural support policy not only would eliminate poverty but also would allow for expanded productivity to meet the growing post-war consumer demand. A national school lunch program, Voorhis argued, would help expand the demand for American commodities by introducing children—and their mothers—to new foods and by creating outlets for surplus products. Elected to the House of Representatives from California's Twelfth District in 1936, Voorhis claimed an "almost religious zeal" for the school lunch program.[28] A Midwesterner by birth, Voorhis was educated at Yale. After graduation, he put aside his elite background to work with the "common man," spending the 1920s working in factories and on the railroad. Finally, he turned to his true passion, education, and opened a home and school for boys. Voorhis's social conscience was evident from his early days in Congress where he consistently championed liberal causes and was a staunch supporter of New Deal welfare measures. Indeed, the congressman's liberalism ultimately became his downfall when he lost his House seat to the young Richard Nixon in 1946. In that heated campaign, Nixon attached Voorhis's "pink" record, particularly his support for labor and his opposition to anti-Communism. At the top of Nixon's list of "bad votes" cast by his opponent was Voorhis's support for the National School Lunch Program.[29]

Beginning in 1944, Russell and Ellender in the Senate, along with Voorhis and others in the House, began a legislative campaign to create a National School Lunch Program. As both the House and Senate debated creating a permanent National School Lunch Program, children's meals became part of a larger struggle over states' rights, federal power, and racial equity. In the case of school lunches, unexpected alliances created space for the creation of a new social program yet also limited the scope of that program. While considerable public support existed for school lunch programs, legislators had to craft a program that would satisfy widely competing constituencies. On the one hand, liberals riding their New Deal and wartime policy successes saw school lunches as an expansion of the social safety net and part of a new civil rights agenda. Optimistic about the ability of the federal government to solve social problems and institute a new era of tolerance and equality, liberal law makers embraced children's welfare and a national school lunch program as emblematic of America's moral and political leadership in the post-war world. Southern Democrats also signed on to the patriotic symbolism of school lunches, but they saw a national program also as a conduit for regional development and agricultural support. For southern legislators, school lunches presented a perfect combination of agricultural relief, regional development, and children's welfare.[30] Although they certainly parted company from liberal Democrats when it came to federal oversight or civil rights, they could happily support federal subsidies to agriculture.

Racial equity and states' rights marked the congressional debate over school lunches from the very start. In 1944 and 1945 both the House and the Senate held hearings on the creation and the shape of a National School Lunch Program. Initially, the legislators considered three versions of a National School Lunch bill. In an unexpected move, a group of southern Democrats, led in the Senate by Allen Ellender and South Carolina's Ellison "Cotton Ed" Smith, proposed to take school lunches out of the Department of Agriculture and place the newly created National School Lunch Program under the control of the Commissioner of Education. Neither Ellender nor Smith were known for their support of federal education policy. Indeed, both men fiercely opposed anything that might open the door to Washington interference in the public schools, particularly when it came to the distribution of resources in the South's segregated school systems. Nor were these men known for their support for social programs in general. While Ellender had supported some New Deal social legislation, Smith was, according to one account, one of its "ardent" foes.[31] It was therefore surprising that Smith and Ellender, both former chairs of the Senate Committee on Agriculture and Forestry with a proprietary interest in the Department of Agriculture, would suggest moving school lunches from their traditional bureaucratic base. Nonetheless, their bill proposed giving the federal Commissioner of Education control over children's school meals. The reason for this sudden interest in making children's nutrition part of an education program was the fact that the wartime Community School Lunch Program, as administered by the Department of Agriculture during the war, had been contracting directly with local school systems. For Smith and Ellender this smacked too much of Washington interference in state affairs. They preferred to keep federal officials away from their region's segregated school systems. Their bill gave the Commissioner of Education control over school lunches but prohibited him from working directly with schools or even with local school systems. Instead, the Smith-Ellender bill established a national school lunch program that could work only through state-level educational offices. State officials—as opposed to local school administrators—would be authorized to distribute federal resources in accord with "local custom." Smith and Ellender did not mind bringing federal resources into the South so long as they could control the distribution of those resources. In this case, they supported the creation of a national school lunch program but insisted that decisions about which schools participated and which children received federally subsidized food be determined by the states and not by Congress.[32]

Smith and Ellender's assurances that their bill would not allow federal officials into the nation's schools did little to assuage conservative suspicions that children's meals represented the entering wedge in a campaign to expand Washington influence. Northern Republicans joined Southern

Democrats in opposing federal authority. Republican senator Robert A. Taft warned against allowing federal "nutrition experts" into the schools. "To set up a new Federal control over the diet and food of the people of this country," he said, "seems to me to go beyond anything we have done heretofore and beyond the existing school-lunch program."[33] Under the Constitution, of course, state governments had authority over public education, and legislators from both parties questioned any expanded federal role in school matters. New York Republican John Taber declared the National School Lunch bill to be "one of the most dangerous bills that has ever been brought to the floor of the House." In his view, it was "designed to wreck the public school system of America."[34] Ohio Republican Cliff Clevenger warned that "if you participate in this thing you will find . . . you have lost control of your free public-school system."[35]

Equally unexpected was the effort by New York's veteran liberal senator Robert Wagner to keep the school lunch program in the Department of Agriculture. Wagner's school lunch bill left the Secretary of Agriculture in charge of children's meals, but also included funds for nutrition education. Children's welfare advocates and liberal reformers generally favored nutrition education programs and severely criticized the Department of Agriculture for its lack of attention to this aspect of school lunches. The reason Wagner failed to gain much support, however, was that his bill allowed and even encouraged the Secretary of Agriculture to negotiate contracts with individual schools and school districts, much as the Community School Lunch Program had been doing. In keeping with the liberal goal of expanding the social safety net, Wagner's bill encouraged federal oversight and involvement in local school lunch programs. Indeed, his bill would have allowed federal officials to bypass state educational administrations and, at least potentially, to work with black and white schools equally.

In the end, Richard Russell introduced what he considered to be a compromise bill. Russell had already made it clear that he would support the program only if it remained in the Department of Agriculture. His bill, however, eliminated federal money for nutrition education and stipulated that the Secretary of Agriculture could operate only through state education departments. As Russell put it, federal officials would have "no authority what-ever over the management of the schools."[36] Russell's bill, which he claimed to have drafted without consulting anyone in the Department of Agriculture, ultimately became the National School Lunch Act passed by Congress in 1946.[37]

Two major arguments were raised in opposition to Russell's bill. Both reflected traditional arguments against the expansion of federal authority as well as new post-war anxieties. The threat of communism and nuclear war, combined with fears of a renewed economic depression, fueled conservative calls for a vigorous national defense despite continuing opposition to the growth of the federal government. The few voices raised in opposition to the creation of a national school lunch program saw it as a dangerous encroachment by the federal government into local affairs. Feeding children in school, the critics believed, would be the first step in the intrusion of government into citizen's kitchens and schools. North Carolina Democratic senator Harold D. Cooley wondered how far the government would go. If Congress began with free lunches for schoolchildren, he asked, then "why not provide medical care and dental care and hospitalization for all poor children who are needing in that regard?"[38] Other lawmakers feared that government-sponsored subsidies of children's meals would weaken the spirit of individualism, the nation's fundamental character strength. In a Congress that was about to pass federal housing legislation and would shortly consider a comprehensive health care bill, government action rankled many conservatives and smacked of creeping socialism. The Republican Whip, Leslie Arends of Illinois, acknowledged that "the objective of hot school lunches is desirable," but said he could not support the creation of a permanent federal program for "all school children."[39] Iowa Republican John Williams Gwynne agreed. "I believe in school lunches," he said, "I believe in children having proper food and proper education." But "whose responsibility is it"? he wondered. For Gwynne and other Republicans, the answer was simple. "The responsibility is first upon the parents." Only if the parents prove unable to meet their duty, he believed, should the government step in.[40]

School lunch opponents clearly viewed government involvement with childhood meals and food habits to be a major threat to the development of individual character and initiative. Closely linked to these concerns were fears that a school meal program would undermine traditional gender roles and turn child-rearing over to the state. Opposition to school lunches was particularly heated because food and meals represented such fundamental, formative experiences for the nation's youth. The idea of communal feeding seemed particularly dangerous for individuals as well as for communities. Michigan Republican congressman Anthony Dondero, for example, feared that the school lunch programs were "destroying local self-government."[41] Others predicted that a government feeding program would signal the triumph of socialism, which "has brought hideous creeping paralysis to the economic life of every country that has ever adopted it." Ohio representative Cliff Clevenger warned that "unnatural mothers" who advocated "turning children of three and one-half and even two years of age over to the state" were behind the push to create institutional school meal centers.[42] Oklahoma Republican Ross Rizley, an inveterate Cold Warrior, feared the emasculating effects of a strong federal government. "I would hate ever to see it come to the place in this Government," he said, "where we just fed kids for the purpose of feeding them, whether they needed it or not." If you subject children to such a program, he warned, "you tear down, to my way of thinking, the very things that I think have made this country and have demonstrated in this war that our kids were better than anybody else's kids when it came to a question of fighting."[43] Fearing that a free school lunch program would destroy national morale, the bill's opponents warned against "inculcating in little children at the most impressionable period of their lives the idea that they can get something for nothing from Uncle Sam."[44]

School lunch advocates clearly had a more positive view of federal programs, particularly children's welfare measures. "I see nothing subversive in the school lunch program," Richard Russell insisted. Indeed, he argued, school lunches would provide an insurance program against creeping socialism. "In my opinion," Russell said, "a school child who has a good bowl of hot soup and a glass of sweet milk for his lunch will be much more able to resist communism or socialism than would one who had for his lunch a hard biscuit which had been baked the day before and which he had brought with him to school in a tin can."[45] Virginia representative John Flannagan, a co-sponsor of the legislation in the House, similarly argued that feeding children would protect national security rather than threaten it. "The dictator nations," Flannagan observed, "exist upon hungry bodies and befuddled minds. If you want to dispel the gloom of Nazism and communism from the face of the earth, the thing to do is to feed and educate the peoples of those nations. A full stomach and a trained mind will never embrace either Nazism or communism."[46]

DISCRIMINATION AND SEGREGATION

Most fundamentally, however, the school lunch debate revealed the beginning of a new civil rights legislative initiative. The post-war Democratic political agenda depended on an increasingly tenuous New Deal coalition of urban liberals and southern conservatives. While conservative southern legislators like Russell and Ellender could support federalism in the name of farmers and children, they fiercely opposed any effort to challenge their region's entrenched system of racial segregation. At the same time, however, a new generation of legislators and reformers, buoyed by the wartime rhetoric of tolerance and freedom, began to push for legal and legislative measures designed to end segregation. Thus, when Congress began debating the school lunch program, first-term New York congressman Adam Clayton Powell, along with the NAACP, was quietly devising a plan to challenge any legislation that sent federal funds to segregated facilities. When the school lunch bill came before Congress in February 1946, Powell had just begun to formulate his strategy. Immediately after taking office that year, he had spearheaded a bruising fight on the floor of Congress over the creation of a permanent Fair Employment Practices Committee (FEPC). This legislation would have permanently funded the wartime agency set up to monitor racial discrimination in employment and extend the federal government's civil rights activities into the post-war period. Knowing that federal school lunch funds would be going to states with segregated school systems, Powell decided to make the school lunch bill his first test case.[47] When the school lunch bill came to the floor of the House two weeks after the FEPC fight, Powell immediately offered an amendment that would prohibit federal funds from going to any state or school if, in carrying out the functions of the bill, "it makes any discrimination because of race, creed, or national origin of children, or, between types of schools, or, with respect to a State which maintains separate schools for minority and for majority children, it discriminates between such schools on this account."[48]

Powell's amendment, like the post-war civil rights movement generally, posed a fundamental challenge to American liberals. For most of the twentieth century, liberal lawmakers had bemoaned racial segregation but had done little to challenge it. In particular, Congress stayed far away from the South's "separate but equal" public school system. By opposing any measure that sent federal resources to segregated institutions or states, Powell's amendment put liberals—as well as conservatives—on notice that the issue could no longer be ignored. Appealing to the post-war liberal rhetoric of humanitarianism and tolerance, Powell pointed out that Congress had just sent funds to the new United Nations refugee administration. He challenged his colleagues to "be humane enough to see that the minority race have the same opportunities in the free-lunch program as do those of the majority race."[49] The question was, how far would liberal Americans be willing to push Congress to dismantle racial segregation? In the case of the school lunch legislation, would the program's liberal supporters be willing to go so far as to withhold funding from racially segregated schools? Powell knew his strategy would not dismantle segregation, but he did hope to insert the principle of nondiscrimination into federal policy. "The purpose of my amendment," he told the House, "is not in any way to alter existing educational patterns." Rather, he said, "the purpose of my amendment is to assure that where there are separate schools or even where there are not separate schools, the money allotted for the school lunch program shall be allocated fairly to all people without regard to race, creed, color, or national origin."[50] By wording his amendment as anti-discrimination rather than anti-segregation, however, Powell inadvertently undermined his own purpose. As far as school lunch advocates, whether from the North or from the South, were concerned, the program already was open equally to all children.

Lawmakers had insisted from the start that surplus food be available to any school wanting to participate. Program administrators, in their turn, had long insisted that there was no discrimination in the program. Of course, the financial and administrative requirements of the school lunch program, by definition, excluded many districts and schools from participating. What is more, while provisions existed on paper requiring all participating schools to offer free lunches for poor children, no one looked very closely at how many (if any) free meals were actually available. Nor had anyone looked into the actual distribution of lunch programs to see how many black schools, North or South, participated. Everyone involved with the school lunch program blithely asserted that there was no discrimination. Liberals were therefore particularly uncomfortable with Powell's amendment. Jerry Voorhis, for example, simply refused to support it. Not only did he believe it to be "not at all necessary," but he also feared that "the controversy and misconceptions arising from it might hurt the bill."[51]

Opposing discrimination rather than segregation, Powell's amendment actually invited the support of southern legislators. Richard Russell, for example, loudly declared that he, too, opposed discrimination and had crafted the school lunch bill to serve all children equally. While Russell and other southerners distrusted Powell's motives and certainly did not want to see Congress move toward dismantling segregation, they took great pains to insist that segregation and the system of racially separate schools in their region in no way constituted discrimination. North Carolina representative John Hamlin Folger declared that segregation "has never been a discrimination in any particular and never will be." Folger supported the school lunch program because, he believed, children's health "is too important to all of our races."[52] Virginia representative John Flannagan, a strong advocate of the school lunch program, declared Powell's amendment "entirely unnecessary." It would, he warned, "alienate some votes that might otherwise be cast for approval." In other words, Flannagan knew he could marshal support for the school lunch program from southern representatives, but would not be able to keep them in line if the bill in any way appeared to endorse federal interference with segregation.

By introducing his amendment in the language of anti-discrimination as opposed to anti-segregation, Powell left open a doorway through which segregationists like Russell and Flannagan could slip. Southerners had long argued that segregation was not a system of racial discrimination, but simply a separation of the races. Indeed, the very language of the Supreme Court's 1890 confirmation of segregation affirmed that separate could be equal. So strong was Richard Russell's conviction that segregation did not equal discrimination that he had actually agreed to a mild anti-discrimination clause in an earlier version of his bill. "The colored people are my friends," Russell insisted, "and I want to see them have the benefit of these funds. I know in the main, they need it more, perhaps, than some of the others do." In Russell's view, segregation was simply a recognition of social reality and racial capacities. Russell warned that Powell's amendment, by withholding federal resources from southern states, would actually end up discriminating against black children. "The inclusion of this clause," Russell warned, "will do that which the author of its amendment does not want, because there are too many states . . . that maintain separate schools for the races."[53] Should Powell's equation of segregation with discrimination hold, Russell predicted, no southern schools would be able to participate in the National School Lunch Program.

Southern conservatives, of course, immediately recognized Powell's amendment as what it was—an attempt to dismantle segregation. Texas representative William Robert Poage, an inveterate defender of states' rights, pointed to Powell's own recent statements arguing that "segregation is discrimination." Poage understood that if the amendment passed, local officials would lose the power to interpret just what constituted discrimination in federal programs. Pointing to a recent case in which a federal judge had ruled against the common practice of stipulating racial preferences in newspaper job-ads, Poage warned that the country was embarking on a slippery slope.[54] Mississippi's deeply conservative representative John Elliot Rankin also saw in Powell's amendment the threat of a new assertion of black rights. Rankin, who rarely bothered to disguise his contempt for minorities, whether black or Jewish, accused Powell of using "the exact language used in the Communist platform" in his amendment. The Communists, Rankin insisted, "want to destroy our separate school system and to force Negro equality upon us." The Powell amendment, Poage warned, "means trouble throughout the Southern States." What "they" mean by discrimination, he observed, "is segregation of the races."[55]

Powell's amendment only reinforced Republican opposition to the school lunch program. Foreshadowing what would become an increasingly common congressional alignment, northern Republicans joined with the most conservative southern Democrats to oppose any expansion of federal power. While some northern Republicans claimed to support the principle of anti-discrimination, they clearly saw Powell's amendment as a good way to kill the entire lunch program. Harold Knutson, a Republican from Minnesota, for example, admitted that he opposed the creation of a National School Lunch Program because he did not want to see any more growth in the federal government. He nonetheless voted in favor of

Figure 4.1. President Truman signing the National School Lunch Act. Congress created the National School Lunch Program in 1946. Also shown: Richard Russell (*third from left*) and Allen Ellender (*fourth from left*). United States Department of Agriculture, photo by Forsythe. Courtesy Harry S Truman Library.

Powell's amendment. Pennsylvania Republican George Harrison Bender introduced his own amendment that specifically prohibited federal funds from going to any state that maintained separate school systems. When confronted, both representatives admitted to being "against the passage of the bill."[56] Powell's amendment finally passed with a vote that reflected the shifting post-war political alliances. Among the votes against the amendment were Jerry Voorhis and the up-and-coming congressman from Texas, Lyndon Baines Johnson.

Southern Democratic party support, so necessary for the success of the school lunch legislation, ensured that the structure and administration of school cafeterias would be left to local officials and, despite the Powell Amendment, would leave existing racial divisions intact.[57] The decentralized administrative structure of the program reflected one of the core characteristics of American welfare and social policy. While social welfare advocates praised the new National School Lunch Program as a victory for children's health and nutrition reformers applauded the new potential for improving American diets, astute observers soberly warned that the school lunch bill was, in truth, severely limited in its scope. Unions, liberal women's organizations, and child welfare advocates, in particular, cautioned against the bill's funding formula that required states to match federal contributions to the program. The matching provisions, they warned, would render poor states less able to match federal dollars and poor districts within states would have difficulty meeting the matching obligation. As a result, the very children who most needed a nutritious lunch would be left out of the program entirely. National Education Association legislative representative Agnes Winn cautioned that bill's funding formula "forces the diversion of available school revenues from one purpose to another—from arithmetic and history and citizenship to the school lunch program." Given that choice, she said, few districts would be willing to pay for free lunches.[58] United Auto Workers' Union representative Anna Berenson warned that unless "ironclad safeguards" were instituted to ensure that poor states "guarantee that all children, regardless of geographical accidents of birth," would benefit from school lunches, the program would inevitably favor more prosperous communities. The spokeswoman of the American Association of University Women concluded that the legislation crafted by Congress ensures that "unto him that hath shall be given."[59] As with much of American welfare state legislation, however, Congress formulated a program that depended heavily on local resources and left the day-to-day administration to the discretion of local officials. Congress did not stipulate how states were to raise their matching contributions nor, despite Powell's amendment, did it establish any enforcement mechanism to ensure that school lunches were offered equally to all children. The most problematic consequence of lax congressional oversight, however, was the fact that while the school lunch legislation required schools to feed poor children for free, no one was charged with enforcing that provision.

The debate and legislation establishing a national school lunch program after World War II revealed both the high ideals of American democracy and the social fissures that would split the country open over the next two decades. Coming out of the war, American optimism ran high. American freedoms would unlock the "iron curtain," and America's consumer prosperity, it seemed, would fuel a world economy devastated by war. In this context, few public voices denied the value of feeding children at school. The New Deal promise of rational social planning and a more equitable distribution of resources seemed logically to point to a national food program for the nation's children. Indeed, most public officials liked to boast that America could well afford to keep all of its children healthy. Commenting that he had received "thousands of letters" from across the country in support of the school lunch bill, Adolph J. Sabath, Democratic representative from Illinois, said, "I do not know of any appropriation we have ever made that has been more humanitarian in nature."[60] At the same time, a persistent fear that the economy would once again sink into depression fueled farmers' desires to protect what they had come to see as a significant outlet for surplus commodities—the nation's school cafeterias. Overall, however, a lingering, if not intensifying, distrust of federal authority combined with the realities of racial and economic equality to make it difficult for law makers to craft a truly universal or egalitarian school lunch program. Indeed, the question of which children would receive lunch, who would decide, and what role state and local officials would play in that process revealed fundamental splits in the post-war American political agenda.

CHAPTER 5

Ideals and Realities in the Lunchroom

During the 1950s the National School Lunch Program became a permanent fixture in the federal budget. It also became a potent symbol for the American promise of equality and prosperity in the post-war world. Popular loyalty to the program reflected a confidence in continued economic growth and in America's new position as "leader of the free world." The affluent society and an expanding middle class became articles of faith in post-war political and popular culture. In 1959, when Vice President Richard Nixon promised the Soviet Union's Nikita Khrushchev that the United States would defeat communism with kitchen appliances, he articulated America's quintessentially optimistic confidence that consumer prosperity would necessarily produce social equality, if not world peace. Central to that vision, of course, was individual health and an abundance of food. Frozen foods, processed foods, and "fast foods" signaled not only seemingly homogenized American tastes but the ability of even those whose incomes did not quite meet middle-class levels to enjoy the benefits of modern life. Poverty and hunger all but disappeared from the pages of newspapers and from the consciousness of most lawmakers. In the Cold War world, the United States claimed not only to support its heartland producers but also to ensure the health and well-being of all its children. Most Americans, if asked, assumed that their government offered school lunches to all children and free lunches to any who could not afford to pay. In 1961 the *New York Times* confidently asserted that "children unable to pay must be served free lunches; and the lunches must meet nutritional standards of the Department of Agriculture."[1]

The fact was, however, that the American public invested the National School Lunch Program with an idealism that far outstripped its capacities. School lunch menus were still based on surplus commodities—apricots one year, olives the next—and many schools chose not to serve "Type A" meals. More significant, however, was the fact that most American children did not, in fact, have access to the program. Although federal school lunches were available in almost every state and U.S. territory (Alaska, Hawaii, Puerto Rico, and the Virgin Islands), only about half of the nation's public and parochial schools actually participated in the program.[2] Similarly, although the number of children participating in the program increased from 8.6 million in 1950 to 14 million a decade later, this constituted only about one-third of all American schoolchildren.[3] The National School Lunch Program, while an agricultural subsidy in content, was administered like a social welfare program in practice. This meant that, as with other welfare benefits, school lunches were administered by states who decided how federal resources were distributed and by local officials who decided which schools participated and how many free meals were offered. Most significantly, school teachers, principals, or social workers determined which children deserved free lunches. The tension between an ideal of universal child nutrition and the ability, indeed, the willingness of either Congress or the states to fund and oversee such a vision revealed the limits of the post-war liberal welfare agenda.[4]

The Truman and Eisenhower years were marked by a relatively prosperous economic growth that enabled both Democratic and Republican administrations to foster expansions of government functions. Those expansions, however, did not alter the decentralization that marked American social policy. For example, in his Fair Deal, Truman promised "full employment and nutritionally sound diets" for all Americans.[5] He happily signed the school lunch bill, noting that "no nation is any healthier than its children or more prosperous than its farmers."[6] In addition to school lunches, his administration endorsed public housing, modestly expanded Social Security coverage, debated national health insurance, and raised the minimum wage.[7] The Truman administration also signaled, at least rhetorically, a new commitment to racial equality. Not only did the president integrate the armed forces, but he also called for the abolition of poll taxes, spoke out against lynching, and opposed discrimination in employment. The words, however, often bespoke ambition more than action. President Truman's housing initiative, for example, promised affordable accommodations for all Americans but, in fact, built very few homes.[8] The Democrats created the National Science Foundation and passed the Atomic Energy Act, but were unable to enact national health insurance or to convince Congress to pass any substantial aid to education. In most cases, the Democratic party's social agenda continued to depend on a New Deal coalition of southern legislators and liberal representatives. During the early 1950s, some southern Democrats began to abandon the party, but stalwart school lunch advocates, including Richard Russell and Allen Ellender, remained loyal. These men supported Truman when it came to defense and agriculture but balked at any hint of a civil rights or labor agenda. After the Dixiecrat revolt of the early 1950s, the Democratic party basically retreated from an expansive social agenda.[9] In deference to its southern wing, the party allowed welfare programs, including Aid to Dependent Children and school lunches, to be administered locally by the states and accepted severe limits on federal

Figure 5.1. Idealized image of the National School Lunch Program. Two children eating their lunches in a school cafeteria. National Library of Medicine.

control.[10] When it came to school lunches, this meant that the program operated differently in each state as local officials decided how to distribute donated commodities and school administrators, welfare workers, or county representatives determined which schools participated in the program. Most notably, for the school lunch program, the Department of Agriculture did nothing to ensure the participation of black schools in racially segregated southern districts, nor did it establish any policies or guidelines to enforce the School Lunch Act's mandate that poor children, north or south, receive free meals.

NUTRITION AND SURPLUS COMMODITIES

During the 1950s, the National School Lunch Program enjoyed bipartisan support in the halls of Congress. The Democratic party regularly pointed to the program as a key element in its post-war agenda. The party's 1952 election platform, for example, promised to "enlarge the school lunch program which has done so much for millions of American school chil-

Figure 5.2. Idealized image of the National School Lunch Program. African American children in a school cafeteria. National Library of Medicine.

dren . . . while at the same time benefiting producers."[11] Richard Russell, who generally opposed any expansion of the federal budget, continued to champion children's meals. He told one skeptical constituent, "I voted against the British loan and have voted to reduce all foreign aid. I may say, however, that I do not propose to vote to reduce the modest amount provided as Federal aid for the school lunch program, for I think this is one of the most worthwhile activities of the government."[12] During the late 1940s, particularly after the Republican congressional victory in 1947, a small group of fiscal conservatives attempted to cut school lunch appropriations. Each time, however, their efforts were defeated. When, for example, President Eisenhower's Secretary of Agriculture, Ezra Taft Benson, recommended a cut of eight million dollars in the School Lunch Program's $75,000,000 budget, he met a formidable opposition led by Allen Ellender, who succeeded in gathering enough votes on both sides of the aisle to quash the cuts.[13] Indeed, Republicans as well as Democrats saw school lunches as part of an expansive post-war agenda. President Eisenhower enlarged the national highway system and increased federal aid for agricultural markets, both domestic and foreign. In 1954, for example, Congress passed the landmark food policy act P.L. 480, authorizing the Department of Agriculture to buy surplus commodities from American farmers and sell (or later donate) them abroad. While Eisenhower generally resisted special assistance for the poor, he actually increased the school lunch budget and started a special school milk program in 1954.[14] By the mid-1950s, both Republicans and Democrats seemed to accept school lunches as a permanent part of federal budget. Indeed, federal appropriations for the program increased every year throughout the 1950s. Cash and commodity assistance to schools increased during the decade, from $65 million to $94 million.[15] Reflecting back on the program's early years, *New York Times* reporter Ben Franklin commented that it had "practically no enemies in Congress."[16]

The National School Lunch Program's political support stemmed as much from its central place in the Department of Agriculture's domestic agenda as from its claims regarding children's health. When he signed the School Lunch Act, for example, President Truman confidently observed that the program "contributed immeasurably" both to children and to farmers.[17] During the 1950s, school lunchrooms were, as they had been since the 1930s, prime sites for the "disposal" of surplus agricultural commodities. Agriculture department officials had always viewed school lunches a means to an end—that is, as an insurance policy against the advent of agricultural surpluses. According to one estimate, school lunch and milk programs accounted for half of all federal food relief programs between 1950 and 1962.[18] The total value of commodities (per child) distributed to all states and territories varied from year to year during the 1950s, ranging from eight to eleven million dollars.[19] The commodities sent to school lunchrooms included processed foods as well as meat, dairy, vegetables, and fruits. In 1951, for example, the government distributed close to two million pounds of food products, including dried beans, cheese, orange juice, and peanut butter, along with apples, pears, cranberries, beets, cabbage, butter, and honey.[20] The Special Milk Program begun in 1954 distributed another 400 million half-pint milk bottles to schools.[21] The total program costs for school lunch and milk programs rose from 367,643 million in 1950 to 1,002,676 million in 1960.[22] North Dakota senator Quentin Burdick summed it up well, noting, "The entire Nation gains from this program because it helps assure a strong well-fed youth, a larger income for the farmer, a huge market for the food trades, jobs for the lunchroom personnel, employment for related industries, constructive outlets for abundant commodities, a well-nourished student who is more receptive to instruction, and a healthier Nation."[23]

Although Department of Agriculture officials maintained that the School Lunch Program was meant to "improve the dietary habits of school children," in truth, the program's bottom line was "to encourage the domestic consumption of nutritious agricultural commodities and other foods."[24] Lunchrooms were an important outlet for surplus products, including meat, milk, eggs, and cheese. If the Secretary of Agriculture determined that a commodity was in surplus, he was allowed by Congress to purchase that food and then donate it to schools for children's lunches. (After 1954 under P.L. 480 he could also sell or donate those commodities abroad.) Food industry groups—and their congressional representatives—were not shy about claiming their commodities to be "in surplus" if market prices were low. Thus, for example, the Florida citrus industry regularly made "strong representations" to the Secretary of Agriculture to convince him that the state was in a "surplus oranges situation."[25] In another case, William L. Lanier, president of the Georgia Farm Bureau Federation enlisted Senator Richard Russell's aid in convincing school lunch officials to substitute peanut butter for the butter requirement in the Type A lunch. In this case, however, the Department of Agriculture resisted. Howard P. Davis, deputy administrator of Consumer Food Programs, told Russell that while peanut butter "makes a significant contribution to the protein-rich food requirement of the lunch," it would not serve as a substitute for butter. No doubt fearing the wrath of the dairy lobby even more than that of peanut growers, Davis assured Russell that "there is a very definite place for both foods in the Type A Lunch."[26]

Children's welfare advocates continued to doubt whether schools could put together nutritious meals from the limited—and inconsistent—choice of foods available as surplus commodities. *McCall's Magazine*, for example, warned, "They're playing politics with our children's health."[27] Schools could expect a regular supply of staples such as dry milk, lard, flour, rice, and cornmeal, but they never knew what other foods might appear. One year, for example, the Department of Agriculture distributed six million dollars' worth of beef but the next year offered only half that amount.[28] Similarly, the department distributed six million dollars' worth of eggs one year, but because the market price went up, eggs were not on the surplus list the following year. Department of Agriculture contracts required schools to accept whatever foods were offered on surplus. This led to loud complaints from school officials and lunchroom supervisors, who were often at a loss as to how to concoct healthy meals from the food they received. As one Maryland principal observed, split peas and ripe olives had "no takers" in his state.[29]

NUTRITION AND THE FOOD SERVICE INDUSTRY

The shape of school meals and cafeteria operations reflected the declining influence of nutritionists and home economists in the Department of Agriculture. During the 1950s, school lunches became big business, and, as such, administration and finance became increasingly important parts of cafeteria operations. Nothing symbolized the priority of agricultural and business interests in the National School Lunch Program more than the fact that the program was administered out of the Consumer Marketing Service (CMS). This division was, as its title indicated, concerned with the marketing and distribution of agricultural products. It was staffed largely by men trained in economics and accounting who had little, if any, interest in or knowledge of nutrition. Indeed, placing the school lunch program in the CMS not only illustrated the ascendancy of economists and administrators, but also revealed the diminished influence of home economists and the declining interest in nutrition within the Department of Agriculture. After World War II, women's employment in the federal government generally declined along with the stature of agencies such as the Children's Bureau, the Women's Bureau—and the Bureau of Home Economics—that had been bastions of female influence in social and welfare policy.[30] In 1953 the Bureau of Home Economics was abolished and its functions transferred to the Agricultural Research Service. Similarly, the Farm Security Administration, which had traditionally been a center for nutrition education, was dramatically cut back, and the Agricultural Extension Division, long a significant employer of women and an important center for nutrition research and education, shifted most of its energy to technical support for industrialized agriculture. According to one estimate, by the end of the 1950s, nutrition research constituted only 4 percent of the Agriculture Department's budget.[31] Anthropologist Margaret Mead, who had worked closely with Bureau of Home Economics nutritionists during the war, noted that, in the past, the Department of Agriculture had been "the motive power for better food and better nutrition practices." By the 1960s, she said, interest at the USDA in the nutritional health of Americans had "withered away."[32]

The decline in interest in nutrition at the federal level had serious consequences for women in home economics. As federal funds for nutrition research dried up, university home economics departments, traditionally supported by the Agricultural Extension Service, began to close their doors or merge into schools of nursing, public health, or human development. Home economists turned to product testing and consumer training and left nutrition research to the chemists. Like other women's professions, home economics began a gradual decline during the 1950s that accelerated into a dramatic crisis during the 1960s. Where, for example, women made up 80 percent of social workers in 1930, they constituted only 65 percent in 1940 and continued to be steadily displaced by men throughout the postwar years. Similarly, men made gains among high school teachers in the post-war years, displacing women from their traditional posts.[33] Although this trend would speed up dramatically during the 1960s as women's educational and professional options expanded, the decline in home economics was well under way by the mid-1950s. High schools continued to offer home economics to girls and shop to boys, but by the end of the decade these gender distinctions began to collapse. Home economists who remained in the schools, furthermore, focused less on nutrition education and more on consumer education and family development. In many high schools, nutrition education (and home economics generally) disappeared from the curriculum, often replaced by physical education programs. While school nurses and social workers still regularly weighed and measured children, few medical researchers, or anyone else for that matter, did much with the data. Harvard nutritionist Jean Mayer observed that no one really knew how many children in the United States suffered from hunger or malnutrition "because not enough attention has been focused" on these problems.[34] No one, it seemed, was monitoring the nation's nutrition.[35]

Despite the declining interest in nutrition research and education, the National School Lunch Program proved to be a boon to the food-service industry. During the 1950s, the profession created by women—home economics—turned into an industry called food service, and what had been a female-dominated occupation gradually shifted to male leadership. Fostered largely by Department of Agriculture contracts and National School Lunch Program guidelines, the new food-service profession expanded dramatically. Federally subsidized school cafeterias had to be operated and supervised by administrators trained in Department of Agriculture fiscal guidelines and administrative procedures as much as in nutrition. Home economists who did not undergo new professional training lost their school lunch positions to a new generation of food-service supervisors—often men—who were as interested in business and administration as in menu planning and nutrition. As school food service became "a career option," rather than a part of the home economics teacher's purview (or the responsibility of PTA volunteers), it became increasingly attractive to men interested in management. As the American School Food Service Association's first president, Thelma Flanagan, observed, the cafeteria manager was not "just a cook" anymore."[36]

School food service as a profession came of age with the creation of the National School Lunch Program. During the 1930s, school cafeteria professionals formed regional School Food Service Associations that met regularly and articulated standards for nutrition and hygiene. These associations distributed recipes and menus, often sponsored by food industry groups using brand-name products. After the National School Lunch Program went into effect, the regional associations formed the nationwide American School Food Service Association (ASFSA) in 1946. In 1955 the ASFSA hired as its first executive director John Perryman, a man more experienced in business than in children's nutrition. Perryman built the organization through a network of state and regional chapters and within four years boasted a national membership of over 17,000.[37] Perryman deftly guided the ASFSA into the modern era in which food service, and school lunches, constituted a key element in the food and agricultural businesses. He centralized the food-service profession, establishing a national office for the ASFSA and organizing annual conventions in which members could meet not only to learn about the latest nutrition theories and federal school lunch regulations but also to see new food products and cafeteria equipment. Perryman maintained close ties to both the Department of Agriculture and to the food-service industry. The ASFSA regularly sold advertising space in its newsletter and invited private companies to exhibit at its annual national conventions. While during its early years, most of the association's advertising revenue came from kitchen and cafeteria equipment manufacturers, by the end of the 1950s, brand-name foods and new food products were commonplace. "I remember the eye-opener of seeing instant potatoes," recalled cafeteria manager, Lucille Barnett. School food service had, in her professional lifetime, "moved from a cracker-barrel, backwoods business to a billion dollar industry."[38] By 1952 school lunch programs constituted a $415 million operation, including large investments in equipment in many schools. In 1961 school lunches accounted for $308 million out of $366 million in federal food dollars.[39] That year, Secretary of Agriculture Orville Freeman boasted that the National School Lunch Program was "the largest single group feeding effort anywhere in the world."[40]

Like other industrial operations, school food service increasingly depended on unskilled workers and distant supervision. Indeed, school cooks were among the lowest paid professionals in the food-service industry. School lunch workers, more often than not, were working women, mothers and housewives who wanted part-time jobs. These women had little formal training, although everyone agreed "they are a splendid group of people. . . . their endeavors are most sincere and valiant."[41] Unlike dietitians and home economists, who were required to hold higher education degrees, school food-service workers' training, when it was not on-the-job, consisted of workshops and in-service programs. Indeed, by the 1960s, only 38 percent of school cafeteria assistants had finished high school, and just 80 percent of managers had earned a high school degree.[42]

As late as 1968, school cafeteria workers earned only $1.60 per hour.[43] In some places wages were even lower. Washington, D.C., cafeteria workers, for example, earned between $1.35 and $1.65 per hour.[44] Chief of Pay Systems and Labor Relations for the district's school lunch programs considered school cooks to be less skilled than their counterparts who worked in hospitals. Hospital cooks, he noted, "must be diet cooks" and were expected to prepare three meals a day, while school cooks only prepared lunch."[45] When schools moved toward pre-packaged meals and central kitchens in the 1960s, trained cooks almost entirely disappeared from the cafeteria. States employed dietitians to oversee school lunch menus, but these professionals spent little time, if any, actually working in the kitchen. In Alabama, for example, one dietitian planned menus for all of the state's lunch programs. She supervised several thousand women who did the actual food preparation. The state's director of food-service operations admitted there was "a common feeling that home economists no longer knew much about school lunch programs."[46]

The Limits of the Lunchroom

In truth, during the 1950s, the National School Lunch Program served up more in rhetoric than in substance. The Department of Agriculture could boast about its school lunch program, and those lawmakers who had an interest in agriculture could feel good about their support for farmers. Despite the generally optimistic tone of domestic politics during the 1950s, however, American social welfare policies, including the National School Lunch Program, were marked by serious limitations. Most notably, the school lunch program's administrative and fiscal structure revealed the influence of southern legislators who insisted on weak federal oversight for social programs and the reluctance of liberal lawmakers to challenge obvious regional and racial inequalities in services and benefits. The popular belief, for example, that any American child who needed a nutritious lunch could get one was largely a myth. The National School Lunch Program's administrative structure fundamentally institutionalized inequality and discrimination and seriously undermined the federal government's claim to be an effective guardian either of national food policy or child nutrition. As with Aid to Dependent Children and other federal welfare programs, federal funds were distributed via state agencies. While this pleased southern legislators who resisted federal involvement, particularly when it came to racial equity, it perpetuated local inequalities when it came to feeding children. Thus, while the National School Lunch Act set nutrition standards for children's meals and insisted that poor children be given free lunches, Congress established no enforce-

TABLE 5.1
Sources of Funding for School Lunch Program, 1947–68*

Year	Total program cost (in thousands)	Children's payment (in thousands/ %)	State and local funds (thousands/ %)	Total federal contribution (%)	Federal food donations (%)	Federal cash appropriation (%)
1947	218,631	52.5/23.56	17.4/7.96	31.1	1.1	30.0
1950	367,643	48.2/13.11	19.2/5.22	32.6	10.5	22.1
1955	611,539	55.0/8.99	20.1/3.29	24.9	11.5	13.4
1960	1,002,676	55.5/55.39	22.0/21.96	22.5	7.1	15.4
1965	1,492,797	53.4/35.79	19.6/13.14	27.0	14.3	12.7
1968	1,872,011	53.2/28.42	23.5/12.55	23.3	11.8	11.5

Source: Hearings, School Lunch, and Child Nutrition Programs, September 29–October 1, 1969, Committee on Agriculture and Forestry, United States Senate, 91st Cong., 1st Sess., 184.
*Does not count local contributions.

ment mechanism—and appropriated no funds—to ensure that these requirements were met.

School lunch funding structures perpetuated America's regional and racial inequalities. In order to encourage local "buy-in" for the school lunch program, congressional appropriations covered only a small fraction of the cost of children's lunches. After the first three years of operation, states were obligated to match federal contributions on a three-to-one basis. Most states, rather than raise local taxes, decided to charge children a small amount for lunch and count those fees as their part of the match. Thus, until the early 1960s, the National School Lunch Program's financial base rested on families who were able to pay the cost of subsidized meals for their children. For this reason, lunches during the 1950s came to be seen as a subsidy for the middle class, broadly defined as families who could afford to pay for school lunches.

Although congressional appropriations for children's lunches increased each year during the 1950s, the federal government's real share of school lunch budgets actually declined (see Tables 5.1 and 5.2). In 1947, the program's first year of operation, federal contributions accounted for 32 cents out of each school lunch dollar, while state and municipal contributions made up about 12 cents. Children's lunch money, along with contributions from PTAs and civic groups, made up the rest of the program's operating budget. In 1952 the federal school lunch contribution fell to only 12 cents and state government payments accounted for just 9 cents.

TABLE 5.2
Local Sources of Financing for National School Lunch Program, Selected States, 1967*

State	Children's fees	State government	Local government	Charities
Alabama	100%			
Arizona	82.0	0.3	17.7	
Arkansas	93.6	2.3	4.1	
Florida**	94.5	0.3	2.5	
Georgia	96.4	0.4	3.2	
Louisiana	49.0	36.0	13.0	0.2
Maine	85.2	1.6	11.4	1.6
Maryland	86.1	0.3	13.9	
Massachusetts	65.5	11.0	22.5	
Minnesota	90.5	2.3	6.9	0.3
Missouri	75.7	20.4	3.9	
Nebraska	97.2	—	2.8	
New Hampshire	89.9	0.6	9.1	
New Jersey	78.0	0.6	21.4	
New York	52.9	20.9	26.2	
North Carolina	90.3	0.8	8.9	
Ohio	79.2	0.2	20.6	
Oklahoma	89.9	5.6	5.4	
Oregon	81.5	0.7	17.8	
Pennsylvania	90.8	0.3	8.9	
South Carolina	89.0	4.3	3.9	
Tennessee	90.2	0.3	7.7	
Texas	96.6	0.4	3.0	
Utah	79.1	19.9	1.0	
Virginia	90.0	0.4	9.6	
Wisconsin	76.9	0.9	22.2	

Source: Committee on School Lunch Participation, *Their Daily Bread: A Study of the National School Lunch Program* (Atlanta, Ga.: McNelley-Rudd Printing Service, 1968), 38–39.

* Some states were not listed because the figures were incomplete at the time of publication.

** This was the first year Florida appropriated funds for school lunches. At the time of the study, the governor had just vetoed it.

In point of fact, the only source of school lunch funding that increased during the 1950s was the amount that parents sent to school for their children's meals. By 1952, parent contributions in the form of lunch fees covered over half of the program's costs. Indeed, between 1947 and 1968, state and local contributions averaged only 21 percent of the total program costs, while children's fees nationwide, accounted for 55 percent.[47] In 1962, Department of Agriculture officials boasted that the states paid nine million dollars in matching contributions. Two-thirds of that nine million, however, came from children's school lunch fees and not from state or local treasuries.[48] Some state legislatures actually passed laws prohibiting the use of local taxes for school lunch programs. Others contributed only to food expenses and refused to pay for operating costs or equipment. In Louisiana, despite Allen Ellender's commitment to the program state funds made up just over one-third of the school lunch operating expenses. In Georgia, the situation was even worse. State funds made up only 0.4 percent of the cost of lunch. Northern states were only somewhat more generous. New York State, for example, paid only 21 percent of the cost of lunch, and Massachusetts contributed only 11 percent.[49] In other words, while the federal government took credit for a National School Lunch Program, it was children's fees that kept the program going.[50]

The consequences of the School Lunch Program's financial structure meant than many American children had no access to subsidized meals. Because states were not obligated to participate in the federal program, as late as 1960 only about half of the nation's public and private schools (64,000) contracted with the department of Agriculture for lunch programs. While the department boasted that it fed over fourteen million children, this was only a third of the nation's public school students.[51] Most of the children eating school lunches during the 1950s came from rural, white school districts in the South and southwest. The program's heavily rural and southern bias clearly reflected the continued influence of legislators like Richard Russell and Allen Ellender, who enthusiastically backed the program well into the 1960s. Not surprisingly, both Georgia and Louisiana claimed among the highest participation rates in the nation (73% and 74%, respectively), this despite the fact that the states themselves contributed little to the program.[52] Indeed, in 1960, not one of the nation's large cities contracted with the Department of Agriculture for school lunch subsidies.[53] As late as 1962, only 5 percent of Philadelphia's schools participated in the federal program. Chicago and Detroit offered subsidized lunch for only 10 percent of their schoolchildren, while Cleveland and San Francisco fed fewer than 20 percent. The only major city boasting even 50 percent participation was Miami (62%), reflecting the program's general Southern tilt[54] (see Table 5.3).

The program's rural bias reflected the structure of urban schools as much as the interests and influence of southern lawmakers. Many city schools had been built during the 1920s' expansion of public education. Designed as neighborhood schools in an era when middle-class mothers had not yet entered the work force in large numbers, most of these schools had no cafeteria facilities—school boards as well as school architects as-

TABLE 5.3
National School Lunch Program Participation in Select Cities, 1962*

City	Number of children participating	Percentage of total attendance participating
Miami	102,718	61.5
Philadelphia	11,585	4.7
Boston	14,896	11.2
Detroit	28,766	9.9
Chicago	49,611	16.5
San Francisco	14,802	17.1

Source: Hearings, National School Lunch Act, June 19, 1962, Subcommittee on Agriculture and Forestry, United States Senate, 87th Cong., 2nd Sess., 25.
*Includes only elementary schools.

sumed children would go home for lunch. Whether this reflected the reality of life in urban, working-class neighborhoods of the 1920s and 1930s is questionable. It is certain, however, that by the 1950s, despite the rise of a post-war "culture of domesticity," large numbers of mothers held jobs outside their homes and could not wait in their kitchens for their children to come home at noon. The domestic ideal, combined with a general disinterest in agricultural programs, however, explains why, until the mid-1960s, most northern politicians as well as liberal civic groups paid little attention to the workings of the school lunch program. Only after 1963, when the civil rights movement looked to the North, and politicians as well as activists "discovered" poverty, did school lunches become an issue for legislators in states such as Illinois, Ohio, California, and Massachusetts. As one historian put it, during the 1950s, the school lunch program worked well in the South and in rural areas but was "no issue at all for big-city liberals."[55]

Like other federal welfare benefits, school lunches depended on the will of local politicians to fund the program. The consequences of this decentralized administration were particularly dramatic when it came to providing free lunches for poor children. The fact that the Department of Agriculture allowed states to use children's fees as the matching requirement meant that even if schools wanted to offer free lunches, they had to come up with local contributions to do so. Most states chose simply to ignore the free lunch mandate. The burden of meeting the full cost of the lunch program rested on local communities, many of which had neither the resources nor the inclination to devote substantial amounts of money to feed poor children. Schools could, admittedly, charge more to paying children in order to subsidize free meals. Most districts, however, felt themselves strained even to meet the costs for children who could pay. Local administrators feared that asking children to pay higher prices would cause them to drop out of the program and thus decrease the overall revenue. One state school lunch director called the program's matching formula "not realistic."[56] The predictable result was that few children received free lunches, and, particularly in the South, racial segregation prevailed. The American School Food Service Association's Rodney Ashby admitted: "Despite successes, achievements, accolades, and unbelievably few criticisms, our pride of accomplishment . . . is not a little dulled when we view what should have been done and what must yet be accomplished."[57]

The fact was, during the 1950s, few policy makers, whether in the Department of Agriculture or in liberal civic organizations, were particularly concerned about feeding poor children. The Department of Agriculture largely ignored the School Lunch Act's provisions requiring participating schools to offer free lunches to children who could not afford to pay. In the end, the number free lunches served actually declined during the 1950s. Just after the program began, 17 percent of lunches were served for free. By 1960, fewer than 10 percent of the National School Lunch Program meals were offered for free.[58] A 1962 survey estimated that half a million low-income children attended schools that participated in the program but offered no free meals.[59] When confronted with the survey results, Secretary of Agriculture Orville Freeman admitted that the findings "jarred any complacency we might have had."[60]

The limits of the program were dramatically illustrated in 1955 when the Los Angeles school district quietly dropped out of the program. When the federal cash subsidy for each meal fell to 4 cents that year, the district decided it was "financially impractical" to remain in the program.[61] No longer contracting for federally subsidized food, the district tried to develop a lunch program based on local resources. According to its own evaluation, however, the nutritional standards for Los Angeles school lunch fell below federal guidelines, providing only one-third of the children's RDAs. Los Angeles school officials then faced the financial conundrum of a school lunch system dependent on children's fees. To serve nutritious meals and at the same time provide free lunches to poor children, the city's lunch administrators realized they would have to either ask for increased local taxes or raise the price of lunch. Believing the former was politically impossible, they announced that the cost of lunch would increase. When the price went up, however, the number of paying children declined and the district ended up losing money in any case. Ultimately, Los Angeles school officials decided to keep the price of lunch low in order to induce children to stay in the lunch line. This meant that they also decided to limit the number of free meals they could offer. Poor children in Los Angeles thus found themselves excluded from the lunch program. While the result was that the city ran a viable lunch program, feeding about one-third of its schoolchildren in 1960, the number of poor children receiving free meals was "microscopically small," less than 1 percent.[62]

Cases like Los Angeles notwithstanding, the National School Lunch Program ended the 1950s as one of the nation's most popular federal programs. No one in the federal government had bothered to tinker with it very much during the fifteen years since its establishment, and most people thought the program worked pretty well. The Department of Agriculture exerted little administrative oversight, largely because of the founders' aversion to federal interference in state affairs. Agriculture officials believed it was up to the states to distribute both cash and commodities as they saw fit. For that reason, the inequities in the system remained largely hidden from public scrutiny. The principle of states' rights guarded local officials from accountability and provided an easy excuse for federal officials to ignore the fact that the program was not meeting its stated goals. The last thing Department of Agriculture officials wanted was to be seen as interfering with local school matters. In principle, as Allen Ellender envisioned it, this would ensure local loyalty to the program. In fact, as the dismal figures on poor children revealed, it reinforced a deep inequality in the American social fabric. That inequality could be masked during the 1950s as relative prosperity combined with a political climate that eschewed critical dissent. By the end of the decade, however, demands for racial equity, along with a growing awareness that many Americans had been left out of the era's economic boom, opened the school lunch program—and other government benefits as well—to new scrutiny.

CHAPTER 6

No Free Lunch

For the first fifteen years of its existence the National School Lunch Program enjoyed widespread support but fed relatively few children. Those children who ate school lunches generally paid a small fee and received a "balanced" hot meal that was prepared on-site at least partly from surplus commodities. Teachers, principals, and social workers might designate certain children to receive free lunches, but on the whole, few schools regularly provided free meals. Indeed, the period between 1946 and 1960 marked a remarkably complacent time when it came to questions of poor people in America. While a new movement for civil rights was quietly brewing, it focused more on dismantling the legal structures of Jim Crow—voting rights, public accommodations, and segregated schools—than on economic conditions. After 1960, however, poverty returned to center stage in national policy and reform circles. Although the "discovery" of poverty during the 1960s took many forms, from President Johnson's War on Poverty and the institutionalization of Great Society welfare programs to the vast expansion of volunteer food pantries and community health clinics, Department of Agriculture officials were slow to grasp the significance of these movements for its long-standing food programs, including the National School Lunch Program. Only gradually did it dawn on policy makers, parents, school officials, and activists that poor children were not being served in school lunchrooms.

Poverty had never, of course, disappeared from American communities. Despite the aura of affluence that characterized the 1950s, large numbers of Americans remained outside the middle-class consumer economy. While blue-collar union wages afforded many working-class families a comfortable living, the benefits were largely confined to white workers in urban, industrial enclaves. Outside the manufacturing sector, rural poverty, combined with large swaths of urban "ghetto" areas, gave lie to the notion that all Americans had achieved middle-class status. Indeed, the post-war economic expansion of the 1950s effectively hid lingering pockets of poverty—rural as well as urban—from public view. By the end of the decade, however, a decline in the manufacturing sector threatened the economic security even many blue-collar families thought they had achieved after World War II. At the same time, a resurgent civil rights movement revealed the underlying racial inequalities in America that encompassed economic status as well as political rights. With the "discovery" of poverty during the early 1960s, federal benefits like the National School Lunch Program appeared increasingly limited, if not downright discriminatory. The program promised, in principle, to feed the nation's children and to provide free meals for those who could not afford to pay. By the end of the 1950s, it was clear that neither goal was being met.

As the election of 1960 approached, Americans seemed to believe that they had conquered the problems of poverty and hunger. Images of undernourished draftees and Depression Era bread lines had long since receded. The nation had plenty of food—so much that tons of commodities were regularly shipped abroad to feed the hungry in the "underdeveloped" world. Indeed, under P.L. 480 the Department of Agriculture set up school lunch programs abroad to bring the bounty of American farms to the world's hungry children.[1] In the midst of abundance, however, nutritionists rather quietly began to warn Americans against "overeating," and doctors began to report an increasing incidence of obesity. American culture focused on diet fads and weight loss—symptoms of too much to eat rather than too little. Margaret Mead observed that "every cocktail party, every school picnic, every coffee-break, the whole articulate verbal section of the American people were trying not to eat something."[2] Hunger and malnutrition seemed a very distant threat to those Americans who, by 1960, enjoyed an unprecedented bounty of consumer goods including an ever-growing assortment of processed, frozen, and prepared foods.[3] Poverty, hunger, and malnutrition appeared to be conditions endemic to foreign countries and remote parts of Africa, Asia, or Latin America, certainly not conditions found in the American heartland.[4]

DISCOVERING HUNGER IN AMERICA

Federal food policy during the 1950s was not predicated on domestic poverty or the fact that there might be hungry children in America. Indeed, the nation's main center for food policy, the Department of Agriculture, spent the decade focused on agricultural productivity, commodity markets, and foreign aid. While the USDA regularly distributed milk and surplus foods to the nation's schools, its primary mission was to support farm incomes and provide technical support to the increasingly industrialized agricultural sector. Similarly, when Congress authorized the Department of Agriculture to send commodities abroad under P.L. 480, its intent was as much to maintain American agricultural prices as to feed hungry people in the "Third World." Just as the Department of Agriculture had used American schools as outlets for surplus food during the 1930s, agriculture officials used farm commodities "to encourage economic development abroad."[5] By the time John F. Kennedy was elected president in 1960, food had become a staple in Cold War diplomatic strategy. Shipments of wheat, corn, and other commodities served as symbols of American democracy and prosperity, shoring up regimes threatened by internal revolutionary movements and external Soviet support. Ultimately, as president, Kennedy codified the use of food as a diplomatic weapon by appointing Senator George McGovern to head the "Food for Peace" program targeted at "developing" nations.[6] Agricultural prosperity and an abundance of food appeared to confirm the success and superiority of American institutions in the Cold War world. Kennedy's Secretary of Agriculture Orville Freeman boasted that "if we were as far ahead of the Russians in the space race as we are in agriculture, we would by now be running a shuttle service to the moon."[7]

So confident were Americans in their abundant food supply that nutritionists and home economists rarely studied domestic food habits and cultures any more. Reporting to Lyndon Johnson on malnutrition among children in the United States, presidential aide, Richard W. Reuter noted, "Our office has been able to find little evidence of study of the nutritional adequacies of U.S. families since New Deal days." He added, "Apparently, little is known of the actual diets of children in our own poverty areas."[8] Unlike earlier generations of food reformers who had been fascinated by the food cultures of immigrants, ethnics, and African Americans, midcentury nutritionists explored eating habits and food-related conditions like rickets and malnutrition only in foreign settings. "We know more about the nutrition of Indians in India than we do about our own people," admitted one malnutrition specialist.[9] When nutritionists, doctors, social workers, or teachers discussed hunger in American at all, they did so through the lens of foreign field research and experience abroad. Indeed, many of the 1960s anti-poverty activists came to domestic concerns after serving in the Peace Corps abroad. Returning home, this generation was shocked to "discover" poverty in their own communities.

As it turned out, the only language food reformers of the 1960s had to describe hunger and malnutrition came from their experience outside the United States. When, for example, anti-hunger activists in John F. Kennedy's presidential campaign found poor communities in the Mississippi Delta, they likened the condition of people there to "those primitive tribal Africans in Kenya and Aden."[10] A group of physicians subsequently told an "incredulous" panel of experts that, after examining black children in South Carolina, they were shocked to find advanced stages of hunger and kwashiorkor, "a protein deficiency disease normally associated with West Africa."[11] Similarly, a child care worker in Hidalgo County, Texas, was shocked to find the conditions there "considerably worse" than any she had seen during her Peace Corps stint in Honduras, "the most backward country in Central America."[12] Urban activists likewise drew on their experiences in places like Ethiopia, West Pakistan, and Southeast Asia to understand the conditions they found in America's inner cities.[13] The specter of hunger in the world's most prosperous nation was profoundly embarrassing. Images of starving children in the Mississippi Delta and in Appalachian valleys and, increasingly, in the nation's poor urban neighborhoods as well unnerved mainstream liberals. As late as 1967, President Johnson's Interagency Task Force on Nutrition and Adequate Diets reported that "at the present time most of the basic and applied work on the relationship of malnutrition to development is being carried on outside of the U.S."[14]

A new, domestic-oriented anti-hunger and anti-poverty movement emerged during the early 1960s. Informed by such striking works as Michael Harrington's scathing expose, *The Other America*, and a powerful and influential review in *The New Yorker* by Dwight MacDonald, poverty began to take center stage among liberal reformers.[15] Led in large part by civil rights activists and liberal church groups, a new "hunger lobby" linked domestic poverty to racial inequality and demanded a reorientation of domestic food and agricultural priorities. As the civil rights movement in the South exposed the realities of economic as well as political discrimination, the media and the American public gradually took notice of hunger and malnutrition in their own midst. Most accounts of the "discovery" of poverty during the early 1960s date the change in public awareness to John F. Kennedy's presidential campaign. During a campaign visit to rural West Virginia, for example, Kennedy promised to pay special attention to social issues at home. After the election, liberal policy makers pushed the new president to address poverty and inequality in the North as well as the South. While the new administration put most of its focus on employment and educational opportunity rather than hunger, one of Kennedy's first executive orders reestablished the Food Stamp Program. By the time of the Kennedy assassination and Lyndon B. Johnson's announcement of his War on Poverty, in 1964, new anti-poverty and anti-hunger groups had begun to appear throughout the country. Chief among the goals of these groups were free lunches for poor children.[16]

Agriculture or Welfare?

Initially, the Department of Agriculture resisted efforts to link its food programs to welfare policy. While the department had always, in a very real sense, provided welfare for the nation's farm sector, Secretary of Agriculture Orville Freeman, much like his predecessors, never envisioned the surplus commodity programs as social welfare more generally. Neither USDA officials nor their congressional supporters had any desire to get into the business of welfare or social services. Throughout both the Kennedy and the Johnson administrations, Freeman contended uneasily with the growing pressure to re-orient the lunch program toward needy children. It was not that he objected to government assistance for poor children or that he opposed a free lunch program. But he believed that these programs belonged elsewhere in the government bureaucracy. Freeman was not unsympathetic to calls for welfare reform; he just did not believe that the Department of Agriculture was the appropriate vehicle for such measures. As a protégé of Minnesota Democratic senator Hubert Humphrey, the Secretary had solid liberal credentials. He chaired Minnesota's Democratic Farmer-Labor Party in the 1950s and served three terms as governor. During a bitter 1959 strike at a meat-packing plant in Albert Lea, for example, he called in the state's national guard, thus alienating the company management, who preferred to wait out the union action, as well as the union who felt it was in a position to win the strike. Freeman's actions nonetheless won him the respect of state as well as national Democratic leaders, and at the 1960 Democratic National Convention, he had the honor of placing Kennedy's name in nomination. After the election, Kennedy tapped him to become Secretary of Agriculture.[17] When Freeman took over the department, he inherited a six-billion-dollar operation with over 96,000 employees. It was second in size and influence only to the Department of Defense.[18] Freeman's view was that the USDA existed for the benefit of American farmers and that it was his job and the job of agriculture programs to keep those interests in the forefront. What is more, the School Lunch Program mission, as Freeman saw it, was to make nutritious meals available to all children, not just those who were poor.

When Freeman became Secretary of Agriculture, the National School Lunch Program was, without doubt, one of the department's most prized achievements. Commanding a loyal backing in Congress, the program had been protected throughout the 1950s by a still-powerful southern farm bloc. Louisiana senator Ellender, who had chaired the Senate Agriculture Committee for over two decades, remained one of the program's staunch protectors. During the early 1960s, however, pressure built to expand the program's reach, particularly, to provide free lunches for poor children. For an increasing number of liberal lawmakers, protecting farmers would no longer suffice. American food policy, they insisted, must serve the needs of all citizens and, most especially, the poor. For the first time since the National School Lunch Program's creation, its fundamental mission came into question. Not only did critics begin to ask why farm surpluses defined school menus, but they also began to question how decisions were made regarding which children received free meals. Ultimately, the critical question was whether the school lunch program could—or would—serve as a universal child nutrition program and also provide free meals to poor children.

Freeman openly admitted that the lunch program had badly neglected the nation's poor children. In 1962 he commissioned a survey of the program. The results, he admitted, "were jarring, to put it mildly."[19] The survey uncovered the fact that poor children were almost entirely excluded from school lunchrooms. "In many areas only a very small percentage of school lunches are free or reduced prices, the heaviest participation in school lunches coming in areas where there is little need."[20] According to Freeman's own estimate, at least half a million needy children attended schools that offered lunch programs but did not serve free meals. As if that were not enough, over nine million American children attended schools that offered no meal program at all. Of those nine million, Freeman estimated that at least one million were "children of poverty."[21] The problem clearly went beyond simple poverty. Schools with the highest proportion of needy children were concentrated in low-income urban areas—neighborhoods that by the early 1960s were heavily black. Similarly, in the South, most of the all-black schools in that region's segregated system had no lunchroom facilities.[22] In 1963, according to White House aide, Harry McPherson, Jr., the school lunch program in Alabama, Georgia, Mississippi, and Virginia reached 62 percent of white children and only 26 percent of non-white. At the same time, McPherson estimated that fewer than one-third of the white children came from low-income families, while "from 50 to 90 percent . . . of the Negro children came from such families." In Maryland, only one out of eight students in "the Negro high school" received school lunches as compared with one in two or one in three in the white schools. The basic reason for the "gross inequities," McPherson admitted, was that "the program is administered as a surplus food distribution activity and the methods of administration largely ignore the question of need."[23]

The Department of Agriculture's dismal record of service to poor children fueled both citizen outrage and intra-governmental rivalries. Lyndon Johnson's War on Poverty quickly spawned both federal and local agencies that threatened the Agriculture Department's monopoly on food policy and children's meals. New York congressman Charles Godell put it bluntly, "I think we can state without much question," he said, "that the commodity distribution program was not a program primarily established to feed the hungry in this country." In Godell's view, the school lunch program should be moved "elsewhere than the Department of Agriculture."[24] Joseph Califano, head of the newly created cabinet Department of Health, Education and Welfare (HEW), saw in the Department of Agriculture's failures an opening for his own programs and began to offer funds to schools wanting to establish free lunch programs for poor children.[25] HEW's pioneering Head Start Program, for example, included free meals in its pre-schools. HEW funds were more flexible than the Department of Agriculture's school lunch appropriations and could be used to pay for labor and equipment as well as for food. Califano went so far as to suggest that all federal child nutrition programs be shifted from the Department of Agriculture to his own agency. As presently structured, the HEW secretary charged, the National School Lunch Program benefited farmers but was of little use to poor children. Furthermore, the Department of Agriculture had neither the will or the desire to turn itself into a welfare agency. Califano's legislative assistant Phillip Hughes argued that the Agriculture Department's "main concern" was to serve farm interests. The special needs of the poor, Hughes said, particularly the need for food, were "more likely to be met sooner" if the federal government turned over responsibility for child feeding to HEW.[26] In fact, among the proposals for "legislation with Civil Rights implications," prepared by President Johnson's advisers in 1965, was a plan to shift all school lunch and milk programs over to HEW.[27]

Nutrition professionals and child welfare advocates had long questioned the Department of Agriculture's control over children's nutrition. Nutritionist Michael Latham took the department to task for its "imperfect job" and its inability to distribute food to the people who really needed it. The USDA"s underlying philosophy, Latham insisted, "is in conflict with what needs to be done." In Latham's view, "a department which has as its main aim the improvement of agriculture and the lot of the farmer suffers a conflict of interests when its second duty is to feed the poor."[28]

Under Califano's leadership, communities across the country began to use education and welfare funds to open new free lunch programs in schools and day-care centers. In particular, states used funds from the 1965 Elementary and Secondary Education Act (ESEA) to start free lunch programs. Often these were considered "emergency" meal programs for poor children in urban areas and predominantly black rural counties as well.[29] ESEA and Head Start free lunch programs operated independently of the Department of Agriculture and appeared where no National School Lunch Programs had existed before. South Carolina, for example, used ESEA funds to provide an estimated 1700 free lunches. Little Rock, Arkansas, used similar funds to serve over 2,000 meals each day. In Minneapolis, 3,000 "inner city" children ate free lunches paid for with ESEA funds, while in Texas, Colorado, and New Mexico, schools drew on these monies to provide meals for the children of migrant workers.[30] By the end of 1965, Agriculture Secretary Freeman, who was not especially happy about the fact that other agencies were infringing on his department's school lunch territory, estimated that as much as $16 million in education funds was being spent "to assist the schools in feeding needy children."[31] Neither Freeman nor Agriculture Department advocates in Congress wanted to lose food programs—whether school lunches, milk, or food stamps—to other authorities.[32] John A. Schnittker, Acting Secretary of Agriculture, insisted that while HEW was making a significant contribution improving the nutritional welfare of poor children, the ultimate "objective" of nutrition for all children would best be served "by centralizing in the Department of Agriculture the basic responsibility" for such activities.[33]

With powerful advocates in both the House and the Senate, the Department of Agriculture enjoyed considerable support in its effort to maintain a hold on school lunch programs. While the push to expand welfare programs, particularly to African Americans, was gaining ground in Congress, however, school lunch advocates hesitated simply to target poor children. Traditional program backers, including Allen Ellender and Richard Russell, were particularly leery of explicitly turning the program into welfare because they feared this would lead to increased federal scrutiny of Jim Crow restrictions on benefits for blacks. These men argued therefore that the program should remain focused on all children and should not shift its emphasis to the poor. Ellender, for example, loudly protested against turning the school lunch program into welfare for poor children. Liberals, he believed, with their commitment to a civil rights agenda, were trying to entirely re-define the school lunch program. "I do not want to mix it in with "Headstart" or "Head-on" or whatever you might call the programs in the poverty program," Ellender complained.[34] Richard Russell similarly insisted that feeding poor children had never been the original bill's central intent.

With increased competition from new agencies and mounting public pressure to serve more poor children, the Department of Agriculture and its congressional backers for the first time had to re-think the fundamental goals of the school lunch program. In an effort to ward off the critics and to answer the increasingly loud demands for more free lunches, Agriculture Department officials, along with the program's professional association, the American School Food Service Association, began to draft major changes in the program's administrative and funding structure. In 1962 Congress for the first time required the Department of Agriculture to enforce the free meal provision in the School Lunch Act. In the school lunch budget appropriation that year, Congress directed the Secretary of Agriculture to provide free lunches to all poor children. The legislators, however, neglected to appropriate any new funds for this purpose. Indeed, the special assistance fund that was supposed to provide an incentive for states to offer more free and reduced price meals went entirely unfunded for two years.[35] Still, Congress put the Department of Agriculture on notice that something needed to be done to re-direct school lunch priorities.

Sensing a looming crisis, and probably hoping to deflect any widespread public or congressional scrutiny of the school lunch program, the Department of Agriculture, under Freeman's direction, developed a small-scale food-based welfare plan. Using the model of foreign aid, Agriculture officials put together a school lunch "CARE package" that included "the essentials for lunch," including nutrition charts and menu suggestions. The CARE packages were distributed to a small number of model schools. This was, Freeman later admitted, "a less than adequate solution."[36] The following year Agriculture Department staff members were dispatched to a few isolated Appalachian communities to help local school officials start lunch programs. Most of the targeted schools, however, had no space to store, prepare, or serve food, and many had only "two-burner hotplates" for cooking. Freeman's heart clearly was not in this new direction. While he admitted that these projects brought much needed nutrition to poor children, he complained to Congress that they required an "enormous effort." If Congress wanted his Department to adequately feed the nation's poor children, Freeman declared, it would have to vote new appropriations and provide "new authority" for the use of surplus food and federal resources.[37]

The "new authority" came in 1966 as the forces for reform gained ground both in Congress and among public advocacy groups. In 1966 Congress passed the Child Nutrition Act that, for the first time, appropriated funds directly for free lunches. The act also established a pilot School Breakfast Program aimed at poor children. The 1966 Child Nutrition act proved to be a milestone in the transformation of school lunches from farm subsidy to welfare. Heralded as "an important landmark in the War on Poverty," the Child Nutrition Act covered public as well as parochial schools and included every state plus Puerto Rico, the Virgin Islands, and Guam.[38] John A. Schnittker told LBJ aide, Harry McPherson that the reason the 1966 Child Nutrition Act passed was that members objected "to doing less for kids, even if some are rich kids."[39]

The 1966 Child Nutrition Act put federal money into free lunches for the first time, but it did not fundamentally alter the National School Lunch Program's basically inequitable financial and administrative structures. The new federal "Special Assistance Funds" earmarked specifically for free meals promised no new matching money to the states and provided no additional federal money for basic school lunch operations, such as new facilities, equipment, or labor. That is, the Special Funds could not be used to expand existing cafeteria facilities, build new lunchrooms, or hire more staff to cover the new free meals that had to be provided. Department of Agriculture officials offered no help to local

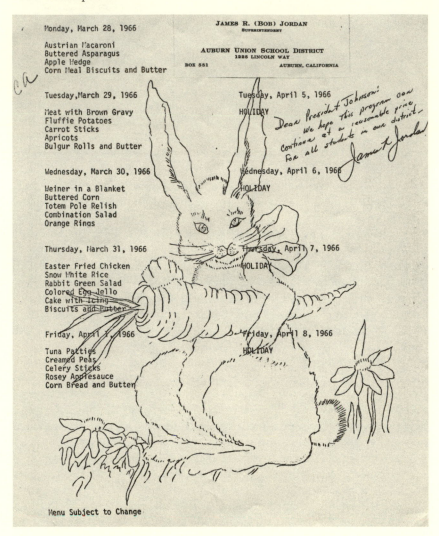

Figure 6.1. School administrators protested cuts in regular school lunch appropriations. Lunch menu with handwritten note addressed to President Johnson, from James R. Jordan, Superintendent of the Auburn Union School District, Auburn, California, April 4, 1966. GEN AG-7-2 School Lunch Program 4/1/66-4/4/66, WHCF Box 11, LBJ Library.

schools, which now had to finance large numbers of free lunches. Because very few states contributed any local taxes or other state resources to school lunchrooms, urban districts, in particular, were caught in a dilemma. Built without cafeteria facilities in the first place, city schools by the 1960s were "plagued with decaying buildings" and had little money to pay for repairs, let alone new cafeterias.[40] City school districts, already in financial crisis, had to raise their own money to build or expand their kitchen and lunchroom facilities. They also had to raise money to pay lunchroom workers, most of whom were low-paid women. Indeed, the ASFSA estimated that the vast majority of its members "are in an income bracket that scarcely lifts each of them above the poverty level."[41] The results were predictably problematic. In Washington, D.C., for example, the price of Type A lunches increased from 35 cents to 42 cents. The district faced an additional crisis when the unionized school cafeteria workers demanded a pay increase but insisted that the increase not come "through raising lunch prices."[42] Nonetheless, Congress now mandated that all schools—whether they had previously participated in the National School Lunch Program or not—provide free lunches to all poor children in the district. The result was, one report noted, a "crazy quilt pattern which bears little relationship to the degree of need."[43] The pattern did, however, bear considerable relationship to the nation's pattern of racial discrimination and clearly allowed states to continue "local custom" with regard to black children.

Ever reluctant to become involved in state-level decisions about school lunch policies, the Department of Agriculture essentially left the provision of free meals up to local and state officials. The result was widespread inequality and inconsistency from state to state and district to district. Some states sent the special assistance funds only to schools that specifically requested aid. Other states targeted one or two schools for pilot programs—leaving the rest without money for free lunches. In Alabama, for example, the state's share of the special assistance fund, almost $60,000, went to fourteen schools. However, Sumter County, the poorest district in the state with a 70 percent black population, received none of the money. Georgia distributed its special funds to almost two dozen schools, but there, too, the poorest county received nothing. Arizona used all of its $20,000 appropriation in one district. Arkansas sent its special fund to nine schools, none of which were in its largest city Little Rock. In Colorado the all of the funds went to one school in Denver, and Florida sent its entire appropriation to just ten schools.[44]

The Agriculture Department funding formula for the special funds only compounded the system's inequalities. Each state's share of the special assistance funds depended on a complicated calculation based on the number of children who had received free lunches during the past year. This meant that states with historically more generous welfare policies received more than other states, regardless of number of poor children in the schools. New York, for example, received over $350,000 in special funds, while California, which actually had more schools but had served fewer free lunches the previous year, received only $100,000. Poor children in California thus received lower school lunch subsidies than did their East Coast counterparts.[45]

Most problematic was the fact that legislators neglected to establish any standards or procedures for determining which children would be eligible for free meals. Like federal welfare policy generally, the Child Nutrition Act left it to state and local officials to determine benefit levels (in this case how many free lunches to offer) and to identify who was eligible for assistance. Great Society welfare policy depended heavily on local standards in the distribution of public benefits. Despite the fact that the Johnson administration initiated the first "serious" reform in Aid to Dependent Children (ADC), for example, including requirements for vocational training in order to push women into the work force, states still set eligibility standards and determined benefit rates.[46] As the inequities of the nation's welfare system became more evident, however, particularly the extent to which African Americans had systematically been excluded from the welfare system, Congress came under increasing pressure to establish national eligibility standards. The debate over eligibility standards for school lunches as well as for food stamps, ADC, and other federal benefits starkly exposed the limits of the American welfare state.

The 1966 Child Nutrition Act, at least in theory, directed the Secretary of Agriculture to establish—and enforce—guidelines for determining which children qualified for free lunches.[47] Neither the USDA nor Congress, however, was eager to alter the unspoken rules of local prerogative when it came to the distribution of welfare benefits. While the department had long established nutrition guidelines—in the form of RDAs, food equivalency charts, and healthy menus—it always left the day-to-day operation of school lunchrooms in the hands of local officials. The program's congressional backers, particularly southerners such as Ellender and Russell, strongly favored the program's decentralized operation in which administration, menus, and eligibility were all determined by people at the local level. Decentralization had clearly had been the intent of the program's founders, who were happy to bring agricultural subsidies to their states but wanted no federal interference with "local custom" when it came to schools. As civil rights leader Ralph Abernathy told Orville Freeman, "Local resistance is an old and sad story."[48] While civil rights demands increasingly challenged states' rights in the South, particularly with regard to voting, public accommodations, and, by 1965 employment as well, education and school funding continued to be local matters. Thus, despite increasing pressure to fund free meals for poor children, the Department of Agriculture had difficulty shifting away from its traditional "hands off" approach to local administration of the National School Lunch Program.[49]

The free lunch mandate, however, forced the Department of Agriculture into a welfare role for which it was ill prepared. Having, up until this point, maintained only minimal oversight on state and local lunch programs, the Agriculture Department was singularly uncomfortable with its new welfare-oriented role. DOA officials initially issued a weak and confusing set of guidelines that basically just reminded local school lunch administrators that they were obligated to provide free meals to all poor children in their districts. Secretary Freeman refused to send specific directions to local administrators telling them how to accomplish this task. Initially, Freeman's directives were so weak that many schools were unaware they even existed. One principal claimed he "had never heard that there were new guidelines," and another called them "a fairly closely guarded secret."[50] Ultimately, confusion over the mandate to serve free meals, combined with the fact that the school lunch budget overall did not increase, set up a series of confrontations not only between federal and state officials but between grass-roots activists and government officials as well. Indeed, for the next two years, Freeman engaged in a battle with school lunch advocates over how to feed poor children in the nation's schools.

The problem, as Orville Freeman saw it, was an issue of federal versus state authority. Congress, he believed, never intended that the Department of Agriculture or the National School Lunch Program interfere with state educational policies. It had simply authorized him to distribute free lunch funds to each state. After that it was up to local officials to determine which schools and which children received benefits. "The law is specific," Freeman said. Only state legislatures, he believed, held the power to determine how food and meal subsidies were distributed. The only thing he could do, Freeman told Congress, was to withhold school lunch funds, but he knew this would spark outrage around the country as all children, rich and poor, would be affected.[51] Freeman knew, furthermore, that if he refused to send food to delinquent states (states that did not make plans to offer free lunches), schools would simply stop feeding children altogether. The dilemma was posed starkly by Alabama representative Glenn Andrews, who pressed school lunch director Howard Davis about what his department would do if districts did not comply with the free lunch mandate. When Davis reluctantly acknowledged that his department would be "bound to carry out the law of the land," Andrews replied tartly, "In other words, for political considerations you would leave a bunch of children hungry if a county failed to integrate properly?"[52] The result would be that neither poor nor middle-class children would get school lunches. Thus the only guidelines the secretary could muster were constant urgings that states follow Department of Agriculture standards of operation. Beyond that, Freeman insisted, his hands were tied.[53]

Because neither Congress nor the Department of Agriculture wanted to alter the unspoken rules of local prerogative, the distribution of federal welfare benefits was notoriously inconsistent. In some school districts only children whose parents were on welfare qualified for free lunches, but in other areas welfare recipients had to pay for their children's lunches. The Washington, D.C., school district, for example, assumed that welfare payments covered food costs and insisted that "parents who received welfare could afford to pay for lunch."[54] The income qualification for free lunches varied widely across the country. In some districts, families earning $2,000 a year qualified for free meals, while in other states the income cut-off was $3,000.[55] In South Carolina, children from families earning under $225 per month could get free meals, while in New Mexico the figure was $110; in Arkansas, children could not eat for free unless their parents' monthly income was less than $85. Florida's free lunch criteria were fairly loose and included children from families receiving county assistance, families on "limited" income, children eligible for ESEA subsidies, as well as families facing "temporary emergencies" and children showing signs of malnutrition or "clear-cut neglect." [56] Eligibility for free lunches often varied from school to school within the same state. In one Georgia county a family with two children and an annual income between $2001 and $2500 had to pay five cents for lunch, while in the neighboring county those children could eat for free.[57]

Local decisions about which children received free lunches revealed a continuing legacy of paternalistic, if not racist, practices. In most cases, eligibility for free meals was determined by school officials—teachers, social workers, or principals—or by other individuals in the community, including PTA members, welfare case workers, or local ministers. School lunch founder, Senator Richard Russell, for one, saw no problem with such a personal approach. Local officials, he believed, were best suited to "determine the ability of the children to pay for lunches, with the free lunches to go to the neediest children."[58] This was, of course, precisely the paternalistic, often discriminatory system that welfare and civil rights activists sought to avoid by establishing objective, national eligibility standards. For one thing, principals and teachers regularly made moral judgments about the behavior of students and parents when deciding which children could eat for free. In Florida, principals, teachers, and social workers oversaw the eligibility process.[59] The result was inconsistent at best and discriminatory at worst. A child in Collier County, Florida, who

Health Department director Charles Bradley admitted was "malnourished," nonetheless did not qualify for the free lunch program. The problem was that the child did not appear thin enough. "Look at the fat arms
and muscles," Bradley said, "that kid's all right."[60] In San Diego, Texas,
school superintendent Bryan P. Taylor was confident that he knew the
children's "mothers and the grandmothers and their fathers and their fathers before them," and would have no trouble deciding which children
needed free lunches.[61] Children in Appalachia were regularly denied free
lunches if their fathers were considered to be alcoholics. A Florida school
lunch supervisor "let" two children have free lunches because she found
out that their father was going into the hospital. However, when she discovered that the family had a television set in their home, she took away
the privilege, saying, "If they could afford a television set, they certainly
could afford good nutrition for their children, so I refused to put them on
the free list." The trouble with "these people," she concluded, "is that
they have no sense of values—they just don't know what's important
and what isn't."[62] Thus, in most states, the decision as to which children
received free lunch was personal and often arbitrary.[63]

Leaving eligibility determinations up to local officials had predictable
results. In some schools poor children were required to carry out the garbage, sweep the floors, or clean the washrooms in return for lunch.[64] One
district went so far as to insist that poor children "clean their plates,"
while paying children were allowed to leave food. Another state required
regular school attendance and insisted that the poor children "apply
themselves well" before they were deemed eligible for free meals. All over
the country free lunch children stood in separate cafeteria lines or paid
for their lunches with special, easily identifiable tokens. Ultimately, neither weak Department of Agriculture guidelines nor the posturing of
elected officials prevented children from experiencing the social stigma
attached to poverty.

The chaos of state and local free lunch eligibility requirements reflected
one of the central tensions in President Johnson's War on Poverty. On
the one hand, public pressure had dramatically altered the context for
discussions of poverty. Grass-roots welfare-rights and anti-poverty movements demanded that poor people be treated with dignity and respect,
particularly from public officials in places like welfare offices and schools.
At the same time, targeted programs separated poor and black people
from middle-class Americans, increasing the distance and the stigma
attached to poverty. While the school lunch program's congressional advocates, including Allen Ellender, for example, insisted that there be no
distinction between poor and paying children, they were unwilling to let
federal officials intervene in local school decisions. Thus, although Ellender insisted that rich and poor children "should play together and

work together and eat together," he believed that community tradition and local officials could best decide which children needed free meals.[65] But local officials simply perpetuated the racial and class discriminations common across the country. Many school officials, north and south, found themselves having to make judgments for which they were neither prepared nor entirely sympathetic. As one former state school superintendent observed, school boards often differed in class, race, and ethnicity from the poor children they were being asked to serve. "I think they had an awakening in the last few years," she said. "They found a lot of people there that I don't think they considered to be people—Mexicans, Negroes, Indians and so forth."[66]

The debate about which children qualified for free lunches quickly became a microcosm of the growing debate about poverty in America. Certainly, no national standard existed in 1966 that defined who was poor, who was near-poor, and who could afford 30 cents a day for lunch. Civil rights and anti-poverty activists increasingly demanded national standards for eligibility and service, but it was not at all clear what such national standards should be. Any "objective" measure of poverty had always been elusive, and measures of hunger similarly subjective. While nutrition scientists could identify conditions that constituted starvation and had successfully identified diseases caused by nutrient deficiencies, judgments about malnutrition in school children remained largely impressionistic.

FOOD AND THE POVERTY LINE

Establishing a measure for poverty in the 1960s, began, as it had earlier in the century, with estimates about family food budgets. Traditionally, the ability to afford a "decent" standard of living hinged on a healthy or "adequate" diet. The line between self-sufficiency and dependence for many families lay in the price of food. The post–World War II economic boom and the success of trade union negotiations solidified the notion that living standards depended on the price of consumer goods, particularly groceries.[67] Even in affluent America, the price of food and the definition of poverty were closely linked. As home economists and others had long argued, the cost of the "market basket" determined the standard of living of most families. It is not surprising, then, that a home economist, working in the Social Security Administration, came up with a formula for measuring the "poverty line." Mollie Orshansky combined a 1955 Bureau of Home Economics household budget survey showing that families generally spent one-third of their incomes on food with the Department of Agriculture's recommended nutrition standards, better known as RDAs. Orshansky estimated how much income a family needed to "provide its members RDA on a regular basis." The formula, as Orshansky later admitted, would provide only the minimum of health and well-being. No family, she said, could live at that level "for any length of time beyond an emergency."[68] Indeed, Orshansky ruefully observed, no one in America would settle for mere subsistence "as the just due for himself or his neighbor, and even the poorest may claim more than bread."[69] Critics such as Michael Harrington dismissed any effort to create a standard poverty line. Such an attempt, he said, merely set "a minimum measure for life at the bottom."[70] Senator George McGovern echoed Harrington's hesitation, pointing out that the problem of defining standards lay in deciding whether adequacy should be based on a minimum, optimum, or intermediate level of need. Nonetheless, Orshansky's formula provided a quick and convenient way for government officials, trying to shape new welfare programs, to determine who would be eligible for benefits. In 1965 the federal government, through the War on Poverty's Office of Economic Opportunity, officially adopted Orshansky's formula as the basis for eligibility for its programs.[71] Other agencies quickly followed suit.[72]

Despite obvious drawbacks, the federal "poverty line" soon became the standard measure of eligibility for welfare benefits, including school lunches. The problem was that poverty remained a relative condition, and no national "poverty line" could realistically describe conditions in every part of the country. Indeed, because any objective measure of poverty was illusory, the "poverty line" quickly became the lowest possible standard of living. Further, because income and cost of living varied considerably from region to region, the actual "line" below which families were deemed to be "poor" varied as well. State guidelines for determining which families qualified for food stamps or which children should eat free or reduced price school meals were thus wildly inconsistent.[73] While the federal poverty line determined minimum eligibility for benefits such as food stamps, states as well as local districts could set their own criteria for local welfare payments as well as for free lunches.

An "objective" measure of poverty did not eliminate the stigma of being poor in America. Throughout the country, children receiving free lunches were routinely treated differently from paying students. Local officials, often the same individuals who had been carrying out discriminatory policies all along, were being asked to alter long-held practices. Some rose to the occasion, others did not. A Palm Beach County, Florida, welfare worker complained that "children receiving free lunches are too frequently reminded that they are not paying and are made to feel guilty if they do not eat all of the food."[74] As one report on the National School

Lunch Program observed, "where teachers who collect school money are overworked, where the principal regards the School Lunch Program as an unnecessary burden, where the community in general is hostile to welfare recipients in any form, those [federal guidelines] are ignored and those instructions are violated with monotonous regularity."[75] While local administrators promised that poor children would not be singled out in the lunchroom, parents and children knew better. The Chicago Board of Education, for example, announced that welfare recipients would "have to identify themselves" if they wanted their children to receive free lunches.[76] In Detroit, families had to list their weekly budget expenditures in their applications for free meals.[77] In Washington, D.C., poor children went through the cafeteria line "like anyone else," but when they got to the food counter, it was another story. The paying students paid 42 cents and received a hot lunch with "a few extra items," including a salad; poor children received a different meal entirely. School lunch administrator Jacobs admitted that "as much as we try, there is no point in my trying to kid anybody there. . . . I don't believe there is a school in the fifty states where everyone doesn't know who is needy."[78] Testifying before the Senate Select Committee on Nutrition and Human Needs, Margaret Mead reprised her role as an expert on American foodways, noting, "It is very foolish to talk about integration and democracy in our schools" and then establish a separate lunch system for poor children. Americans, she said, "are willing to face the fact that everybody does not have a Cadillac . . . but on food, which is the necessary basis of life, the fact that someone cannot provide it for his children is very stigmatizing."[79] The stigma associated with free lunch programs would not disappear, ASFSA executive director John Perryman predicted, until "food for thought and food for stomach are made available equally to one and all."[80]

When it came to poverty policy, anti-hunger activists, like other 1960s liberal reformers, could not decide whether they were dealing with economic inequality or cultural disability. In the case of food policy, the line between cultural practice and economic decisions was even more problematic. Reformers and policy makers had long questioned the food choices of poor and working-class people. Since at least the late nineteenth century, nutrition scientists insisted that rational food choices would alleviate the worst effects of low wages and economic deprivation. In the 1960s, the notion that cultural attitudes were responsible for economic status gained new credence as "the poor" increasingly became a distinct, and racially marked, class. Attempts to alter the "culture of poverty" appealed to a generation of liberal policy makers who resisted the idea that American inequality might stem from deep-seated racial discrimination and institutional bias. Democratic advisers to President Kennedy, notably, Daniel Patrick Moynihan, insisted that in affluent

America, poverty and malnutrition were products of cultural deprivation as much as material want. In the past, Moynihan observed, "the
poor were poor, no more than that." In the modern period, however,
Moynihan argued, poverty had became a decidedly cultural (often racial) liability. Adopting anthropologist Oscar Lewis's notion that cultural attitudes (like "bad" food habits) associated with poverty could
be transmitted from one generation to the next, Moynihan and others
promoted the notion that a "culture of poverty" had developed that
influenced urban racial ghettoes as well as rural America. Poverty, Moynihan argued, caused "structural changes in personality and behavior."[81]
In this view, malnutrition in particular had to do not with scarcity of
resources—everyone agreed that the country produced an abundance of
food—but rather with poor choices and lack of education. Moynihan's
Harvard colleague and leading nutritionist Jean Mayer went so far as
to suggest that the term "malnutrition" should precisely "refer to the
consumption of the wrong sort of food," rather than to the more general
notion of insufficient nutrition.[82] Columbia nutritionist William H.
Sebrell similarly asserted that in the United States, malnutrition was
largely due to "ignorance of the importance of certain foods." Food
choices, Sebrell insisted, were as much the result of "cultural patterns"
as scarcity or low wages.[83] In a world of consumer abundance and economic growth, hunger and malnutrition boiled down (so to speak) to
cultural choices. The poor, it seemed, simply needed more—or at any
rate better—education. It was an argument that food reformers had been
making for almost half a century.

Poverty and hunger gradually emerged as focal points for social activists of the 1960s. While the "culture of poverty" thesis suggested a need
for things like education and job training, civil rights activists expanded
their agenda to include access to government services as well as respect
from public officials and others charged with delivering benefits to poor
people, particularly poor blacks. Calls for welfare rights, food stamps,
and free school lunches took on increasing importance, particularly after
passage of the 1964 Civil Rights Act that, at least formally, ensured voting
rights and equal opportunity in employment and education. In the highly
charged and increasingly polarized atmosphere of the 1960s, anti-poverty
and anti-hunger movements appealed to liberal sensibilities. Tackling
these issues seemed to call less for a radical restructuring of American
society than for a more equitable distribution of existing resources and
opportunities. The anti-poverty and anti-hunger groups came together
during the mid-1960s largely in an effort to shift public resources toward
the poor and to demand that poor people, most of whom were assumed
to be black, be treated fairly by public officials. The civil rights movement
ultimately forced the federal government, albeit reluctantly, to assert na-

tional standards in matters ranging from voting and employment rights to housing and education and to set eligibility standards for government benefits. National standards, however, proved more difficult when it came to education and children's welfare, traditionally the purview of the individual states. This was not simply a problem of countering racial discrimination in the South. Indeed, states in other regions turned out to be as reluctant as Old Dixie to provide resources for poor people.[84]

Deeply ingrained notions of family self-reliance and personal independence complicated efforts to expand the free lunch program. In many communities there was the conviction that parents should pay at least minimal fees for lunch and resentment against those who could not. That resentment was only intensified as poverty became associated with race. Indeed, in many communities, liberal attempts to expand government benefits to the poor, whether black or white, were met with substantial resistance. Warning President Johnson that the costs of free lunches would bankrupt her lunchroom, Helen A. Davis, school lunch director in Todd County, Kentucky, observed, "It is unfair to the students and parents of this nation who strive to help themselves to withdraw aid to the school lunch and milk programs that will help *all* students in order to help only those who have learned to be parasites on the economy of the nation."[85] Vella Bellinger, a housewife from Berwyn, Nebraska, similarly believed that programs for the poor would discriminate against the middle class. "How can we stress using our ability to provide for oneself and then practice deprivation because one has succeeded in acquiring a modest means of self support?" she asked the president.[86]

In many communities people believed that requiring poor children to work for their meals was a good thing. Ohio's eligibility guidelines declared, "It is good character-building education to have the child perform some work in return for his lunch."[87] C. L. Mooney, president of the Lockney, Texas, Independent School District, similarly observed, "In our district we have had a long-standing policy that no free lunches will be served unless the student is willing to work for his meal." The chore, he said, was usually "token," but the knowledge that they "earned their meat by the sweat of the brow" built pride in the students.[88] A principal in Tucson, Arizona, on the other hand, decided that no one deserved a free lunch. "Everyone should pay something," he believed, "for the family's self-respect." Besides, he added, "the cost of a free lunch program in a school as poor as this would be prohibitive."[89] He did, however, let some children eat for free "on a short term basis," if, for example, a parent was temporarily out of work. In return for their lunch, these children might be asked to help out in the school kitchen.[90]

For the better part of the century, nutritionists and children's advocates had insisted that the public had an interest in healthy children—not just healthy poor children. Indeed, the widespread popularity of the National School Lunch Program rested on the assumption that the government had a role to play in ensuring the health of the next generation. Turning the school lunch program into a free lunch program for the poor, however, risked weakening that popular support. Genevieve Olkiewicz, director of food services for the Montebello, California, Unified School District, worried, "In our recent enthusiasm to help the needy we seem to be forgetting the vast majority of Americans."[91] School lunch advocates of course applauded the effort to feed poor children. But at the same time, they did not want to see the lunch program serve only the poor. ASFSA executive director John Perryman cautioned against re-orienting the lunch program. If the schools were forced to serve only poor children, Perryman warned, the idea of "better nutrition for all children" would be left behind.[92] National Educational Association legislative representative Mary Condon Gereau similarly insisted that while her organization "heartily" favored providing all needy children with lunch and milk, those children should not be fed "at the expense of the other children in the schools."[93]

The debate about free school lunches for poor children revealed a fundamental ambivalence about food, family responsibility, and social policy. Since its inception, the school lunch program had operated in theory (if not in practice) as a universal subsidy. Like school supplies, books, and, indeed, public education itself, many Americans had come to see school lunches almost as a democratic necessity. New York representative James Scheuer argued that "if it is logical to say to a child who can afford it that he can pay for the soup, why is it not proper to say to that child . . . you are going to use so many dollars worth of paper, crayons, and chalk. . . . We think you should pay for that."[94] Deputy Secretary of Agriculture Howard Davis admitted that, in principle, there was no difference. But school lunches, Davis suggested, were not the same as school books. Parents, he observed, "would normally pay for [lunch] if the children went home . . . or if they had lunch at the corner drugstore."[95] Families should, Davis believed, "pay part or all of the cost of these lunches" whenever possible.[96] For many Americans, food and meals remained, at base, a family responsibility.[97] C. L Mooney, president of the Lockney, Texas, Independent School District, for example, told the president that federal assistance providing breakfast and lunch in school raised a moral question. The school's main responsibility, Mooney insisted, was to teach. "May I ask," he wondered, "when the parent's responsibility is going to begin?"[98] Liberal as well as conservative policy makers worried that universal child nutrition programs might "sound like the replacement of the American home." Senator Eugene McCarthy, a staunch liberal, agreed that food was most appropriately provided in the home. Still, McCarthy insisted, it was time for Americans to develop a more comprehensive child nutrition program. Even McCarthy, however, to propose a universal free lunch program.[99] By the mid-1960s, a sense of social crisis overwhelmed any lingering thoughts about a universal lunch program for all children. Indeed, the National School Lunch Program was becoming, for all intents and purposes, a poverty program.

CHAPTER 7

A Right to Lunch

Once the 1966 Child Nutrition Act promised every poor child in America a free school lunch, a nationwide grass-roots movement quickly emerged, demanding fundamental changes in the National School Lunch Program. During the late 1960s, the widespread activism sparked by the civil rights and anti-war movements spawned a new militancy among northern blacks and students. But civil rights, peace, and hunger also motivated a wide swath of mainstream liberal activism as well. National women's organizations, long involved in education, welfare, peace, and equal rights, emerged as leaders in the anti-hunger movement formulating what ultimately became the blueprint for school lunch reform. For liberal groups, in particular, the anti-poverty movement and related calls for free school lunches, free food stamps, and welfare rights pointed to concrete social programs that promised to address both racial and social inequalities. In many ways, hunger was an easier issue to address than the seemingly intractable inequities of race in American life. Tackling food policy called less for a radical restructuring of American society than for a more equitable distribution of existing resources and opportunities.

Civil rights activism, combined with a resurgence of liberal anti-poverty reform, dramatically altered the political context in which the National School Lunch Program had operated for the first two decades of its existence. In the process, school lunchrooms became sites of intense battles over who was poor and where public responsibility for poverty rested. For the first time since the Depression the nation's food policies took center stage both in defining and in combating poverty. Lyndon Johnson's War on Poverty ultimately forced a reorientation of the nation's food policy, turning school lunches and food stamps—essential elements in agricultural policy since the New Deal—into the centerpieces of domestic social welfare. Grass-roots pressure forced the Department of Agriculture, albeit reluctantly, to respond to the nutrition and food needs of the poor. Where historically the central purpose of the department's food aid programs, whether domestic or foreign, had been the disposal of surplus farm produce and the maintenance of commodity prices, during the 1960s food and nutrition became, as one commentator noted, "leading tools in fighting poverty."[1]

One of the fundamental questions raised by the civil rights movement and the "discovery" of poverty in America during the 1960s was what role government welfare programs should play in alleviating economic and social inequality. At its base, the social movements of the 1960s were profoundly ambivalent about whether public benefits like school lunches should be available universally or should be targeted to the poor (and increasingly that meant to African Americans). In the crisis atmosphere that pervaded the late 1960s, however, feeding poor children rose to the top of the public agenda. The resulting shift in the National School Lunch Program had significant consequences for all children. While grass-roots pressure to feed poor children succeeded in vastly expanding the number of free meals offered, the unwillingness of legislators (and, ultimately, the public) to invest more heavily in children's nutrition significantly limited the scope of the program and reduced the number of non-poor children eating lunch at school.

THE FREE LUNCH MANDATE

Although the 1966 Child Nutrition Act promised federal funds for free school lunches, for the next six years community activists, teachers, and local administrators fought with the Department of Agriculture to translate those funds into actual meals for poor children. By the department's own reckoning, through either "intent, ineptness, or inadequate resources" it was slow to feed the nation's poor children.[2] The USDA preferred, of course, to blame local communities for not taking advantage of the available resources, but the Secretary of Agriculture as well as school lunch administrators acknowledged that Washington needed to do more. The American School Food Service Association, the school lunch program's major national professional association, estimated in 1968 that at least six and a half million poor children, mostly in cities or isolated rural areas, still had no access to free lunches.[3] While over two-thirds of America's public schools by then participated in the National School Lunch Program, fewer than 10 percent of children in poor, urban neighborhoods could expect to find a noon meal at school.[4] Most urban schools still had no cafeteria or kitchen facilities and few had budgets that could encompass a free meal program. Philadelphia, for example, fed only 8 percent of its poor children, while in St. Louis only 4 percent of all lunches served were free. Examples of hungry school children came from all parts of the country. A teacher in Green Bay, Wisconsin, told a Senate Committee in 1968 that in her class, "five out of six children are getting no lunch."[5] In Sumter County, Alabama, the principal of the black high school admitted, "We know there are fifty or more children who cannot afford to buy lunch but we don't have enough money to feed them all."[6] On the Marysville, Washington, Indian reservation, the local school lunch director said that out of almost four thousand children, "only 40 receive free or reduced price lunches."[7]

The evident failure of the American welfare system to feed poor children fueled the increasing sense of social crisis that characterized the late 1960s. While the civil rights movement's early faith in integration gave way to militant calls for "black power," and the student anti-war movement adopted ever more revolutionary rhetoric, the anti-hunger/anti-poverty movement also found itself questioning whether American institutions could meet the challenge of reform. For liberal Americans, however, poverty and hunger loomed as the most curable of the nation's woes. Surely, the plentiful supplies of food could be better distributed. The hunger lobby found ready congressional allies in liberal legislators. Most notably, for the first time, urban Democrats, who were in the midst of challenging their party's intransigent southern wing, began to focus on food policy.

The mounting calls to end poverty and hunger spurred a series congressional hearings and media reports. In April 1967, New York senator Robert Kennedy, along with Pennsylvania senator Joseph Clark, led a highly publicized congressional visit to the Mississippi Delta. The senators' description of rural poverty and hunger among that region's mostly black population shocked mainstream America. Not long afterward, the Citizens' Crusade Against Poverty, a liberal coalition largely representing labor unions and religious groups, sponsored a physicians' tour of the same delta area.[8] The Citizens' Crusade (soon re-named the Citizens' Board of Inquiry) published its findings in a widely distributed volume, *Hunger U.S.A.*[9] Most disturbing to the physicians was the extent of hunger among the Delta residents. Families living on $15 a week, surviving on "biscuit for breakfast, boiled beans for lunch, and bread and molasses for dinner," contrasted sharply with the comfort and affluence of middle-class America. "We do not want to quibble over words," the doctor's report asserted, "the boys and girls we saw were hungry—weak, in pain, sick, their lives are being shortened."[10]

The physicians' accounts of "pitiful" Mississippi children living in "alarming," "unbelievable," and "appalling" conditions elicited moral outrage among the nation's editorial writers and sparked the formation of grass-roots anti-hunger groups all across the country. *Hunger U.S.A.* became the basis for a controversial CBS television report of the same name. By the spring of 1968, exposes, including a Pulitzer Prize-winning series on conditions in poor communities by journalist Nick Kotz, prompted more Senate and congressional hearings on poverty, hunger, and malnutrition. Finally, in late 1968 George McGovern, former head of the Food for Peace Program, convened a Senate Select Committee on Nutrition and Human Needs. McGovern expressed his shock and dismay at the fact that "every American does not have the food, medical assistance, and other related necessities essential to life and health."[11] He urged "bold emergency action" to combat hunger and poverty.[12] Meeting in venues across the country, the committee provided a platform for poverty activists, welfare mothers, and community organizers to air their grievances. The widely publicized hearings also became an arena in which representatives from the Departments of Agriculture and Health, Education and Welfare (HEW), along with local officials, attempted to defend their programs and justify their practices. Among the most contentious topics to be aired was the National School Lunch Program's failure to provide free meals for poor children.[13]

The anti-hunger lobby focused special ire on the Department of Agriculture. Most particularly, the hunger lobby insisted that the department had botched the task of feeding the nation's poor. Food and agriculture policy, the activists insisted, should provide food for hungry people, not market subsidies for farmers. In effect, the hunger lobby was asking the Department of Agriculture to re-orient its food programs and re-define its central mission. John Kramer, a leading hunger activist, called the department's oversight of food programs "an acknowledged farce."[14] Leslie Dunbar, head of the Citizens' Crusade, declared that food programs are "welfare programs" and should not be administered by a department "which has as its key purpose maximizing income for producers of major crops."[15] The implications for the lunch program were clear. The hunger activists challenged the Department of Agriculture to abandon its traditional mode of using lunch programs as outlets for surplus commodities and to expand the program's capacity to provide free lunches for the poor.

THE WOMEN'S CAMPAIGN

At the heart of the hunger lobby was a group of mainstream liberal women's organizations who insisted that the Department of Agriculture had a moral obligation to feed poor children. Immediately after Congress passed the 1966 Child Nutrition Act promising school lunches to poor children, five national women's groups—the National Council of Catholic Women (NCCW), the National Council of Jewish Women (NCJW), the National Council of Negro Women (NCNW), Church Women United (CWU), and the Young Women's Christian Association (Y.W.C.A.)—formed the Committee on School Lunch Participation (CSLP). Initially, the women's intent was simply to help start free meal programs in their communities. Their purpose quickly shifted, however, once they began to realize the extent to which poor children were left out of the National School Lunch Program. While a militant women's liberation movement was gaining strength during the late 1960s, the CSLP represented the liberal mainstream of women's politics. The CSLP constituent organizations embraced what historians have labeled a "maternalist" politics based on family and child welfare. Ultimately, the CLSP, with its moderate approach and seemingly conservative style, forced a radical restructuring of the National School Lunch Program.[16]

The CSLP was, in many ways, a classic example of women's civic participation. The five national organizations shared a long history of cooperation on social and educational issues and for decades had worked in coalition on both the local and national levels. While the middle years of the twentieth century have often been characterized as the "doldrums" in terms of women's political activity, in fact, women's organizations, including those forming the CSLP, actively pursued political agendas including equal rights, education, housing, race relations, and children's welfare.[17] Women in cities as well as small towns ran parent-teacher groups, served on school boards, campaigned for jury duty and repeal of the poll tax, and lobbied for women to be appointed to public boards and commissions. In the context of the increasingly militant movements for civil rights and against the Vietnam War, liberal women's organizations optimistically believed that nation's social problems could be solved by rational leadership, citizen participation, and compassionate legislation. Eschewing any "divisive" political agenda, the CSLP women embraced rather "a religious orientation" and a concern for social problems that was "neither that of a useful political tool or a passing fancy."[18] Not unlike women reformers in the early twentieth-century Progressive Era, the CSLP women believed the government could and should be a positive force for public welfare. At the same time, they believed American democracy needed a universal system of welfare, health, and education to ensure informed participation by all citizens. The CSLP groups could all proudly claim decades of "practical experience on the local level dealing with the great social issues of our day."[19] Indeed, these groups had provided key advocates for the School Lunch Program since its inception and had lobbied extensively for the 1966 Child Nutrition Act guaranteeing poor children access to free lunches.

In the tradition of women's voluntary activities, the first instinct of the women of the CSLP was to organize a service project that would, as NCJW representative Olya Margolin said, provide free lunches "where needed." As it became clear, however, that the need was much greater than the capacity of volunteer projects, the women began to reconsider their strategy. After considerable debate, the CSLP steering committee decided to undertake a nationwide survey of the school lunch program.

With a sizable grant of $25,000 from the Field Foundation, a Chicago-based philanthropic organization that focused on civil rights, community development, and children's issues, the CSLP hired NAACP staff member Jean Fairfax to coordinate the survey project. Over the next eighteen months, under Fairfax's direction, women from each of the sponsoring organizations interviewed school lunch administrators, principals, teachers, and parents in their communities. They asked direct and pointed questions aimed to uncover exactly how the lunch program operated, where the funding for school meals came from, and precisely which children were served—and which were left out.[20] The result was a carefully researched and shockingly frank report entitled *Their Daily Bread*. In essence, *Their Daily Bread* was a manifesto in favor of a government-sponsored universal free lunch program for all American children. In practical terms, the report provided unassailable evidence of the need for a free lunch program for poor children. If a universal lunch program was not feasible, the women insisted, the National School Lunch Program should become a key element in a national anti-poverty agenda.

Their Daily Bread presented a scathing indictment of the National School Lunch Program. The 1966 Child Nutrition Act, the CSLP charged, by not changing the school lunch program's fiscal and administrative structure, had left "the root of the problem"—free lunches for poor children—un-addressed.[21] There simply were not very many free lunches available in the National School Lunch Program. The CSLP's most damaging finding was its documentation of how little states and local communities contributed to the program. In a careful analysis of the sources of school lunch funding in each state, *Their Daily Bread* made it clear that every state relied on children's fees, often for over 90 percent of the program's operating budget. But the women's report found abuses in the program that went beyond structural problems. Evidence from all parts of the country pointed to widespread discrimination against poor children and poor communities. The women documented inconsistent standards used to identify poor children and practices that singled them out in insidious ways, including different meals, separate lines, work expectations, and dress codes. "Over and over again," they wrote, "we heard parents say that although their need is great they would not subject their children to the humiliation of being pointed out" in the school lunch line.[22]

The results of the CSLP project galvanized a widespread movement for school lunch reform. The "most cherished myth" about school lunches in the United States, the women reported, "is that no child who really needs a lunch is allowed to go hungry." Pulling no punches, the CSLP declared, "We flatly say that this is not so." The committee's conclusions were stark. Two out of three American children did not participate in the National School Lunch Program. Fewer than 4 percent of the nation's fifty million school children were able to get free or reduced price lunches. Eligibility for free lunch was determined "not by any universally accepted formula" but by "local decisions about administration and financing which may or may not have anything to do with the need of the individual child." The school lunch program, the CSLP report concluded, was not simply inadequately funded, rather, its entire administrative and financial structure was "both unjust and harmful." Four fundamental problems lay at the heart of the program. First, the federal financing was inadequate and "the gap between available Federal money and the needs of the program grows bigger every year." Second, the funding formula that allowed states and local school districts to count children's meal payments as their matching contribution meant that few schools could afford to offer free meals. Third, those schools that did offer free lunches had no "uniform method of determining who shall be eligible," resulting in "unequal and unfair decisions on the local level." Finally, many older, urban schools, built without cafeteria facilities, could not afford to participate in the program. This meant, the CSLP concluded, "that the slum child, who needs good nutrition most, has the least chance of getting a school lunch." Like the women who carried out the school lunch study, "most of middle-class America," they found, assumed that school lunches were universally available. These "comfortable assumptions," the CSLP discovered, "are unrealistic."[23]

The National School Lunch Program's fundamental inadequacy stemmed from its reliance on local initiative and "custom." Just as the civil rights movement doubted that local communities would, on their own, enact measures to eliminate racial discrimination, so the CSLP women doubted that states, counties, or cities would—or could—solve the problem of poverty without federal intervention. The federal government, the CSLP concluded, was the only institution that could equitably and effectively care for the nation's poor children. The problem was that the federal government—and the Department of Agriculture—had left school lunch funding up to state legislators, and these bodies, almost uniformly, threw the cost of lunch back on to the children themselves. According to the 1946 School Lunch Act, states were required to match every dollar of federal funds with three dollars "from sources within the State." Neither Congress nor the Department of Agriculture, however, had ever spelled out what those sources should be. Thus, from the start, the CSLP found, "the only substantial non-Federal contribution is what the children pay for lunches." The figures were startling. Between 1962 and 1967, states contributed less than 25 percent of the operating costs for school lunches. On the whole, children's fees accounted for between 75 and 100 percent of the program's financing.[24]

No matter which region of the country the CSLP looked at, they found state legislators, school boards, and county commissioners reluctant to pay for school lunch programs. In Alabama, for example, the state and local governments contributed nothing at all. But Alabama was only the most extreme case. In Arkansas, Georgia, North Carolina, and Virginia, children paid over 90 percent of the program costs. Missouri children paid 76 percent, Wisconsin's students paid 77 percent, and in Utah, children's fees made up 79 percent. In most cases, state legislatures appropriated less than 10 percent of the total lunch costs. Florida, Georgia, Maryland, North Carolina, and Texas contributed less than 1 percent. The most generous state was Allen Ellender's Louisiana, which contributed 36 percent of the costs. No other state even approached this amount, New York and Missouri came in at around 20 percent. While local contributions were also skimpy, they frequently exceeded the amounts contributed by state legislatures. In Arizona, for example, the legislature put in only 0.3 percent, while counties and school boards contributed a total of over 17 percent. In Massachusetts, where the legislature contributed 11 percent of the cost of lunch, counties, towns, and school boards added another 23 percent. Richard Russell's home state of Georgia contributed a mere 0.4 percent, and localities there only 3.2 percent beyond that. It could be fairly said that children paid for the National School Lunch Program. The CSLP recommended that states and local communities not be allowed to use children's fees or private charity to meet their matching responsibilities. Children's health and nutrition, the women believed, was a public and a national responsibility.[25]

Overall, *Their Daily Bread* reported that few poor children participated in the National School Lunch Program, and those who did were often discriminated against or embarrassed in the lunch line. "The odds are against the hungry child whether he goes to school in a rural Southern County or a large Northern industrial city," the report concluded. New Jersey, for example, offered free lunches to only 12,933 of its 108,767 poor children. In Alabama, only 38,149 of the state's 244,311 poor children received free lunches. On the Marysville, Washington, Indian reservation, no free lunches were offered in the district's only high school." The principal of a St. Louis, Missouri, "slum elementary school" told the CSLP that of the 1,045 children in his school, the majority of whom were on welfare, "twelve are given free lunches." "There are no reduced price lunches," he added.[26]

The heart of the problem, the CSLP reported, was the fact that there were no enforceable federal standards governing school lunch programs. "Local custom," *Their Daily Bread* stated, ended up perpetuating racial discrimination, mistreating poor children, and neglecting poor communities. The women uncovered wide disparities across the country. Because the federal government left it up to local officials to decide which children were eligible for free lunches, eligibility requirements often differed from school to school or county to county within the same state. In Reno, Nevada, for example, one principal offered free lunches to children's whose family income was under $200 per month, while at another school the principal set the figure at $300. In neither case did family size enter the equation. Some principals let any child whose parents were on welfare eat for free, while others insisted on a minimum income, regardless of the state welfare standard. In Sumter County, Alabama, for example, families earning less than $2,000 were eligible for free lunches, while in Palm Beach County, Florida, mothers on AFDC had to request free lunches from the welfare department. In some states parents had to submit evidence of income; in others, teachers decided which children were eligible by their clothing. The worst element of "local choice" for the CSLP was the fact that the Department of Agriculture did nothing to prevent discrimination against black children and all-black schools. The state of Georgia, for example, sent no federal money to Tailaferro County, which not only was one of the poorest areas of the state but had no white public schools. Ultimately, local officials had complete leeway over which children ate lunch at school. While most school principals and teachers probably tried to be fair and just in their decisions, the system was left open to individuals like the Tucson principal who said, "I don't believe in free lunches for welfare people.[27] Despite the fact that Congress formally banned discrimination in the program and Department of Agriculture officials insisted that there was none, the CSLP found that poor children were, in fact, treated differently from paying children.

What disturbed the CSLP's liberal sensibilities most was the fact that minority children, "Negro, Puerto Rican, Mexican-American, and American Indian," were left out of the National School Lunch Program altogether. "We did not design our questionnaires to find out about racial and ethnic discrimination," they wrote, but "the material in this report amply documents wholesale economic discrimination." While the women were not surprised to find discrimination in the South where racial segregation had for so long characterized public education, they were stunned to discover widespread discrimination in the North as well. Although northern cities did not have the same history of legal segregation, housing and employment discrimination resulted in highly segregated neighborhoods and schools. "The exclusion of urban slum schools" the CSLP found, meant that millions of poor, black children were left out of the program. Sixty percent of Cleveland's children, for example, attended schools without lunchrooms. In Detroit only 79 of the city's 224 elementary schools participated in the school lunch program. One-quarter of the schools not participating, the CSLP found, "are located in the slums." In Philadelphia, "not a single one of the 12 slum schools" surveyed had lunch facilities.[28]

There was only one conclusion the women could come to. "Our chief recommendation," the CSLP declared, "calls for a universal, free school lunch program." Understanding, however, that such an idea was utopian, at best, the women made two practical and politically appealing suggestions. First, they recommended that the price and funding formula for school lunches be revised, and second, they insisted that the federal government issue unequivocal guidelines and standards for free lunches. Every school district, *Their Daily Bread* declared, should be obligated to feed all of its needy children, and those children should be identified "according to a uniform Federal standard."[29]

School Lunch and Civil Rights

The release of *Their Daily Bread* in the spring of 1968 coincided with the assassination of Martin Luther King, Jr., and underscored the increasing sense of political and social crisis pervading the nation. Believing in the good faith of government officials, the CSLP had arranged to meet with Secretary of Agriculture Orville Freeman on April 4 to present their findings and provide him with the opportunity to respond before they publicly released *Their Daily Bread* at a news conference scheduled for the next day. On the morning of the news conference, however, CSLP spokeswomen Jean Fairfax and Olya Margolin awoke to the news of King's death. Margolin's first instinct was to cancel the news conference. "I feel all this seems somehow irrelevant in the wake of the tragic events," she confided to Fairfax. In the end, however, the women decided to proceed, because, as Margolin put it, "perhaps the most judicious thing we can do is to persevere in our efforts."[30] Margolin's caution stood in sharp contrast to Jean Fairfax's view of the situation. Without the knowledge of the CSLP executive committee, Fairfax invited the NAACP Legal Defense Fund (LDF) to appear at their news conference. The LDF took the opportunity to announce that, based on the findings revealed in *Their Daily Bread*, it planned to sue the Department of Agriculture if the National School Lunch Program was not brought into compliance with civil rights laws. The LDF threat appalled and embarrassed the CSLP sponsoring organizations. The entire executive committee immediately sent a telegram to Secretary Freeman apologizing and distancing themselves from the LDF's confrontational politics. Thanking the secretary for his "very cooperative attitude," the CSLP assured him that the LDF threat was made without their prior knowledge or endorsement. A legal suit, the women assured Freeman, "is not part of our program."[31] Still, the moment of the King assassination marked a shift in mainstream liberal politics as activists increasingly moved toward a more militant, if more despairing, politics of confrontation. For CSLP women and others in the civil rights and anti-hunger campaigns, the moment also marked an intensified sense of impending social upheaval.[32]

In fact, from the start, Jean Fairfax had an agenda slightly different from the CSLP sponsoring organizations. Where the CSLP groups believed that their research and the facts they uncovered would surely move legislators toward fairness and equity, Fairfax was less confident. Indeed, she had been Dean of Women at Kentucky State College and at Tuskegee Institute and worked for the YWCA during the 1940s. After World War II, Fairfax worked with the American Friends Service Committee and then the NAACP Legal Defense Fund. She had seen first-hand the intransigence of racism, both north and south. Fairfax was happy to present the CSLP findings to the press, to congressional committees, and before community forums, but she also wanted immediate and concrete change. Although she had promised the CSLP executive board to keep "the tone of the project . . . constructive," Fairfax clearly had doubts about how effective liberal persuasion would ultimately be. After the debacle of the news conference, Fairfax warned the CSLP women that the time for caution had passed. While it appears that Fairfax herself had been caught off-guard by announcement of the LDF suit, she nonetheless reminded the CSLP that "a suit against a public official is neither a personal attack nor a hostile act." Where Margolin and others on the CSLP executive board clearly felt the action had been a breach of "good faith and etiquette" because it occurred immediately after what had been a "pleasant" meeting with the Secretary of Agriculture, Fairfax insisted that the meeting with Freeman had not been intended as "a social occasion." Indeed, she said, "we were in his office on serious business relating to starving children." The point, Fairfax insisted, was that Freeman's department was guilty of inaction and neglect. A lawsuit in such cases, she said, "is the most conservative and traditional" way for American citizens to claim their rights.[33] Questions of style masked important strategic differences among the women. At the same time, however, conventional, "lady-like" behavior afforded the CSLP women a certain legitimacy and an entrée into the halls of government. For mainstream liberal women during the late 1960s, style and polite behavior proved to be powerful weapons.

The CSLP women were hardly prepared for the impact their report had on policy makers and activists alike. They modestly hoped their report would offer "enough evidence of discrimination in the School Lunch Program to warrant a thorough study" and speedy reform. As it turned out, the CSLP project would become the centerpiece of an increasingly acrimonious debate about welfare rights and the fate of poor children in

America. At the moment that the CSLP findings reached headlines in newspapers across the country, Martin Luther King's followers in the Poor People's Campaign (PPC) camped out in front of the Department of Agriculture and vowed not to leave until Congress and the president did something about poverty and discrimination. In the aftermath of King's death, the PPC brought several thousand protesters to Washington to dramatize the economic dimensions of the civil rights movement and to channel the energies evident in the growing urban unrest. When Ralph Abernathy, spokesman for the encampment dubbed "Resurrection City," presented the Secretary of Agriculture with the PPC's demands, free food stamps and free school lunches were at the top of the list. The Department of Agriculture, he charged, has "let our people starve."[34] Although Jean Fairfax assured the CSLP Executive Board that King's lieutenants would "do everything they can to prevent violence," she also warned that "poor people are desperate and angry" and worried that things could quickly spin out of control. Much of the anger, Fairfax knew, was directed at Freeman and the failures of the National School Lunch Program. Fairfax urged the CSLP women to use their influence to convince Secretary Freeman "to join with us in a militant effort to implement the recommendations" of *Their Daily Bread*. "If our efforts can produce some tangible results soon," she assured the women, "we may help not only to prevent violence but to give the poor some reason to believe that our system can become responsive to their needs."[35] This was precisely the appeal that CSLP women intended to make. Eschewing the tactics of the street, these women believed that solid evidence and reasoned debate would move lawmakers to action. In 1968, however, liberal confidence in the democratic process was severely challenged.

During the months following the release of *Their Daily Bread*, social tensions deepened the divisions in American political life. The image of hungry children in the midst of affluent America seemed to represent the heartlessness and inequities of a system in which increasing numbers of people were feeling left out of the mainstream. *Their Daily Bread* became the authoritative evidence for a broad-based anti-hunger movement that coalesced as the civil rights and anti-war movements intensified during the summer of 1968. Illinois representative Roman Pucinski praised *Their Daily Bread* but deflected blame away from his fellow congressmen. "You women and your organizations have made a monumental contribution in calling attention to one of the main reasons of why there is unrest in America," he said. However, he believed that the unrest stemmed from the fact that "we in Congress pass programs in good faith, but then those programs don't get down to the local level."[36] In the context of urban riots, an escalation of the Vietnam War, and the assassination of Robert Kennedy, a polarized political climate led even the most optimistic liberals to doubt the sincerity of public officials and the ability of the federal government to ensure racial equality and economic opportunity. As liberal policy makers desperately sought ways to address the public anger and discontent through traditional political channels, community groups, often funded by President Johnson's War on Poverty community development funds, became increasing politicized and militant. Radical and liberal groups alike used the CSLP report to buttress calls for welfare reform and an end to poverty.

Free school lunches fit with the radical agendas of groups like the Black Panther Party as well as with liberal efforts to "make the system work." Organizations as disparate as the Catholic Church and the Black Panthers used the CSLP findings to bolster demands for more free lunches. The Catholic Conference, for example, used the women's interview model to survey school lunch programs in Catholic schools. The Poor People's Campaign demanded that the Department of Agriculture immediately open food programs in counties where none existed. Free food stamps, better consumer education for the poor, and free lunches, PPC leaders agreed, should be the department's focus—not aid to farmers. The Citizen's Board similarly demanded that the Department of Agriculture "immediately provide free and reduced price lunches for every needy child."[37] Even government agencies outside the USDA took up the call. HEW, long eyeing the school lunch program for its own, convened a task force on nutrition and children's meals. Finally, some states began, for the first time, to enact new tax laws to pay for free lunches.[38] While the CSLP women intended their report to point toward the need for a universal school lunch program for all American children, the crisis atmosphere of the time made them admit this goal was a long way off. Instead, the demand for free lunches for poor children held center stage.

For radicals like the Black Panther Party, free lunches represented not only a useful rhetorical demand but a concrete social service as well. The Black Panther free breakfast program in Oakland, California, formed the party's central organizing strategy and stood as its most enduring legacy. When Senator George McGovern asked school lunch program administrator Rodney Leonard whether the Panthers fed more poor children than did the state of California, Leonard admitted that it was "probably true."[39] Even more moderate civil rights leaders such as Jesse Jackson saw the Black Panther free breakfast program as one of the most "creative and revolutionary" food programs in the country. Unlike the National School Lunch Program in which, as the CSLP discovered, poor children were regularly embarrassed or humiliated, Jackson observed that "the only prerequisite to eat a Black Panther breakfast is to be hungry."[40] Jackson adopted the free lunch demand as part of his own Operation Breadbasket agenda. Leading demonstrators to the Illinois state capitol in 1968, he charged that legislators who sent "sons and fathers" to fight in Vietnam neglected the children in their own country. Unlike the Black Panther strategy of building independent community institutions, however, Jackson's Poor People's Campaign focused its energies toward wresting resources out of federal and state governments.[41]

In response to mounting grass-roots pressure, Agriculture Secretary Freeman promised quick action to bring free lunches to poor children. Freeman clearly preferred to work with the women's groups than to deal with more militant anti-hunger activists. He praised *Their Daily Bread* as "by all odds the most accurate and constructive" report.[42] Other critics, he charged, including the CBS program *Hunger USA*, promoted "misinformation" and "misunderstanding" and distorted the department's achievements. Freeman demanded that the network air corrections to its "oversimplified, and misleading picture." The secretary similarly accused reporter Nick Kotz of "making a major muck-raking enterprise out of picking at our programs." Kotz's reports, Freeman said, were "pathetic word pictures of the people we are not yet reaching." He declared that he and his department were "doing everything we can" to reach those children but admitted that there was room for change in the program. He conspicuously invited CSLP representatives, rather than PPC leaders, to serve on a liaison committee to help draft new school lunch guidelines.[43] Over the course of the next twelve months, debate both inside and outside Congress focused on transforming the scope and operation of the National School Lunch Program. The CSLP's Jean Fairfax, along with NCJW representative Florence Robins, regularly appeared at congressional hearings and public forums to promote their report and to lobby for increased funding for free lunches. The women were given a warm welcome by legislators. Even liberal stalwart George McGovern opined that the women's report was reasoned and that critics such as those who produced "Hunger USA" were "a little long in the criticism of the adequacy of the human welfare job Agriculture has done and short on praise of the agriculture sector for doing all it has done."[44] The Department of Agriculture, McGovern said, "is not a welfare agency in the sense of immediate and direct aid to the poor." This, of course, was the heart of the matter.

Ultimately, grass-roots pressure resulted in a dramatic increase in the number of poor children receiving free or reduced price meals. Although Congress kept level the federal overall school lunch appropriation (i.e., operating costs, meal subsidies, and food donations), in the spring of 1968 it approved $32 million to be used to expand the school lunch program in impoverished areas and those with "a high concentration of working mothers or mothers enrolled in job training programs."[45] A month later the Senate approved funds for pre-school lunch programs in poverty areas as well. Finally, in January 1969, the annual school lunch appropriation for regular lunches was increased to $50 million and an additional $5 million was authorized for "needy" children.[46] From a fund-

TABLE 7.1
Children Participating in the National School Lunch Program, 1947–85 (in millions)

Year	Total number of participants	Number of free and reduced-price participants	Percentage of free and reduced-price participants	School enrollment (all schools, total)	Percentage of enrollment participating
1941	4.6	n/a		26.80	17
1947	6.6	n/a		27.18	25
1955	12.0	n/a		35.89	33
1960	14.1	n/a		43.07	33
1965	18.7	n/a		48.37	39
1970	22.6	5.6	25	51.27	44
1975	24.9	9.1	37	49.81	50
1979	27.1	11.7	43	46.85	58
1980	26.6	11.9	45	46.21	58
1985	23.6	11.5	49	44.98	52

Source: "Child Nutrition Programs: Issues for the 101st Congress," *School Food Service Research Review* 13, no. 1 (Spring 1989): Table 11, p. 38. United States Census Bureau, The 2007 Statistical Abstract, The National Data Book, School Enrollment, No. HS-20, Education Summary, Enrollment, 1900–2001 and Projections, 2001.

ing level of $146 million in 1965, the National School Lunch Program appropriation grew to $226 million in 1973, and the School Breakfast Program grew from $3.5 million in 1969 to $18 million in 1973.[47] Congress declared that all children below the federal poverty level should receive free lunches. The states now had to provide free meals for children whose family incomes were up to 25 percent above the poverty line, and reduced price meals for those families with incomes up to 50 percent above poverty level.[48]

The impact of the new lunch budget was dramatic. To continue receiving federal subsidies, local school districts, particularly those in low-income communities, had to vastly increase their free meal service. In Pennsylvania, for example, the number of free meals jumped from 25,000 per month to almost 2.8 million.[49] Philadelphia provided 10,000 meals in fifty schools. The city of Dallas increased the number of free lunches from a mere 2,000 to over 14,000 within a year.[50] In St. Louis, the percentage of free lunches increased from four to over 60 within a year.[51] Providence added 1,000 free meals a day; Wilmington, Delaware, 600; and Portland, Oregon, 2,400. Washington, D.C., Indianapolis, and Oklahoma City began to serve free lunches to poor children. Chicago opened a central kitchen to provide lunches for thirty-eight inner-city schools without cafeteria facilities (see Table 7.1).[52]

But increased federal funding for free lunches did not immediately alter the way school lunchrooms operated. For one thing, the federal mandate did not contain sufficient new funds for general lunchroom operation. This meant that local districts and states had to come up with their own funding sources in order to be able to feed all children identified as poor in their districts. Because most school lunch programs relied on children's fees to cover costs, many administrators simply tried to raise meal prices for paying children. Under the new federal rules, however, the maximum that any school could charge for lunch was 20 cents.[53] The second problem was that while the federal government mandated that free lunches be available to all poor children, the Department of Agriculture was slow to articulate eligibility standards and even slower to issue operating guidelines about how poor children were to be treated.[54]

Grass-roots activists, taking up the CSLP findings, demanded that the states assume a more prominent role in providing free lunches to poor children. States for too long had relied on surplus food and children's fees. "The real secret to expanding the ability of schools to serve lunch to all those who need it but cannot afford it, and ultimately perhaps to make school food service universal," John Kramer, executive director of the National Council on Hunger and Malnutrition in the United States, noted, "is to prompt State governments to put up their fair share of the cost." This would happen, he believed, only if state and local governments "are either confronted by an outraged, politically potent citizenry or are subject to federally imposed stringent matching rules."[55] Most states, however, dragged their feet when it came to appropriating funds for school lunches. As a result, anti-poverty groups across the country mounted demands for new state funding. In Illinois, Jesse Jackson led the Southern Christian Leadership Conference's Operation Breadbasket in a demonstration to the state legislature in Springfield. The Committee for the Hungry Child in Detroit, the Mingo County, West Virginia, Hot Lunch Strike Committee, and the Tucson, Arizona, Free Lunch Committee challenged local officials to feed poor children. In Houston, high school students organized themselves and threatened to boycott the schools. Coalitions in Arizona, California, Oregon, Washington, Kansas, Nebraska, and Iowa launched coordinated campaigns during the summer of 1969 to demand state funding for free lunch programs.[56]

ELIGIBILITY STANDARDS AND THE RIGHT TO LUNCH

Frustrated by the slow pace of change in school lunchrooms, the Poor People's Campaign, along with the Citizen's Crusade, threatened a national mobilization for the "right to lunch" and promised "an endless string of litigation directed at securing a meal for every needy pupil in every community in the Country."[57] Across the country grass-roots groups began to agitate for free lunch programs. By the end of 1969, the National Council on Hunger and Malnutrition documented lawsuits throughout the country. These suits focused national attention on two issues: the reluctance of local officials to put resources into school lunches and the continued paternalism and discrimination that characterized rules regarding which children were eligible for free lunches. Even moderate anti-hunger groups were frustrated with local and state officials who refused to supplement federal dollars with local funds in order to provide services for poor children. At the same time, anti-hunger activists, influenced by a newly emerging welfare rights movement, focused increasingly on issues of dignity and fair treatment by public officials.[58]

The call for a right to lunch mirrored a growing welfare rights movement during the late 1960s. Demanding not only access to government benefits but respect and dignity as well, this movement directly challenged federal bureaucratic offices and regulations. Women on welfare organized the National Welfare Rights Organization (NWRO) to mobilize welfare recipients and to educate women regarding eligibility standards and application procedures for food stamps, Aid to Dependent Children, and other federal benefits. In 1969 the group put out a pamphlet entitled "The New School Lunch Program Bill of Rights," which listed the following "rights":

1. The right to have every school operate a school lunch program.
2. The right that all poor school children receive their lunches for free or at a reduced price.
3. The right to make sure that children receiving free or reduced price lunches and breakfasts will not be discriminated against in any way.
4. The right to be told by school district officials about the rules and administration of the school lunch program.
5. The right to prevent school administrators from prying into your personal life, or asking irrelevant questions when your children apply for free lunches.
6. The right to get your free lunches immediately, without being investigated or forced to prove eligibility.
7. The right to appeal a denial of free lunch benefits or any other administrative decision that adversely affects a student.
8. The right to have the appeal decided fairly and by an impartial referee.
9. The right to a good and nutritious school lunch.

10. The right to fair and equal treatment, free from discrimination based on race, poverty, color or religion.
11. The right to assure that children and families of children receiving free school lunches have the same constitutional rights as everyone else.

The pamphlet offered specific information on free lunch eligibility including income and family size, provided guidelines for filling out the federal application forms, and gave phone numbers to call if federal or state officials did not comply or if applicants were not treated with dignity and respect. It also suggested things to do "in case your rights are violated," including organizing hearings and pressuring local politicians and state agencies. If all else failed, the Bill of Rights advised, "bring law suits."[59]

The results of the widespread mobilization for free lunches were mixed. In Illinois, Jesse Jackson's coalition forced the state legislature to appropriate $5.4 million for free lunches. The Baltimore, Maryland, FOOD (Feeding Our Own Deprived) Committee, made up of "clergy, junior leaguers, and just plain folks," pressured the governor to contribute $1.5 million in state funds for free lunch programs. In Memphis, where the school board had never contributed local funds to children's lunches, a broad-based citizens' coalition ranging from welfare rights activists to Junior Leaguers forced the school board to appropriate $150,000 of its Title I funds to provide lunches for poor children.[60] Gary, Indiana, and Wichita, Kansas, began entirely new free lunch programs, and Detroit promised to provide food service in seventy schools where no lunch programs had existed before.[61] John Perryman, lauding the grass-roots efforts, said, "For the first time in history we have had the courage to say that matching funds for the federal dollars shall not come alone from the nickels and dimes of the children, but also from state matching funds."[62]

The free lunch mandate challenged longstanding interpretations of the National School Lunch Program's mission. In California, for example, a newly emboldened conservative movement pushed for dramatic reductions in state spending. When the state legislature overwhelmingly passed a $4 million subsidy for school breakfast and lunch programs, the recently elected governor, Ronald Reagan, cut all but $500,000 and earmarked this for a pilot program rather than for general use by poor children.[63] California Rural Legal Assistance immediately sued the state in U.S. District Court, contending that the 1946 School Lunch Act promised every needy child a free lunch. T. W. Martz, Stanislaus County counsel, rejected that interpretation, insisting that the state was under no obligation to provide free lunches to all children on welfare. It had never been the intent of the School Lunch Act, Martz asserted, to provide free meals to all needy children. Martz appealed to the School Lunch Act's now aging sponsor,

Richard Russell, who agreed that free lunches had been intended "to go to the neediest children" only "to the extent of available funds." Russell bemoaned the program's recent transformation, saying, "I have always favored leaving as much control as possible to the local school boards and it never occurred to me that the welfare department or the courts would undertake to classify the individual children as participants."[64] The California Rural Legal Assistance attorney declared this interpretation to be an example of "insensitivity, indifference, ineptness, and inertia." The only way a needy child could be assured of a free, nutritious lunch in California, he asserted, "is to be arrested for a serious crime and confined to a juvenile detention center" where meals were provided.[65] Ultimately, the free lunch provisions were upheld and the court ordered the Secretary of Agriculture to provide food for children in sixteen California counties that had refused to establish lunch programs.

Securing state funding for school lunches solved only half of the problem. Eigibility and dignity were different matters entirely. Free lunch children in all parts of the country were still required to stand in separate lines, eat different meals, and, in some instances, work for their lunches. In Kansas City, hunger activists took the school board to court, challenging its policy of requiring poor children to work for their meals.[66] In Chicago, Jesse Jackson charged that local officials "established eligibility rules, administrative policies, budgetary limitations, and school reimbursement procedures" that were inconsistent with the federal requirement of providing free meals to all needy children. In a similar lawsuit, the Boston Lawyers' Committee for Civil Rights charged the school board with "non-response" to federal guidelines.[67]

The major stumbling block in the way of enforcing national standards for eligibility and service in school lunch programs were entrenched patterns of racism and states' rights interests. When it came to public schools and education, even congressional liberals were reluctant to go very far with federal standards. The Department of Agriculture and its congressional oversight committees had long refrained from becoming involved in the behavior of school officials. When anti-hunger activist Charles Remsberg questioned Department of Agriculture official Keith Keely about the "obvious departures" from federal guidelines, Keely replied, "We don't tell them [local officials] how to do it. We can't dictate to them."[68] The program's founders, Allen Ellender and Richard Russell, in particular, had insisted that school lunch programs steer clear of any involvement in educational issues for fear of threats to the racially segregated school system. Both Russell and Ellender still sat on key committees and did what they could to contain calls to turn school lunches into poverty programs.

Allen Ellender now chaired the Senate Agriculture Committee and vigorously rejected the idea that a federal agency should set the terms for local operation of school lunch programs. He insisted that local officials knew best how to administer the program and how to decide which children were needy. In a revealing exchange with Martha Grass, a Marland, Oklahoma, welfare rights activist, Ellender clearly found her demands incomprehensible. When Grass asked the senator why poor kids were not receiving free lunches, Ellender told her it was a matter of state assistance. Grass refused to accept that argument. Ellender admitted that "there is something out of place at the local level." But, he added, "don't blame the Federal government." Grass pressed him on who was responsible for feeding poor children, but Ellender responded with a constitutional disquisition saying it was the executive branch, not Congress, that had the responsibility to administer the laws. Grass clearly did not care which branch of government provided free lunches as long as poor children were fed at school. "You have so many branches," she told the senator, "no wonder we are going hungry."[69] Ellender was frustrated and confounded by local authorities who, as he saw it, simply chose not to sufficiently supplement federal resources. When, for example, the Boston School Board failed to meet federal guidelines for free lunches, Ellender could not understand why an affluent city like Boston did not put sufficient funds into "helping the poor." Why, he asked welfare rights activist Patrice Twigg, would "you expect the Federal Government to barge in and force the States to operate school lunch programs?" Twigg tried to explain the city's at-large electoral system in which advocates for the poor had little chance of winning electoral majorities. What is more, she said, local administrators often do not recognize the poor "as being people." Ellender dismissed Twigg's complaint asking why, if local activists were unhappy with local officials, they did not simply "throw them out of office?" Twigg fired back, "We need someone from the Federal level."[70]

Despite Ellender's long support for the National School Lunch Program, he had never intended to see it turn into a poverty program. Indeed, in his view, the new demands for free lunches were undermining what had been a highly successful agricultural surplus program that also provided nutrition for children. In truth, Ellender did not believe in free lunches. He was convinced that people who demanded free meals were basically free-loading on the government. This attitude, predictably, drew the ire of welfare activists and free lunch advocates. Gloria Atchinson, a member of the Detroit Committee for the Hungry Child, for example, challenged the senator's characterization of poor people as free-loaders. "Most people," she said, "have a lot of pride and they want to be able to pay for their lunches." However, she insisted, even if poor parents could not pay for their children's lunches, they deserved to be treated respectfully by their government and by public officials.[71]

Reports of free lunch protests and lawsuits revealed that discrimination in school lunchrooms was a national problem. Lawsuits against urban school districts, in particular, dramatically illustrated the extent to which public resources were unequally distributed even outside the racially segregated South. Particularly when it came to education, northern cities found themselves accused of "de facto" segregation and racial discrimination. In Boston, for example, a new city-wide electoral system, inaugurated during the 1950s, resulted in racial exclusion just as the black population of the city increased. By the middle 1960s, school desegregation proved as divisive in the North as it had been in southern states. As Detroit's Superintendent of Public Schools, William Simons, observed, "there is only one local unit of government where the welfare of children is dependent upon the whims of the voters and that is the public schools."[72] Still, Leslie Dunbar, co-chair of the Citizens Board of Inquiry, insisted that the school lunch critiques, including "Hunger USA," were pro-states' rights. The reports, he pointed out, "might even stimulate states to do more for their needy citizens than the law requires." At the very least, Dunbar hoped federal standards of eligibility would "require the observance of necessary minimums and would vest in every individual the right to such."[73]

Despite ever more direct criticism by anti-hunger and civil rights activists, the Department of Agriculture only reluctantly issued standards and guidelines for free lunch programs. Indeed, it was not until 1971 that the Secretary of Agriculture released a clear set of guidelines. Reiterating the responsibility of every school participating in the National School Lunch Program to serve free meals to all poor children in its district, the department finally enumerated minimum income standards for free lunch eligibility and uniform reimbursement rates for federally subsidized meals.[74] The initial income requirements for free meals was set at 100 percent of the federal poverty line. The federal standards, however, actually threatened to exclude many of the "near poor" from receiving free meals. In New York, for example, with one of the nation's most generous free meal programs, the income eligibility cut-off was $4,250. Because federal funds would reimburse the state only for families under federal "poverty line," which was only $3,940 that year, school officials estimated that several thousand children would be left out of the program. Harvard nutritionist Jean Mayer warned, "No one who has followed this issue would have expected the Administration to interpret 'needy' to exclude people who are poor but not quite that destitute."[75] This, combined with the declining participation of full-paying children as the price of meals went up, threatened the entire structure of the school lunch program.

School lunch administrators greeted the free lunch guidelines with considerable ambivalence. While they generally endorsed the expansion of meal offerings to poor children, they feared lawmakers—and the public—would lose sight of the nutrition needs of all children, regardless of social status. Echoing the sentiments of early twentieth-century nutritionists and home economists, school administrators reminded lawmakers that malnutrition threatened all children, whether their families were rich or poor. Norma Goff, director of food service for Ridley Township, Pennsylvania, for example, told President Johnson that "children from families in an income bracket that can afford the school lunch frequently have poorer food habits than those coming from low income families."[76] Indeed, school lunch professionals increasingly worried that the attention to poor children was threatening the idea of universal child nutrition. When President Johnson threatened to cut the general school lunch budget, even as he approved funds for free meals, the ASFSA and the American Parents Committee mounted a national lobbying campaign urging the president not to feed the poor at the expense of other children. John Gehn, superintendent of the Gilman, Wisconsin, Joint School District No. 2, warned LBJ that "changing these fine programs to include only needy children would be a big mistake." Gehn worried that the new guidelines would lead more children to be identified as "needy," but that "it has been my experience that the less identification of this type the better it is for all concerned."[77] Jerry Peterson, superintendent of the Story City, Iowa, Community Schools, told the president, "It doesn't make sense to create new programs . . . by taking money out of one pocket and putting it into another."[78] The message from school administrators was clear. They did not want the National School Lunch Program to turn into a program for poor children. In their view, all children needed a nutritious lunch.

The threat to paying children revealed a fundamental tension within the program and within American social programs generally. The National School Lunch Program's remarkable popular support rested on the assumption that every child who wanted a nutritious meal could receive one. Indeed, the program was designed as a welfare program for farmers and had traditionally operated as a benefit for middle- and working-class families who could pay a subsidized price for their children's meals. Senate sponsor Richard Russell, for one, insisted that "the School Lunch Act was passed for all children (not just the needy)."[79] Russell's liberal Senate colleagues similarly asserted the program's universal intent. New York's Jacob Javits, for example, declared that the School Lunch Act of 1946 "was never intended to be a poor person's lunch program." The purpose, Javits said, was to ensure adequate nutrition for children regardless of whether they were rich or poor. Children's health, Javits believed, "is an important national asset."[80] Congressional advocates as well as school lunch professionals feared that a singular focus on the needy would spell the end of the program's "traditional" goal of providing nutrition for all children. Liberal Senator and anti-poverty advocate Carl Perkins warned, "We have to be most careful not to price the middle-class child out of the lunchroom."[81] ASFSA executive director John Perryman similarly worried that if child nutrition programs became part of overall educational or welfare appropriations, it would spell "a total disaster" for the school lunch program.[82] Perryman opposed turning the program into welfare. "Our nation's educational history abounds with evidence that public education . . . faltered and failed so long as it confined itself to the pauper's offspring," he said.[83] Holding to the ideal of a universal school lunch program, the ASFSA fought against shifting the program's focus to welfare.[84] The National Education Association also favored a universal system. In 1970, NEA president George Fisher observed, "I don't distinguish between money for school lunches and money for all other things we need in education. . . . A hot lunch program shouldn't be a free lunch for the poor. It should be a free lunch for all children."[85] Nonetheless, the trend was set. By the early 1970s, as one historian noted, the school lunch program had moved "from an outlet for farm surpluses to a small convenience for part of the middle class to an important welfare benefit for children of the poor."[86]

The fundamental dilemma confronting free lunch advocates was whether the program could exist as a means of ensuring the nutritional health of all children or whether it would become an entitlement program for the poor. Scholars have suggested that one of the underlying tensions marking President Johnson's War on Poverty as well as American social welfare policies generally has been the fact that some programs, like Social Security, at least in theory offered universal benefits and therefore garnered widespread popular support. Other programs, most notably Aid to Dependent Children and Food Stamps, targeted the poor and therefore gained weaker support among middle-class tax payers. Of course, Social Security was not, in any real sense, a universal benefit—farm workers, domestic servants, and service workers were long excluded. Still, the program remained a bedrock of the nation's social safety net. Other scholars argue that the key to public support for welfare lies less in the claim to universality but, rather, in the institutional structure of the program. In this case, federal programs fail not because of the group of clients served but, rather, because the American welfare system has relied too heavily on states and entrenched local interests to administer the benefits. In the case of school lunches both interpretations are important. The National School Lunch Program had strong public support exactly because of its universal claims. The push to re-direct the program's focus to poor children threatened that universal claim. But what threatened the program even more was its administrative weakness and the continued reliance on local officials to shape and distribute the benefits. During the late 1960s, school lunch advocates understood the risks of turning the program into one targeted only to poor children. They understood even more the continued risks of leaving the administration of school lunches in the hands of local officials. Between 1968 and 1970, however, all other considerations paled beside the sense of social crisis that informed local activists as well as federal policy makers.

In the context of growing social unrest, the question of universal school lunch versus a free lunch program for poor children became moot. Neither public officials nor grass-roots activists felt they could afford to push for idealistic goals. Instead, pragmatic politics won the day. Given that few lawmakers were prepared to spend the estimated $15 million or more that it would take to feed all school children, school lunch advocates pushed for an expanded free lunch program targeted at the poor. Most reformers viewed this as a practical, short-term solution to a crisis rather than an ideal long-term federal policy solution to the twin problems of poverty and malnutrition. *Their Daily Bread*, for example, urged that "the school lunch should be a basic part of free public school education to which every child has a right."[87] The San Diego, Texas, superintendent of schools went further, advocating free meals for all children. "I would not charge a student a dime for a meal," he said, "I think it is as important as English, and history, and math."[88] When asked whether he would give a millionaire's child a free lunch, he replied, "Yes sir. I would think that it is important that they eat at the cafeteria." Just because the family is rich, he reminded the senator, "does not prove that he has the proper food."[89] Yet given the political realities, both the CSLP and the San Diego school board conceded that, in the short run, the most they could hope for would be free lunches for the poor.[90] Everyone involved with school lunches understood that pushing for a universal program would, in effect, spell its doom. They agreed instead to targeted funds that, they hoped would ultimately be expanded to cover all children. It was a vain hope.

CHAPTER 8

Let Them Eat Ketchup

Between 1968 and 1972 the National School Lunch Program was transformed from being primarily an agricultural subsidy into one of the nation's premier poverty programs. This was not entirely what school lunch and children's welfare reformers had in mind nor was it what the program's original political sponsors had intended. The 1940s school lunch advocates imagined a program that would offer healthy, low-priced meals to children and free lunches to those (assumed to be few in number) who could not afford to pay. What happened as a result of mounting pressure to feed the poor, however, was a fundamental shift in school lunch priorities. This shift had significant unintended consequences for the demographics of school lunchrooms and the quality of school meals. Put simply, as the number of free meals soared, the number of paying children precipitously declined. By the middle of the 1970s relatively few children who had any choice ate school lunches. The exodus of paying children from school cafeterias, however, created a huge shortfall in lunchroom budgets. Federal subsidies did not shrink, but they were increasingly earmarked for free lunches. Indeed, it was Richard Nixon who most decisively transformed the National School Lunch Program into a free lunch subsidy.

Just as poor children won a "right to lunch," the quality of school meals declined and the democratic ideal of the school lunchroom disappeared. As free and reduced price lunches became an ever more important part of federal welfare entitlements, the search for financial stability eroded both the nutritional integrity and the public nature of the National School Lunch Program. Although the federal government finally established eligibility criteria for free and reduced price meals and articulated nutrition standards, the administration of the program and the distribution of federal resources still resided in local hands. Most of the time, public funds—federal, state, or local—for free lunches were woefully insufficient to cover the costs of running large-scale lunchroom operations. Despite a seemingly intense public loyalty to the school lunch program, neither state legislators nor local communities were willing to pick up the budget slack. In an effort to maintain the viability of free meal programs, both school administrators and liberal reformers began to look to the private food service industry to keep school cafeterias afloat. At the same

time, the Department of Agriculture began to modify its nutrition standards for children's meals, making it easier for the food industry to enter
the school lunch market. ASFSA executive director John Perryman ruefully observed that the National School Lunch Program had shifted its
focus "from the nutritionally needy to the economically needy."[1] The difference would have seriously disturbed Ellen Richards and the home economists who initiated school lunch programs during the early twentieth
century. For them, every child was, in some sense, "nutritionally needy."

Believing that they had no other choice, however, school lunch administrators across the country began to invite food-service corporations and
fast-food franchises to supply the food and in some cases to actually run
their meal programs. By the end of the 1970s school cafeterias came more
and more to resemble fast-food restaurants. Although nutritionists and
health professionals decried the turn to privatization, many free lunch
advocates ended up lauding the move. Liberals who generally eschewed
big business and criticized corporate values were willing to go along with
at least limited privatization if it meant that poor children could eat for
free. What emerged in many school districts by the end of the 1970s was
a public/private partnership shaped fundamentally by business concerns
such as profitability and efficiency. Nutrition, health, and education all
became subsumed into a model of consumer choice and market share.
While public resources continued to underwrite the National School
Lunch Program, few lunchrooms could stay in business without bowing
in some way or other to the brand names, fast food, and corporate models
of efficiency, productivity, and profit.

WHO PAYS FOR FREE LUNCH?

Richard Nixon took office in the midst of crises both foreign and domestic. While the Vietnam War spiraled out of control during the last months
of Lyndon Johnson's presidency, anti-war, civil rights, and anti-poverty
movements drew thousands of Americans into street demonstrations,
grass-roots coalitions, and community organizations. In one of his first
official acts, President Nixon appointed Harvard nutritionist Jean Mayer
to head a White House Conference on Food, Nutrition and Health.
Mayer, a well-respected nutrition researcher with bipartisan credentials,
wanted the conference to highlight "a nutritional rights counterpart to
civil voting rights."[2] The White House conference brought together a vast
array of players, from anti-hunger activists and community leaders to
educators, nutrition and health professionals, food industry representatives, and Department of Agriculture officials.[3] Chief among the conference child welfare recommendations was a universal school lunch pro-

gram "as a basic school service to promote the learning potential of all children."[4] Admitting that this was a long-term ideal, even in a nation as affluent as the United States, the conference recommended instead that the free lunch program be expanded and that the Department of Agriculture improve the nutrition content of school meals generally. "Every child has a right to the nutritional resources he needs," asserted the conference report. This could only be accomplished, the report concluded, via the public schools, "historically the vehicle through which Americans implement important national and community goals."[5] At the end of the conference, President Nixon promised that his administration would eliminate hunger in America before Thanksgiving 1970.

Jean Mayer proved to be a key figure in shaping the Nixon administration's food policies. Born in France, Mayer was lauded as a World War II hero before becoming one of the world's leading nutritionists. Although he did extensive nutrition work on hunger and malnutrition in Africa and India, during the 1960s he began to warn of an obesity crisis at home. Despite his role as Nixon's spokesman on issues of hunger, Mayer remained a non-partisan figure, gaining the respect of hunger activists as well as legislators of both parties.[6] Mayer was not an uncritical recruit for the Nixon administration. In 1968, testifying before the Senate Select Committee on Nutrition and Human Needs, he took the Department of Agriculture to task for its lack of attention to the problems of poverty and malnutrition. "We cannot," he said, "continue to have the nutritional policy of this Nation be an indirect consequence of such programs as price support subsidies."[7]

While ending hunger before the following Thanksgiving was, perhaps, too lofty a goal, the new president oversaw an unprecedented expansion in food and nutrition programs. Food relief budgets, including school lunches and food stamps, soared from less than $500 million in 1969 to an estimated $8 billion in 1975.[8] In May 1970, the Senate extended free meal service, immediately doubling the number of poor children participating in the program. Where the total federal appropriation for school lunches from 1946 to 1969 had been $3.6 billion, in 1970 alone, the Republican administration put in over one billion dollars. By 1972, Secretary of Agriculture Earl Butz claimed to be feeding over 8.1 million children a year. Most of these new meals were free or reduced-price lunches. In 1971 the *New York Times* reported a record 7.1 million children nationwide receiving free or reduced priced lunches at school.[9] In 1975, the Republican administration put the free School Breakfast Program on permanent authorization.

During the Nixon administration, food as welfare became an institutional part of the federal budget. By the 1970s, Department of Agriculture spending on domestic food programs "quickly exceeded total spending on farm programs."[10] According to one estimate, food programs increased from 11 percent of the department's budget in 1970 to 40 percent ten years later. At the same time, spending on surplus commodities declined.[11] Department of Agriculture admitted that its "Type A meal" nutrition system could not "be used efficiently in the development of commodity agricultural production nor can it be used effectively in determining annual national and local requirements for food procurement."[12] School lunchrooms no longer operated as a significant outlet for surplus agricultural commodities. Indeed, most federal resources now came to schools through cash reimbursements rather than donated food. Large farm interests continued to receive substantial subsidies, but public and congressional debates focused on free lunches and food stamps.[13] Embracing the school lunch program as no other president before him, Richard Nixon declared, "I not only accept the responsibility" for ending hunger and malnutrition, "I claim the responsibility."[14] But Nixon's sense of responsibility did not, in fact, reach all children. Although his administration increased funding for the National School Lunch Program, the president carefully targeted where the money went. "Government support for food programs," Nixon insisted, "should concentrate on helping the needy rather than subsidizing rich and poor alike."[15] With congressional support, under Richard Nixon the two major federal food programs, food stamps and school lunches, actually received increased appropriations.[16] In fact, however, the president's carefully targeted policy signaled an important shift in the philosophy and structure of the National School Lunch Program.[17]

The federal free lunch mandate threw school lunchrooms across the country into ever deepening financial crises. As it turned out, pouring federal money into free and reduced price lunches only exacerbated the local funding problem. Traditionally, states had used children's fees to make up the difference between federal subsidies and the actual cost of meals. Initially, therefore, when Congress mandated more free meals, schools raised the cost of full price lunches. In 1975, when President Gerald Ford proposed cutbacks in school lunch funding, the ASFSA mounted a vocal opposition, saying, "In a vast majority of schools, the poverty program alone would not support a viable school food service." The ASFSA estimated that lunch prices were soaring to "eighty cents and higher" and warned that pupil participation "would be forced down dramatically."[18] The result was predictable. As school lunches became associated with the poor, the paying children, long the financial backbone of the school lunch program, began to drop out. Between 1970 and 1973 an estimated one million paying children dropped out of the program.[19] During the early 1980s school lunch participation overall continued to

TABLE 8.1
Federal Cash Assistance to Children's Nutrition Programs,
1947–85 (in thousands)*

Fiscal year	Basic NSLP authorization	Special assistance (free lunches)
1947	59,900	
1950	64,500	
1955	68,900	
1960	93,600	
1965	130,400	
1966	139,000	1,866
1970	167,900	132,012
1975	466,800	818,373
1980	724,300	1,379,465
1982	425,000	1,620,300
1985	532,085	2,123,946

Source:"Child Nutrition Programs: Issues for the 101st Congress,"
School Food Service Research Review 13, no. 1 (Spring 1989): Table
11, p. 37; Robert H. Haveman, ed., *A Decade of Federal Antipoverty
Programs* (New York: Academic Press, 1977); and USDA, Production
and Marketing Administration, Food Distribution Branch, "Supplement to School Lunch and Food Distribution Programs: Selected Statistics, Fiscal Years 1939–51."
 *Does not include value of commodity donations.

decline from 15 to 35 percent, depending on the state. While the total
number of children participating in the school lunch program increased
from about 22 million in 1970 to 27 million in 1980, most of the new
eaters were poor children who received free or reduced price meals (see
Table 8.1).[20]

Increasing the number of free lunches without substantially increasing
the overall resources meant that states had to bolster their contributions
or local administrators had to raise the price of lunch. School administrators across the country balked at "coping with this financial burden which
grows larger every year."[21] California state officials, for example, responded to a lawsuit demanding free lunches for all welfare children by
asserting that such a measure would, in effect, "force the paying children
to subsidize the needy."[22] Because Congress was unwilling to order states
to cover the true costs of lunch, federal policy simply shifted the burden
of free lunches onto paying children. Despite the urging of congressmen
such as Illinois's Roman Pucinski, who told the Department of Agricul-

ture to "use a little more imagination and come up with answers," it was, as Orville Freeman had warned, the "near poor" who suffered most under the new funding schemes; children whose families could afford full-price meals simply stopped eating school lunches at all. Pucinski correctly predicted that unless substantially more money was put into the overall program, expanding the number of free lunches would actually limit who would be eating at school.

Indeed, the distance between poor and non-poor children grew as school lunchrooms became places inhabited by children labeled "low-income," "disadvantaged," or "at-risk." By the mid-1970s, public schools in most major cities had majority black and majority poor populations. As an indication of the level of poverty among children in the nation's schools, the Department of Agriculture estimated that in 1976 about one-quarter of all children in public schools received their meals free or at reduced price. Put another way, in 1976 poor children made up almost 40 percent of all school lunch participants, and within ten years that figure reached 50 percent.[23] The School Breakfast Program was entirely oriented toward the poor, particularly urban, black children.[24] School cafeterias became racially and economically segregated zones. As one historian observed about the welfare system more generally and Aid to Dependent Children specifically, "this transformation poses something of a historical paradox." Aid to Dependent Children, according to this analysis, while intended to serve poor children, was, like the National School Lunch Program, administratively structured so as to discriminate, particularly against African Americans. Both ADC and the School Lunch Program by the 1970s, however, had become programs that did not just include African American children, but served them "disproportionately." In the case of ADC, the perception of "disproportion" created a "growing backlash against the racial profile of public assistance."[25] In the case of school lunches, however, overall public support remained relatively strong albeit not in the form of either state or local financial commitments.

The economic climate of the 1970s only exacerbated school lunchroom fiscal difficulties. The period's inflation meant that overall food prices went up and operating costs increased. By the end of 1972, food prices were at all-time high levels. Beef, pork, and chicken, as well as fruits and vegetables, all saw record increases. According to one USDA report, the price of food went up by 12.5 percent in one year.[26] At the same time, surplus commodities, long a staple resource for school lunches, disappeared and commodity donations to school lunch programs dried up. Predictably, as the price of lunch increased, fewer families could afford the cost of full-price meals. By the end of the 1970s the nationwide average full price lunch had gone up between 15 and 30 cents. In Connecticut, elementary school children saw the price of lunch jump from 60 to 75 cents. High school students had to pay 90 cents. New York children paying full price faced an 80 cent lunch. While some of the National School Lunch Program's critics charged that students dropped out because they "did not like the taste of lunch," school food-service administrators believed it was because the price had gone up. The other factor, ASFSA representatives noted, was that federal income eligibility levels for free lunches went up during the early 1970s as well. The result was that fewer children overall could afford to eat at school.[27]

Children's nutrition was caught in an ongoing struggle for resources that pitted state and local communities against federal mandates. School lunch advocates insisted, as they had since the 1940s, that children's nutrition was a national responsibility. Harvard Medical School's Julius Richmond, for example, argued that "nutrition is a national not a state issue." All children needed a well-balanced lunch, he said, regardless of where they lived. Leaving school lunches up to local communities, Richmond believed, would mean that "children in states with less resources . . . will not be served as well."[28] Richmond had substantial historical grounds for this fear. As late as 1980 few states compensated for overall reductions in federal school meal budgets. Indeed, according to *New York Times* reporter, Robert Pear, "Such states as Oklahoma and Louisiana, which have the resources to increase spending, generally lack the desire to do so."[29] Department of Agriculture officials, who viewed federal resources as just one part of the school lunch budget, had little sympathy for school lunch officials who complained about dwindling resources. If school cafeterias faced a fiscal crisis, the Department of Agriculture maintained, blame rested with local communities that refused to contribute to children's welfare. G. William Hoagland, head of the Food and Nutrition Service, charged that local authorities had raised the price of lunch "much more than the 11 cents they had lost in Federal subsidy."[30] Hoagland admitted, however, that his department had not anticipated the extent to which paying students would leave the program once the price of lunch increased. This was despite the conventional wisdom in the field that held that for each nickel the price went up, participation rates would drop by one percent.

Beginning with the Nixon-era free lunch expansion and continuing through the Reagan and Clinton administrations, Congress began to pull back on funding for welfare programs. With the budding tax revolt and the rise of a militant conservative movement, local support for public spending, particularly on education and welfare, began to erode. States and school districts thus began to search for new sources of revenue to keep school lunchrooms going. The Department of Agriculture, which had always been reluctant to enforce nutrition or eligibility standards in the school lunch program, nonetheless housed an ever expanding school lunch bureaucracy charged with administering meals for the nation's poor children. Finding unenthusiastic partners in state legislators, the National School Lunch Program gradually began to rely ever more heavily on the commercial food-service industry. School lunch officials found eager allies in a rapidly growing food-service industry, and among the ever more ubiquitous fast-food companies, including McDonald's, Pizza Hut, and Taco Bell.

Privatization gained unexpected allies in the push to feed poor children. Since the program's founding, nutritionists and school food-service professionals had carefully guarded the cafeteria boundaries, resisting efforts to allow commercial operators into school kitchens. The new free lunch mandate, however, challenged those boundaries. The 1969 White House Conference, for one, recommended easing the ban on private companies operating in school lunchrooms. Asserting every child's right to "equal access to nutrition," the conference report acknowledged that existing school lunchrooms were unable to provide meals "at fair cost or reduced cost" to children who most needed the nutrition. The conference majority agreed that the most practical solution in light of the continued reluctance or inability of states to increase their contributions to school lunch budgets was to begin dealing with commercial food-service operations. As long as private companies agreed to meet "all quantitative and qualitative nutritional requirements," the White House Conference Report recommended that schools be permitted either to contract with private companies to bring meals into their schools or to "have the lunches provided elsewhere by the private sector."[31] Department of Agriculture officials welcomed the suggestion. The future for children's lunches, Agriculture Department representative Aaron M. Altschul predicted, lay in "convenience foods" and other industry innovations. "School feeding," he said "does not differ in principle from any other kind of institutional feeding."[32] Because institutions like the military, the airlines, and hospitals increasingly relied on food-service management companies for their meal service, Altschul believed schools could—and should—easily follow suit.[33] The only voice dissenting from this recommendation was American School Foodservice Association executive director, John Perryman.[34]

The first step in the public-private school lunch partnership required nutrition professionals like Perryman to relax their traditional mistrust of commercial food operations. With over 50,000 members nationwide, the ASFSA membership maintained an ambivalent attitude toward the privatization of school lunches. Although many women who found careers in home economics happily landed positions in the private food industry, school lunch advocates, by and large, viewed commercial enterprises with suspicion. Fearing that restaurant or food-service corporations would be concerned more with profit than with children's health, National School Lunch Program planners, since the 1920s, tried to keep private interests out of school lunchrooms. School food-service professionals, in particular, the ASFSA, may have welcomed corporate sponsors at conventions and brand-name food ads in their newsletters, but they resisted direct involvement of restaurants or food-service corporations in school lunchrooms. "My experience," noted Santa Barbara superintendent Norman Scharer, when asked about how to best equip school kitchens, "has been that it is much better to get a food service consultant who has no equipment to sell."[35] At the same time, the ASFSA and school lunchrooms depended on the food industry in significant ways. Food advertisements funded the association's publications, and revenues from food industry displays underwrote their annual national conventions. The ASFSA rank and file viewed the incursion of private companies with mixed feelings. Alfreda Jacobsen spoke for many in her profession when she worried that private food companies would be "interested *only* in making a profit." Corporations, she said, "will sell anything to the child as long as he has the money to pay for it."[36] Jacobson, the school lunch director in Perry, Iowa, protested to President Johnson both as a professional food-service worker and as a mother against legislation "that would allow any food company the benefits of money and commodities from the National School Lunch Program." As a mother, she said, "the fact that my own children would be exposed to the possibility of choosing hamburgers, French fries, and a bottle of pop for every noon school lunch is reason enough to protest." Jacobson told the president, "if we are ever going to have a healthy race of people we are going to have to educate our children to accept only foods that are best for growth and health and not give them a chance to choose only foods that they like."[37]

Professional protestations against private involvement in school lunches increasingly rang hollow, however, in the face of state and local resistance to fund free lunches. Children's Foundation head Rodney Leonard observed wryly that any time the suggestion was made that private food management companies might be a way to bring school lunches to areas not yet served, particularly "within the urban ghetto where facilities do not exist," school food-service professionals "immediately claim the non-profit ideal of the school lunch program is about to be raped."[38] While Leonard acknowledged that the commercial food industry was often known more for "sharp operators and poor service" than for professional management and nutrition, it was, in his view, an "undeniable fact" that private companies, not the Department of Agriculture or local school districts, had made significant technological advances in efficient and inexpensive food-service practices. It would be "an absurd waste of money," Leonard insisted, for states and school districts to invest in buildings and equipment "when food service technology now available are already eliminating the need for these facilities." Food-service companies clearly had the capacity to prepare, freeze, and deliver meals more efficiently than did the schools. Rather than invest in new cafeterias, Leonard suggested, schools should simply buy freezers and microwave ovens.[39] The fact was, Leonard argued, private companies might be able to run lunch programs in areas where the professionals, the government, and the Department of Agriculture had failed.

Privatization of school lunchrooms was a particularly attractive solution to the problem of providing large numbers of free meals to poor children. During the 1970s, an unexpected alliance formed between community activists and corporate America in an effort to bring economic resources into poor communities. Some anti-poverty leaders saw the potential for the development of local school food-service operations that would foster businesses and expand the resources in poor communities. Committee on School Lunch Participation spokeswoman Jean Fairfax, for example, believed that commercial kitchens could become community-controlled corporations "in the ghetto" and could not only provide food for needy children but also create jobs and skills training for neighborhood residents.[40] Anti-hunger activist and chair of the Citizen's Board of Inquiry John Kramer saw privatization as a way to lessen the hold of the Department of Agriculture on school lunches and at the same time enhance opportunities in poor districts. "Nobody is asking that there be a wholesale invitation" to private companies, Kramer said; "we are instead asking that the door be opened." Kramer took the Department of Agriculture to task for its sluggish response to demands for free lunches and for being too slow to see the value in allowing private companies into school lunchrooms. Because neither the federal government nor the states were willing to put sufficient resources into school lunchrooms, Kramer thought, perhaps private food service might be able to turn cafeterias into more viable operations. The issue was not about supplying books or equipment to public schools, he insisted; "we are talking about feeding children."[41] Congressional representatives from districts with large populations of poor children likewise saw private investment as a way to fund free lunches. Illinois congressman Roman Pucinski, for example, became excited at the prospect of bringing private food-service companies into Chicago's poorest school districts. This, Pucinski believed, would offer the perfect solution for schools in his district that had no cafeteria facilities on site. In the Senate, liberal Democrat George McGovern picked up the call for privatization. "If we are going to solve the nutrition problem in the United States," he said, "we have got to have the cooperation of private industry."[42] In effect, once free lunches were mandated for all poor children, public officials and hunger activists alike began to cede the program to the private sector. Because neither Congress nor the public in general seemed willing to fund children's "right to lunch," perhaps the corporate market might be better suited to ensuring equal opportunity for all.

In 1969, as one of his last acts as Secretary of Agriculture, Orville Freeman announced a new set of regulations that would, for the first time, allow school districts to contract with private companies to run, operate, and manage their lunchrooms. Freeman estimated that at least nine million children attended schools in areas that had no lunch facilities. Most of these, he noted, were in "urban ghetto" or rural areas, both home to large numbers of poor black children. Under existing funding restrictions, schools had to raise local money to build new kitchen facilities. If the federal government undertook to finance new cafeterias, Freeman argued, not only would the costs be "astronomical" but such action would destroy the traditional separation between federal and state educational responsibilities. "We are going to have to develop some new delivery systems," he said, particularly in order to expand the availability of free lunches.[43] Working with state nutrition administrators and food management companies, Freeman proposed elaborate contracts that allowed private companies to prepare, transport, and serve meals but also stipulated that all management and administrative responsibilities for the lunch program would remain in the hands of a professional school lunch supervisor. The Agriculture Secretary invited six urban schools that lacked lunch facilities to enter into private contracts on an "experimental" basis. Admitting that he faced a "a strong emotional feeling" about maintaining the public character of the school lunch program, Freeman promised that he would not allow the program to be "exploited for commercial purposes." Although private food-service companies had to operate under the "profit motive," Freeman believed that they could nonetheless keep children's welfare as their main goal. "I see nothing to be lost and lots to be gained by testing under carefully controlled circumstances," he said.[44] Calling the new contracts a "service company approach," Freeman assured his critics that privatization was "simply another tool to help assure every child an opportunity for a nutritious meal in school."[45] Indeed, Freeman went so far as to suggest that the "market strategy" might actually provide better service than his department had been able to provide.

As the professionals feared, however, the "service company approach" did not remain limited to food preparation and delivery. Three years after Freeman's initial foray into private food-service contracts, Congress opened the door to soft drink vending machines in schools. The 1946 National School Lunch Act definitively restricted the sale of "competitive foods" in the schools. To protect lunchroom revenues and also to ensure that children actually ate their lunch (rather than fill up on cakes and candy), the School Lunch Act reflected the influence of professionals who wanted to maintain control over the nutrition content of school food. For years, however, private industry had longingly eyed the school market. Until the free lunch campaign and the budget crisis of the early 1970s, however, there had been little incentive for schools to engage with commercial businesses. The pressure to serve more free lunches and the persistent refusal of states to take up the school lunch budget slack pushed school officials into a desperate search for new revenue sources. In 1972, the National Soft Drink Association finally succeeded in securing an amendment to the school lunch reauthorization bill that would eliminate the restriction on "competitive food." Although the amendment received little attention at the time, the consequences were far-reaching.

School lunch administrators, nutritionists, and newspaper columnists loudly protested vending machines in the schools, but when they realized the true nature of the legislation it was all but too late. *New York Times* columnist Jack Anderson accused the vending machine companies of pulling "a sleeper." The amendment, he said, would only increase private profits "at the expense of children's eating habits." For the first time, Anderson warned, "candy bars, potato chips and soda pop" would be allowed to directly compete with nutritious meals.[46] In an effort to repeal the amendment the following year, Gretchen Plagge, director of food services for the Santa Fe schools, accused the vending industry of duping Congress with its "advertising efforts" and said that no one in the professional community, including medical authorities, nutritionists, and PTA members, "sought such a law." Plagge warned that vending machines would provide students with "countless opportunities for the purchase of foods with little or limited nutritional value." A vending machine snack, she said, was a poor substitute for a "balanced, well-prepared meal." In Plagg's view, Congress had a "moral as well as legal responsibility" to protect children's health, and it would be unethical for schools to exploit children's "desire for sweet, high calorie foods."[47] Children, Plagg believed, simply should not be allowed to choose unhealthy foods. The problem, nutritionists feared, was that the "junk food" would compete not only with more healthful food choices but also for children's lunch money. Columbia University nutritionist Jean Gussow warned that American taxpayers supported the school lunch program in order to provide nutritious food for children—not to supply snacks. The vending industry, however, insisted that any restriction on its access to children was an attempt to "federally control" the market.[48]

The snack and soft drink industry, in a new move, however, claimed that their products, in fact, contributed to children's health. Asserting that "there is more to nutrition than vitamins," industry spokesmen told a congressional panel that "quick energy, assimilation of liquid," and "enjoyment" contributed as much to children's well-being as vitamins and minerals.[49] Nutrition arguments held little sway in the face of shrinking budgets, and within a short time school vending machine contracts were worth millions of dollars.[50] Realizing that it would be almost impossible to legislate snack food out of children's lives, school lunch professionals suggested a compromise. If Congress allowed vending machines in schools, their use should be limited to non-lunch hours so as not to compete with the "non-profit" school lunch program.

Claiming that children had a "right to candy," food industry spokesmen defended the sale of snacks as a legitimate source of extra revenue for cash-strapped school systems.[51] Despite professional and public protest, soft drink "pouring rights contracts" were seductively appealing, particularly for poor schools. In exchange for pouring rights, schools received hundreds of dollars' worth of athletic equipment and other supplies. In addition to revenue from the machines themselves, schools received sports equipment (shirts with the company logo), educational materials (math posters with the company logos), and other resources. Despite the warnings and protests of professionals, snack foods gained a solid footing in the schools. Indeed, within a few years at least one-quarter of all middle schools and 42 percent of all high schools regularly sold soda and candy, and by the end of the century 43 percent of elementary, 74 percent of middle schools, and 98 percent of senior high schools had contracts with vending machine companies and soft-drink distributors.[52] While many of the vending machines were closed during lunch hours, according to one report, one in five high school students could access snack food at any time during the school day.[53]

COMBO MEALS AND NUTRITION STANDARDS

Once private industry had a foot in the door of the school building, it was only a matter of time before the cafeteria lines opened as well. Food-service giant Sodexho vice president Tom Callahan predicted that as long as federal reimbursements did not keep up with "food and labor cost" and state contributions continued to be "embarrassingly low," schools would either have to drop out of the National School Lunch Program or find "creative ways" to meet their costs. The easiest route, he predicted, would be private contacts.[54]

The free-lunch mandate ultimately altered the menu as much as it altered the demographics of the school lunchroom. While never known for being tasty, school lunches had, in general, been prepared on site and, until the late 1960s expansion, were almost always hot, three-course meals that included the major food groups. The Department of

Agriculture's nutrition standards mandating that the Type A, fully subsi-dized lunch provide at least one-third of a child's nutritional require-ments over the course of the week defined the meals that had appeared on children's lunch trays since the 1950s. Although the Department of Agriculture admitted that only about 37 percent of the children partici-pating in the National School Lunch Program actually ate a Type A meal, this menu served as the model for school lunches across the country.[55] Chicken breast with gravy biscuits and honey butter, celery and carrot sticks, a piece of orange, and an oatmeal and raisin cookie with milk could be found, however, only in schools that had kitchens or school districts that could afford to invest in new cafeterias. Faced with provid-ing large numbers of free or reduced price lunches, many schools turned to "bag lunches" or pre-packaged meals delivered by private contrac-tors. Predictably, given more choice in menu options, children chose hamburgers, French fries, or pizza over the three-course balanced meal of meat, vegetable, and potatoes.[56]

At the very moment when large numbers of poor children finally gained the right to free school meals, the Department of Agriculture began to modify its recommended nutrition standards. In 1970 the department eliminated the traditional Type A, B, and C meal designations and an-nounced that henceforth it would reimburse only Type A meals. While requiring all schools to serve the nutritional equivalent of a Type A meal appeared on the surface to be an improvement in the regulations, in fact the change allowed for the introduction of fast foods, snacks, and "a la carte" offerings that easily added up to a less than nutritious meal.[57] In 1979 the rules were loosened even more when the Department of Agricul-ture issued new guidelines allowing for the sale of "foods of minimum nutritional value" in school lunchrooms. Designed specifically to sell candy and snacks in the lunch line, the rules stipulated that if the "food" supplied more than 5 percent of the RDA of just one basic nutrient in a 100 calorie serving, the item could be served for lunch. If the nutrition value fell below that already low bar, then sale of the product was re-stricted to after lunch hours. What was more, the new rules put no restric-tions on the amount of salt, sugar, or fat those products could contain. Assistant Secretary of Agriculture for Food and Consumer Affairs Carol Tucker Foreman admitted that "any manufacturer of candy bars, snack foods, cakes or soft drinks could simply fortify his product with the required 5 percent of any one of the eight nutrients and so have the product declared minimally nutritious." Foreman's assistant, Jody Levin-Epstein, went further, acknowledging that "if a candy bar has only one nut in it, we feel it is above our minimal nutrient standards." Lunch super-visors, nutritionists, and PTAs across the country loudly protested. "I think it's almost a total cave-in to the snack-food industry," wrote

Michael Jacobson, director of the Center for Science in the Public Interest. Jean Gussow lambasted the rules, declaring that "they are really banning nothing—not even jelly beans—when you consider how cheap and easy it is to fortify any food with a little vitamin C and so qualify."[58]

As soon as federal nutrition standards changed and restrictions on private contracts were eased, school districts invited private food-service corporations into their lunchrooms. In the face of continuing fiscal shortfalls, school lunch administrators felt they had little choice but to turn to private companies that promised efficient service and lower costs. The Department of Agriculture justified opening school cafeterias to private food companies as a way to provide new revenues to ailing lunch programs. At the same time, the food industry was entirely eager to enter the school lunch market.[59] Commercial interests promised to supply meals at lower costs and more efficiently than the local, state, and federal government "partnership" that had characterized the program since its inception. Large cities, in particular, eagerly contracted with companies that offered city-wide service. Because urban schools often lacked cafeterias, centralized kitchen facilities were a cheaper option than adding lunchrooms to existing schools. Contractors hired truckers, supplies, food, and cooks and delivered pre-packaged meals to each school. The Buffalo, New York, school board for example, signed a contract with Service Systems Corporation, a subsidiary of Del Monte, to provide lunches in their low-income schools. Service Systems delivered 9,000 "packaged school lunches" every day and hot lunches once or twice a week. According to Buffalo School Board officials, this arrangement allowed them to serve lunches for the first time to children in inner city schools. In Tulsa, Oklahoma, the district contracted with a central warehouse that offered to supply over a hundred schools that then "bid" for food that was stored in large coolers and freezers. The Tulsa warehouse purchased food in large quantities but took the brand names off the products before sending it to the schools.[60] Economies of scale in food delivery, storage, and preparation all appealed to school lunch operators, who saw no new influx of public resources coming their way.

By the 1970s food service, and lunch in particular, had become big business. Lunch, noted one report, "has become the daily institutional meal, and more than half of the nation's population now eats the noon meal" at work, at school, in a hospital, prison, or in the Army.[61] Within a decade the lunch business mounted to $23 million each year. School cafeterias formed a major part of the food-service industry, with annual receipts worth an estimated $4.5 billion by the mid-1970s. As federal restrictions on private contracts eased, one report noted, "more and more companies are zeroing in on this market."[62] By 1975, the National School

Lunch Program operated the third largest food service program in the nation, larger than the Army and trailing only McDonald's and KFC.[63]

Major national food corporations increased their school-focused operations significantly as Department of Agriculture restrictions were lifted. In 1969, for example, the Automatic Retailers of America reported that it added the school market to its already lucrative college, hospital, business, and airline operations. A company spokesman boasted that ARA served "more people daily than any other organization in the world."[64] The company's lunch operations included the Montreal Olympics, while its vending machine business supplied cigarettes, music, games, and snacks to Holiday Inns, Gino's and Denny's restaurants, and flight kitchens for fifty airlines. Other corporations followed suit. Sysco Corporation, for example, entered the school food-service business in the early 1970s and saw its net worth skyrocket from $115 million to over $23 billion in two decades.[65] By the early 1970s, food industry giants such as Morton's, Glidden-Durkee, and Pronto, a division of Hershey Foods, held school lunch contracts.[66] These were highly diversified industries in which schools were only a part of the overall operation. In addition to centralized school cafeterias, the Ogden Corporation, for example, also dealt in transportation, metals, service to theaters and recreational centers, and race tracks. Armour, the venerable meatpacking company with origins in the nineteenth century, entered the school market during the 1970s. The company, then a subsidiary of the Greyhound Corporation, supplied meats, poultry, and dairy products to other food-service businesses as well as to school lunchrooms. Among Armour's specialties were pre-packaged airline meals. Entrees such as beef stroganoff, stuffed peppers, and "Salisbury steak with Polynesian sauce" catapulted the company into the leading ranks of the new prepared food industry.[67]

Fast food and "convenience" foods transformed the form and the content of American meals, whether at home or at school. The American food industry had changed dramatically since the early days of school lunches. While American agriculture continued to enjoy large tax subsidies, by the 1970s, the traditional family farm all but disappeared. The food industry was no longer characterized by small farmers whose concern was growing and marketing their produce. The industrialization of agriculture in the years after World War II resulted in what one critic described as "a gigantic, highly integrated service system in which the object is not to nourish or even to feed, but to force an ever-increasing consumption of fabricated products."[68] Industrial farming, large-scale food processing plants, and national networks of food-service providers characterized the industry. Frozen food, dehydrated mixes, and pre-heated or re-heatable entrees found an increasingly important place at the American table. According to one estimate, the spectacular rise in potato consumption in the United States was due "almost entirely to the purchase of French fries at franchised restaurants."[69] Particularly after the introduction of the home-kitchen microwave oven, convenience foods claimed an ever increasing share of the food market.[70] These new products were key to the ability of schools, particularly those without existing kitchen facilities, to serve large numbers of free lunches. The use of frozen and dehydrated foods, observed Richard Flambert, a San Francisco food-service consultant and designer, "is certainly the most important thing that has happened recently." Mashed potatoes, for example, Flambert said, can now be made without the need for peeling or cooking the raw potatoes. Packaged mashed potato mixes could easily be "poured into a kettle without being touched by human hands." Within five years, he predicted, dehydrated foods would be so common that schools would not even need freezers or refrigerators for food storage. "All that will be required," he was certain, would be "cold or hot water to prepare our foods."[71] Indeed, by 1978, according to one report, over half of all institutions serving meals relied on pre-prepared convenience foods.[72]

School lunch administrators played an important role in introducing new foods to American schoolchildren. Regional and ethnic dishes had become nationalized in a school food market that spanned the continent. "Tacos have moved east and fried clams moved west," noted one reporter.[73] National norms for the size and shape of hamburgers, fish sandwiches, and French fries defined American food culture. While the children may have already discovered hamburgers as fast food, during the 1970s, the ethnic food market had not yet captured the national market.[74] In 1976, for example, Henrietta Green, district school food service director in Colorado, decided to introduce her children to Jewish food to pay tribute to the Jewish New Year. The suburban Denver district featured bagels, baked chicken, red cabbage, and honey cake for its holiday meal. Unable to prepare the bagels in the traditional manner (boiling them in salt water), Green decided to use biscuit dough with eggs and sugar and then bake the "bagels" in the oven. Unfortunately, the special occasion selected for the Jewish meal was Yom Kippur, which Green belatedly discovered was a fast day. Another problem arose when Green discovered that Jewish dietary laws prohibited serving milk and meat at the same meal. Because the Type A lunch required milk, she had to adjust her offerings. Undeterred, Green said, "I'm sure we'll make a lot more mistakes . . . but at least we're getting an education." Indeed, Green went on to plan other ethnic offerings, including pretzels (Germany), fish and chips (Scotland), chicken curry (India), and quiche Lorraine (France). "I'm hoping someone will come up with a lunch representative of the American Indian," she said.[75]

For school lunch administrators, the new food technology presented a perfect solution to the problem of feeding large numbers of poor children without having to invest in new equipment and facilities. Schoolchildren became a captive market for "pre-plated" pre-packaged, and pre-heated meals. Using the model of airline meals and TV dinners, school districts around the country contracted with central kitchens to prepare and deliver pre-cooked meals. Like airplane passengers, school children were offered a plastic "cold-pac" and an aluminum "hot-pak." Unlike airline travelers, however, children still received a carton of milk with their meal.[76] Washington, D.C.'s Bruce Elementary school, for example, employed the new food technology to switch from cold sandwiches, "which everyone agreed were tasteless," to new Styrofoam "traypacks." The precooked meal trays included a napkin and disposable plastic utensils. While children enjoyed the novelty of the new lunches, the meals they ate were no doubt bland and not much tastier than the cold sandwiches, because the central kitchen maintained a policy of using very few spices in its food preparation.[77]

The food delivery model that most attracted school lunch operators was the growing fast-food industry. Indeed, fast foods claimed an increasingly large share of the nation's food budget. According to one estimate, "the palatable, fat-rich hamburger, pizza, fried chicken, and ethnic take-out cuisines rose from 3 to 16 percent of US food outlays between 1963 and 1993."[78] By the early 1970s, school food service increasingly adopted the fast-food model in school cafeterias. While acknowledging the Department of Agriculture nutritional guidelines for children's meals, most school lunch administrators were under pressure to run their operations on business and management principles. This meant that sales and participation rates took precedence over nutrition. In practice, both the Department of Agriculture and the ASFSA encouraged the business model. School lunch operators claimed that fast food drew paying children into the lunchroom and thus provided key program revenue. Tacos, pizza, and French fries, they believed, would be the only offerings that could bring in enough business to shore up what could only be described as failing enterprises.

The most highly publicized and replicated example of the fast-food school lunch model came from the Las Vegas school system. There, in 1972, local businessman Len Frederick, a retired supermarket executive, offered to save the city's school lunch program by instituting fast-food restaurant practices. Boasting that he could "sell better, fresher food . . . for less money," Frederick set out to revive the city's school cafeterias that had been languishing from lack of funds and low participation rates. Paying children, it seemed, flatly rejected the traditional Type A hot meal. Frederick was "appalled" at the school lunch program's high deficits, poor food, and disgruntled employees. Predicting that he could compete successfully with local fast-food chains for children's dollars, Frederick replaced the traditional school lunch menu with "super shakes" and "combo meals." When he began his reformation, only about 10 percent of the city's students participated in the school lunch program, and the city's school cafeterias were running a $200,000 deficit. Within a year Frederick boasted a participation rate of 90 percent and claimed a profit of over a million dollars.[79]

To meet Department of Agriculture nutrition standards, Len Frederick's combo meals had to be fortified and enriched. The school lunch guidelines required that reimbursable meals provide children with at least one-third of their RDAs over the course of a week. Frederick therefore made sure that his tacos, pizzas, hot dogs, and French fries were all enriched to meet USDA standards. The Las Vegas "combo meals" provided the required two ounces of protein, three-quarters of a cup of vegetables, a slice of bread, and a half-pint of milk, for the Type A lunch reimbursement. Frederick developed a recipe for "shakes," for example, that contained the required eight ounces of milk. The shakes also, however, were high in fat and chemical additives. Frederick counted the pickles and lettuce in his hamburger sandwiches as the vegetable requirement, and he used buns that contained wheat germ. The combo meal French fries were fortified with vitamin A and iron. Despite Frederick's claims to business success, however, his nutritional achievements may have been overrated. After visiting the Las Vegas experiment, for example, New York Times food critic Mimi Sheraton reported that fewer than half of Las Vegas students actually chose complete combo meals. She noticed students choosing "two cinnamon buns and a Coke, four sugar cookies and a Sprite," or "two bags of French-fries and a milk shake" for lunch. Even if fortified, these items hardly constituted a balanced meal. Nonetheless, Sheraton noted, the Las Vegas schools counted all of those students as school lunch participants—and thus claimed reimbursements for all of their lunches.[80]

While Frederick's success may have been inflated, his menu inspired school systems across the country. New York, for example, quickly tested the fast-food model in three high schools. Dubbed "the Energy Factory," New York's experiment promised to supplement the Las Vegas–style fast-food combos with "homemade soups, salad bars, and a steam table of conventional main dishes." In an effort to appeal to children's tastes and to attract paying students into the cafeteria, New York planned to expand the program throughout its schools. Cheeseburgers and French fries began to appear regularly on the city's school menu. "I love the shakes," one student told Mimi Sheraton.[81] Despite her general dislike of fast food, however, Sheraton admitted that the new menu had increased school lunch participation in New York from under half to over 65 percent.[82] Dade County, Florida, similarly initiated a fast-food menu at Miami Beach high school. The beef and cheese tacos, cheese pizzas, meat-and-bean filled burritos, corn dogs, and fried chicken all supplemented traditional offerings like grilled cheese sandwiches, turkey rolls, and cottage cheese. Many of the choices were, according to one report, "secretly" fortified. Wheat germ was added to the buns and pizza crust, while "non-degerminated corn" was added to the tacos. Under pressure to increase the number of paying children, lunchroom supervisors incorporated popular items like French fries and pizza into their menu choices. As one pizza industry representative put it, school food-service operators "are learning from their commercial counterparts to be customer driven."[83]

School food service supervisors who had previously eschewed commercialism came to embrace brand names and advertising techniques in order to attract paying children into their lunchrooms. Frances Pietrangelo, school food-service supervisor in East Greenwich, New Jersey, pointed out that her lunchroom had to compete with television advertisements for the food dollars of children who could pay full price for meals. Pietrangelo tried to entice children into the school lunchroom with games and prizes by disguising vegetables in desserts like "beetnik cake" and "carrot cookies." This was, she feared, a losing proposition. Even poor children who received free or reduced-price lunches and had no alternatives preferred fast food.[84] Like the East Greenwich district, schools across the country found themselves competing with food industry advertisements for children's money and attention. St. Louis tried to attract children with a "Vita-lunch" that was essentially an assembly-line cold lunch prepared in a central kitchen and delivered to the elementary schools. The city's high schools served a "Gateway Special" billed as the "gateway to good nutrition, gateway to a good food bargain."[85] Indeed, school lunch administrators conceded that offering fast food was the only way to attract children—particularly paying children—into the lunchroom. ASFSA representative Tami Cline found herself touting pizza as offering "a substantial nutritional value." In addition to protein and carbohydrates, Cline insisted, pizza crust offered vitamin B, and the tomato sauce "has a lot of vitamin C in it."[86]

Private food-service corporations had no trouble tailoring their products to the school market. During the late 1960s, for example, Hostess cakes developed "Astrofood," a vitamin-fortified (and sugar-filled) cake offered for school breakfasts in cities including St. Louis, Memphis, Buffalo, Los Angeles, Seattle, and New York.[87] The problem with fortification, observed Thomas Farley, director of Milwaukee's school lunch program, was that it encouraged children to believe that fast food was healthy. Although Len Frederick's combo meals, for example, were fortified with vitamins and protein, they were still high in carbohydrates and relatively low on vegetables. What is more, some nutritionists warned that fortification masked the underlying content of fast foods and lulled students into thinking they were making healthy food choices. What was worse for nutrition educators was the fact that by mimicking commercial meals, fast-food lunches reinforced "bad eating habits." With fast food in school, nutritionists feared, children would simply never learn "what a balanced meal consists of."[88]

KETCHUP AND OTHER VEGETABLES

At the very moment when the government began to heavily subsidize nutrition for poor children, physicians and nutritionists began to sound the alarm about the general state of American diets. The ubiquitous presence of fast-food restaurants combined with the industrialization of agriculture and the growth of the food-service industry seemed to have the ironic effect of providing Americans with more food choices than ever before while at the same time resulting in poorer diets overall. Americans, rich and poor, had come under the sway of food industry advertisements and fast-food restaurants. According to one estimate, for example, the average American consumed far more soft drinks each year than milk.[89] Another study suggested that in 1955, 60 percent of Americans ate a good diet, but by 1965 that figure was down to 50 percent.[90] As early as 1973, President Nixon's nutrition adviser, Jean Mayer, warned that a national epidemic of obesity threatened the state of American health. A report that year ominously estimated that as many as 50 million Americans were overweight.[91] Another study reported that the percentage of high school students who exercised had declined "greatly" between 1979 and 2001. Yet another report suggested that "the average ten-year-old American boy" weighed fourteen pounds more than he had in 1960.[92] As in the past, the 1970s "malnutrition scare" focused particularly on the diets of poor children. This time, however, school lunches, intended to provide needy children with nutrition they would otherwise not get, appeared the culprits—or at least the allies—in promoting poor food habits.

Some experts trotted out the old explanation that blamed the decline in American nutrition on the fact that more mothers were in the work force and were hence unable to prepare nutritious meals for their families. Spartanburg, South Carolina, school food-service supervisor Lucille Barnett, for example, opined that with 18 million mothers working outside the home, "they have insufficient time to prepare adequate meals." The mother's income provides "plenty of money for snacking," Barnett complained, but "too little training in eating for their health's sake."[93] Other researchers pointed to the lack of nutrition education in the schools. Neither the food industry nor the USDA, it seemed, provided substantial nutrition education to the American public. Indeed, the National School Lunch Program, which was intended, at least in theory, to teach children nutritious food habits, had never developed much of a nutrition education program to go along with lunch. Most experts, however, echoing the traditional lament of nutrition reformers, blamed people for simply choosing "the wrong kind of food."[94]

The 1970s concern with diet differed in important respects from earlier malnutrition debates. In the past, physicians and nutritionists alike believed malnutrition resulted from a lack of essential nutrients, vitamins, and, most particularly, calories. That is, the poor had always been assumed to lack sufficient food in both quantity and quality. Poverty and malnutrition, it was thought, could be detected by deficiencies in weight and height. Now, however, the chronic diseases formerly associated with malnutrition—rickets, pellagra, and anemia—were largely replaced by heart problems, diabetes, high blood pressure, and obesity.[95] The issue was no longer calories; children were getting plenty of those. Rather, doctors, nutritionists, and food writers alike now focused on things like fat, sodium, and cholesterol. Where nutritionists—not to mention physicians, pundits, and politicians as well—assumed that abundance would temper working-class eating habits and encourage the consumption of nutritious foods, instead, the more foods people had access to, the poorer their diets seemed to become.[96]

If the late twentieth-century poor no longer suffered from insufficient quantities of food, they nonetheless, according to the experts, persisted in exercising poor choices when it came to diet. The language of obesity itself revealed this new attitude. As one nutritionist observed, "how often today do we describe a fat person as 'corpulent,' 'portly,' or 'stout'?" Instead, we use words like "obese" or "overweight," which have distinctly negative connotations.[97] Where an earlier generation of home economists criticized poor and immigrant housewives for squandering their meager incomes on steak and butter, 1970s nutrition experts accused them of eating "junk food." As one historian observed, "not only did this make it difficult to think of the poor as hungry, it also put any blame for their inadequate nutrition back on their shoulders: on their ignorance, or, more commonly, their inability to resist temptation and postpone gratification."[98]

Nutritionists and children's welfare advocates blamed the Department of Agriculture as much as fast-food restaurants for children's obesity. As the number of children, particularly poor children, eating school lunches increased, the critics focused particular attention on the quality of food served. In theory, of course, school lunches provided a significant portion of each child's nutritional needs. But the fact was, nutritional standards had changed very little since Lydia Roberts first estimated RDAs during World War II. In 1946, when the National School Lunch Program began, nutritionists worried that children's diets did not provide sufficient calories to maintain health and vigor. The goal of the Department of Agriculture's "Type A" meal had been to ensure that children received at least one-third of the recommended nutritional requirement over the course of a week's school lunches. Government nutrition guidelines mandated that the Type A meal include whole milk and that each lunch regularly include butter, creamed soups, creamed sauces, and puddings. In 1968, however, these foods loomed as the major culprits in children's obesity.

School menus reflected the Department of Agriculture's reliance on the food industry in setting nutrition standards for the nation's children. Despite growing concerns about obesity, school diets were still heavy on fat, salt, and carbohydrates.[99] As late as 1998, according to one report, the school lunch program *was required to offer* as one of its fluid milk options 'whole milk' containing nearly four percent butterfat."[100] It was not until the mid-1970s that the USDA required schools to offer low-fat or skim milk as an option. What is more, it was not until 1976 that the Agriculture Department removed its requirement that butter be served with each school lunch.[101] "There is a profound reluctance," noted Jean Mayer, to use other (polyunsaturated) fats in school lunches, even though studies had firmly established the dangers in butter-based diets. As far as Mayer could see, as long as the National School Lunch Program continued to be an outlet for surplus food, there would be no incentive to move toward a healthier diet. It was, he said, the department's continuing policy of sending surplus commodities to school lunchrooms that skewed children's diets so dramatically toward unhealthy foods. The school lunch program, he charged, "does not deal with what is desirable nutritionally. Rather, it deals with the fact that we have 'too much' of certain foods.[102] The Department of Agriculture proved particularly lax when it came to enforcing its own nutrition standards in school lunchrooms. While the USDA published extensive nutrition tables, recipes, and menus to help housewives as well as institutional food-service managers—and school lunch administrators—meet the recommendations, actual adherence to the nutrition standards was largely self-reported. The department only asked schools to make "a good faith effort" to meet nutrition standards when they applied for federal reimbursements.

By the end of the 1970s, the National School Lunch Program suffered from both financial and nutritional shortfalls. Despite private contracts and fast-food options, school lunchrooms continued to run significant deficits. They could not seem to attract enough paying children to keep their enterprises afloat. Nor could school administrators drum up sufficient local support to supplement federal reimbursements to cover operating expenses. Although school lunchrooms certainly might have operated more efficiently, when it came to feeding children, efficiency often failed. The vast majority of children eating lunch at school were poor, and the vast majority of lunches served were free or reduced-price. While the American public continued to support the school lunch program in theory, taxpayers refused to foot the bill. The inflation of the 1970s combined with a declining supply of surplus food meant that school lunchrooms continued to operate in crisis mode.

When Ronald Reagan took office in 1980 he promised to "downsize" government and eliminate waste in public programs. One of the first targets in the downsizing effort were child nutrition programs, particularly school lunches. At the time, the National School Lunch Program was one of four major non-cash federal programs available to low-income households. (The others were food stamps, housing subsidies, and Medicaid.)[103] The Reagan budget eliminated $400 million of the school lunch program's $4.6 billion budget. The following year's budget eliminated $35 billion from all domestic programs, including $1.4 billion in child nutrition programs. This amounted to about a quarter of the National School Lunch Program's budget. The school lunch program received the largest cut of all child nutrition programs, reducing reimbursement rates, lowering eligibility criteria for free and reduced price lunches, and excluding many private schools from government subsidies. The budget cuts disproportionately affected black children. According to one study, three million fewer black children qualified for free lunches, and 500,000 fewer received free breakfasts.[104]

When it came to school lunches, the Reagan administration hoped to "narrow the focus of federal support" by eliminating all subsidies for meals served to non-needy children.[105] Indeed, Reagan's budget director David Stockman argued that the school lunch program was "wasteful" because it subsidized children whose families could afford to pay for lunch.[106] Reagan administration officials were convinced, furthermore, that thousands of federal dollars could be saved by identifying and eliminating families who fraudulently applied for government subsidies, including school lunches. To root out those children who, in the administration's view, did not deserve a free or reduced price lunch, the Department of Agriculture revised the application procedures for free meals and made the process "look more like a traditional welfare program."[107] As one report put it, the old application was "simple, and the emphasis was on feeding children rather than on ensuring that benefits were being awarded correctly."[108] In the past, school officials simply accepted self-declarations of income and family size. Now, however, schools were required to verify the information on free lunch applications. What is more, school lunch applications now required parents to provide the names and social security numbers for each adult in the household. Although the new, more rigorous application procedures were designed to eliminate abuse in the system, in fact, relatively little fraud turned up. One study concluded that discrepancies in reported income levels were due not to fraud but to the fact that low-income families often experienced irregular earnings. The study found that families usually filled out free lunch applications in August, but schools did not verify the forms until October or November. It was this time lag, which revealed "normal changes in income and household size between the time of application and the time of verification," and not fraud, that accounted for the "misreporting" on school lunch application forms.[109]

The question of who could afford to pay for school lunches, however, remained a tricky one. According to one estimate, the Reagan cuts doubled the cost of breakfast and lunch for four million black children in families earning between $13,000 and $19,000 a year.[110] After the Reagan cuts, an estimated 2,700 schools dropped out of the National School Lunch Program, and the number of children participating declined by 3 million.[111] The Reagan food program budgets instituted during the early 1980s were, according to one report, "the sharpest and most severe [cuts] in our nation's history."[112] Searching for fraud in the school lunch program clearly seemed to penalize poor children for their parents' irregular earnings and for a cumbersome bureaucratic verification system. Ultimately, it proved difficult if not impossible to distinguish the children who "truly" deserved free meals from those who were less needy or "near poor."

President Reagan's budget plans might have finally and definitively limited school lunch subsidies to poor children. As one report put it, "in effect, the Administration wanted to make the school lunch program a low-income program and eliminate its broad-based nutritional support for all school children."[113] The problem was, however, that neither the president nor his budget staff took into account the depth of public loyalty to the National School Lunch Program. In particular, protests against the notion that children who were "near poor" might go without lunch revealed the extent to which Americans still believed that the public had a responsibility to protect children's health and welfare. After all, the line between the "poor" and everyone else was no clearer in 1980 than it had been when Molly Orshansky drew a poverty line fifteen years earlier. Neither Congress nor the public, it seemed, were willing to abandon the possibility (or the illusion) that America had the potential to feed all its children. As one budget analyst observed, "Congress could easily have accomplished [Reagan administration] funding reductions by eliminating all federal support for meals served to non-poor children. That it chose instead to make a variety of other program revisions to avoid this suggested continued Congressional resistance to the idea that federal support for the school lunch program should not be available to all children, regardless of their family income."[114] Ultimately, Congress refused to go along with the president's recommended budget cuts. Even members of Reagan's own party broke with the president to defend school lunch subsidies.[115] Bill Goodling, Republican representative from Pennsylvania, for example, argued that subsidies for poor children and those just above the poverty line were closely linked, particularly when it came to being able to afford the price of lunch. While it agreed to reduce meal subsidies substantially, Congress maintained at least minimal federal support for children's school lunches.[116]

Minimal support, however, proved to be almost worse than outright elimination of school lunch subsidies. In September 1980, under pressure from Congress as well as the medical community, the Department of Agriculture issued a new set of nutritional guidelines for the National School Lunch Program. To be reviewed every five years, these "Dietary Guidelines for Americans" were more specific than the old RDAs that had guided nutrition policy since World War II. Although the new guidelines differed in particulars from early proscriptions, the tone of the recommendations was familiar. Americans were advised to "eat a variety of foods," to exercise, and to limit their intake of fat. Schools were now required to lower the fat and salt content of children's lunches.[117] The problem was, of course, that schools participating in the National School Lunch Program were still required to accept surplus commodities. As in the past, the Department of Agriculture periodically determined which foods were in surplus and designated those items for donation to the schools. Approximately 17 percent of the food served in school cafeterias came from these donated commodities. Although the Department of Agriculture promised to ensure that the donated food met its own dietary standards, many of the items on the surplus list exceeded those recommendations. The fat content of USDA frozen ground beef, for example, dropped from 17–19 percent to between 15 and 17 percent. The fat content of mozzarella cheese used in school pizzas was cut in half but still stood at 10 percent. The salt content of USDA canned vegetables went down, and fruits were now to be packed in juice instead of syrup.[118] It was an improvement but only by degree.

The most egregious (and infamous) of the new dietary regulations was a provision that allowed ketchup to be counted as a vegetable serving on children's lunch trays. In the summer of 1981, President Reagan's Secretary of Agriculture, John R. Block, approved new nutrition guidelines aimed as much at saving money as at providing healthy meals. According to the new guidelines, the ingredients in tomato ketchup conformed to the vegetable requirements in the school lunch standards. Substituting ketchup for more expensive lunch-time vegetable servings, therefore, could potentially save the government millions of dollars. The Department of Agriculture, Block explained, was simply trying to help schools provide free meals to poor children in the wake of the impending billion dollar cut in federal funds.[119] Confronted by an unprecedented public outcry, Block insisted that the regulations had been "misunderstood and misinterpreted." It would be a mistake, he declared, "to say that ketchup per se was classified as a vegetable." Rather, "ketchup in combination with other things was classified as a vegetable." When asked for examples of the "other things," the Secretary listed "French fries or hamburgers."

Ketchup was not the only shortcut in the Department of Agriculture's modified nutrition guidelines. The new school lunch menu signaled the extent to which children's meals had come to depend on processed, packaged, and "fast-food" choices. Under the new regulations, schools could be reimbursed for serving children only six ounces of milk as opposed to the half-pint traditionally offered with school lunches. Hamburgers were reduced from two to 1.5 ounces and fruit servings went from three-quarters to one-half cup. What is more, the juice in jam could now be counted toward the fruit serving and the eggs used in making cakes would be "credited toward the allotment of meat and meat substitutes."[120] Cakes, cookies, and corn chips now all counted as bread servings. Finally, ketchup and pickle relish now counted as vegetable servings. Even ketchup magnate Henry J. Heinz III, Republican senator from Pennsylvania, ridiculed the new regulations. "Ketchup is a condiment," he said, "this is one of the most ridiculous regulations I ever heard of."[121]

A storm of public outrage met the Department of Agriculture announcement of the ketchup regulations. President Reagan and his Secretary of Agriculture quickly discovered the truth in agricultural economist Don Paarlberg's observation that "there are few government activities more popular with all parties than the School Lunch Program."[122] Arguably the most embarrassing, if not memorable moment of the Reagan administration's efforts to "downsize government," the ketchup controversy revealed both the deep loyalty Americans still felt for their school lunch program and the equally deep flaws in the system. Secretary Block declared ketchup to be a vegetable not because of a newly discovered theory of nutrition but because he hoped to save money for a program that was torn between offering free meals to poor children and making a nutritious lunch available to all students.

The ketchup controversy during the summer of 1981 was, in theory, part of an effort to keep the National School Lunch Program afloat in the midst of drastic budget reductions. To reduce the cost of lunches and ensure that poor children continued to receive free meals, the Department of Agriculture decided to reduce the amount of food in each meal. Smaller portions and reduced nutritional requirements were justified, department officials insisted, because American children were healthier than ever before. If anything, children now suffered from obesity—too much food rather than not enough. For the first time, the USDA abandoned the requirement that school lunches supply one-third of a child's nutritional needs over the course of a week. Instead, under a new set of guidelines, school meals could now supply just one-quarter of a child's overall nutrition. While insisting that the "neediest children" would still receive free lunches, the Department of Agriculture estimated that reducing the size of school meals would "result in immediate cost savings." Admitting that smaller meal size might mean "less nutrition" for some children, the program spokesman insisted that school lunches would still be balanced and nutritious. "This doesn't undermine the nutritional integrity of the program," he maintained.[123] Former Assistant Agriculture Secretary Carol Tucker Foreman, however, predicted that farmers as well as children would be affected by the cuts in school lunch standards. According to Foreman, the school lunch program still relied on federal surplus commodity donations. The rest came from local purchases. If lunch portions were downsized, Foreman feared, "both farmers and local economies" would suffer.[124] Popular sentiment saved the school lunch program from the axe of the Reagan budget cuts but could not save it from the fiscal problems tht made priatization the only viable option for many schools around the country.

Fast Food and Poor Children

In June 2003, Congress considered three Child Nutrition bills. The first, a "Healthy Schools and Beverages in School" bill, introduced by Democratic congresswoman Lois Capps, from California, encouraged schools to "improve the nutritional quality of food available in vending machines." Her bill imposed no new restrictions on vending machines in schools but, rather, aimed to offer "healthy choices" in the machines. The second bill, entitled the "Obesity Prevention Act," was introduced by Republican congressman Mike Castle, from Delaware, and aimed to encourage school-based programs to "help reduce and prevent obesity among children." Finally, the third bill, entitled the "IMPACT Act" (short for "Improved Nutrition and Physical Activity Act"), was introduced by Tennessee Republican Senate Majority Leader Bill Frist. For anyone who had been following children's nutrition and the fate of the National School Lunch Program, it was, as America's master of malapropism, Yogi Berra, would have said, "deja vu all over again."[1]

At the end of the twentieth century the National School Lunch Program ranked as the nation's second largest domestic food program after Food Stamps. In 1996 the federal government spent $5.4 billion on the National School Lunch Program and another $1.1 billion on school breakfasts.[2] While participation had declined considerably during the Reagan era cuts, millions of children continued to eat subsidized school meals. [3] Indeed, participation had dropped from about 28.8 million children in 1983 to 24.5 million ten years later but rose again at the turn of the century.[4] Over half of all lunches served in American schools were free or reduced-price. The National School Lunch Program operated in almost every public school, although that did not, by any means, mean that a majority of the nation's children participated. A 1983 study found that only three-quarters of all eligible children actually ate lunch at school. What was more revealing was the fact that 96 percent of the children qualifying for free meals took advantage of the program but only 69 percent of children who could afford to pay for lunch chose to buy school meals.[5] According to a 1980 Census Bureau report, 5.9 million households received food stamps, half of all black households used the National School Lunch Program, and 43 percent of Hispanic households participated.[6] Twenty years later the profile of school lunch children had not changed substantially. A USDA study of school lunch participants found that two-thirds were from female-headed households, and between one-third and one-half lived in households below the poverty level. The study found, further, that "compared with the population of all students, Whites and Asians were less likely to participate." Still, the study found that one-quarter of the white children participating in the program qualified for free lunches, along with 66 percent of African American children, 77 percent of Hispanic children, and 78 percent of Native American children.[7] The lunch program could not escape the fact that it was, indeed, a poverty program.

For American agriculture, the significance of the National School Lunch Program by the 1990s had shifted from surplus commodity outlets to major markets for the food and food-service industries. In 1990, surplus products equaled about 17 percent of the overall value of the food used in the lunch program.[8] That did not mean, however, that surplus food was unimportant in children's diets. By one estimate, the Department of Agriculture distributed almost one billion dollars' worth of cheese, butter, and dry milk to schools.[9] The USDA's Economic Research Service continued to value schools as outlets for agricultural products, estimating that "demand rose significantly for red meats, poultry, and milk" because of federal commodity donations to schools.[10] Regardless of the real impact, the perceived significance of school lunches remained powerful. When, for example, in an effort to address the fat content of children's meals, Department of Agriculture nutritionists suggested that schools serve less beef, the National Cattlemen's Beef Association lobbied heavily against the move.[11]

If school lunches no longer played a significant role in agricultural surplus markets, their role in the health of children, particularly poor children, was more important than ever. By 1990 the National School Lunch Program was "the largest federal child nutrition program and the second largest source of federal funding for elementary and secondary schools."[12] What is more, school lunches became a significant measure by which the federal government judged the resources and needs of American communities. Schools received federal subsidies based on the number of children in their district qualifying for free and reduced-price lunches.[13] Indeed, national estimates of poverty levels in neighborhoods, political wards, towns, and cities were often based on the number of children in the school district who qualified for free or reduced-price lunches. Free lunch had become an indicator of broad social needs and was used to allocate an array of federal and state benefits to schools as well as to other institutions. Indeed, as political attacks on racial affirmative action plans gained traction by the end of the 1990s, the number of children qualifying for free lunch began to serve as a proxy for the racial composition of the school.[14] In 2002, after a series of court rulings called into question the use of race in school attendance plans, districts began to use income—measured by the free lunch eligibility guidelines—to achieve diversity. Cambridge, Massachusetts, Raleigh, North Carolina, and San Francisco all instituted income-based attendance plans during the fall of 2002. Children in these states were "sorted into schools" based on whether they were eligible for free lunches. "Economic integration is a route to racial diversity that may avoid legal challenges," opined one reporter. Century Foundation senior fellow Richard D. Kahlenberg predicted this would be "the next big movement in school reform."[15] The point was to increase student diversity by ensuring an economic mix of students. The easiest way schools could determine the economic status of students was by counting up how many children in the district qualified for free and reduced-price lunches. Given the other federal and state welfare benefits that would accrue to schools and districts claiming a large population of "at risk" students, there was clearly an incentive for schools to count as many children as possible in their lunch program statistics.

Despite the enhanced significance of free lunches, schools depended ever more heavily on the private food-service industry. Few states had stepped in to pick up the slack as the federal contribution to school meals declined during the 1980s. At the end of the century, 260 of Chicago's 592 school cafeterias were managed by either Marriott International or Aramark. In 1997 a report estimated that 110 more of the city's cafeterias would be privatized by the end of the year. "Privatization has introduced new variety and quality of food products to our students," boasted Chicago's food-service manager, Susan Susanke. Claiming that privatized cafeterias brought in as much as a 12 percent increase in participation for lunch and 9 percent for breakfast, Susanke praised the food-service industry for its "extensive experience in sales and marketing," which could not be matched by city school resources.[16] Chicago was not the only city to rely on commercial food operations. All of Rhode Island's 330 public schools, for example, were run by private companies. The state claimed that the partnership with private industry had resulted in a 31 percent rise in participation rates and a dramatic decline in waste. In Oregon and California, school districts similarly contracted with food-service companies. The South Pasadena school district, for example, reported saving $50,000 a year after contracting with the Marriott Corporation to run its lunch program.[17]

Lunch was, indeed, big business. School food service represented a $15 billion market, or "ten percent of all food purchased away from home."[18] By the mid-1990s Marriott Corporation alone managed lunch programs in over 350 school districts (and an estimated 3,500 schools) nationwide and was expanding at a rate of 20 percent each year. Aramark, Sodexho, and Dakara followed Marriott in the school food-service market. Sodexho, for example, claimed to serve 360 million school lunches in 2002.[19] It was the Marriott company that pioneered in bringing the "food court" into the school cafeteria. With this strategy, dubbed, the "Grand Marketplace," school children visited food centers offering specialized choices such as pizza, bagels, tacos, salads, and hamburgers.[20] "Gone are the scary platters of khaki-colored chop suey or glutinous creamed chipped beef," noted *Consumer Reports*. But, the journal added, "the most reliable customers are the children eligible for free and reduced price lunches."[21] Indeed, the children with the least choice formed the largest market for brand-name products and fast-food school meals.

Poor children formed the major target for food industry advertisements and new school lunch products. But paying children were still critical to school lunch budgets. To maintain a solid cadre of paying students, school cafeterias offered what they assumed the market desired. Lunchroom operators basically capitulated to the appeal and the lure of the consumer market in order to keep students—whether paying or free—in the lunchroom. In the mid-1990s, for the first time, federal rules allowed nine fast food chains to operate in the schools. These included Pizza Hut, Little Caesar's, Domino's, Taco Bell, Subway, Chic-Fil-A, McDonald's, Blimpie's, and Arby's. PepsiCo, which owned Pizza Hut, opened business in about 5,000 of the nation's 94,000 schools.[22] Schools also began to offer "brand days" in which the fast-food chains competed with one another for children's lunch money. Brand-name products and fast foods promised to keep school lunchrooms financially solvent.[23] Indeed, by the year 2000, the Centers for Disease Control estimated that one in five schools participating in the National School Lunch Program had brand-name fast foods in their lunchrooms.[24]

The strategy appeared to work. School lunch operators reported that participation rates soared when brand-name fast foods were offered.[25] One Delaware school district claimed that lunch participation went up by 18 percent when Pizza Hut was brought in. The Henrico County School District, which included Richmond, Virginia, actually dropped out of the National School Lunch Program and began to contract exclusively with private companies, including Domino's, Subway, and Taco Bell. According to the district's food service director, Tim Mertz, "branded concepts" accounted for ever increasing portions of school food sales. Mertz's goal was to "have branded food courts in all of its high schools by the turn of the century."[26] The lure of the market was difficult to resist, particularly when public funds were insufficient to maintain lunchroom operations.

School children also provided a potential long-term market for food industry products. Food-service industry advertisers viewed school lunchrooms as the perfect place to create and solidify brand loyalty. "Marketing surveys say the younger generation is brand conscious," said one pizza industry representative in what could only be characterized as an understatement. The ads, said Tim Wellenzohn, product manager at Rich Products Corporation, "helps us get a foot in the door to give the school food service operator an option." Domino's Pizza encouraged franchisers to enter the school lunch market, offering a royalty rebate to any of their businesses participating in the school lunch program. Admitting that "the profit margin is not very good on school lunch sales," Domino's spokeswoman Maggie Proctor nonetheless encouraged the company's franchises to get into the program "for the product exposure—to get our relatively new thin crust and deep dish products out there to kids." One foodservice manager commented that by the time children entered school they were already "intimately familiar" with the different pizza brands. Families eat pizza at home, he pointed out, almost as often as they eat potatoes.[27] The children were, in effect, a captive audience for corporate advertisements, and the schools implicitly endorsed the products. As San Francisco school board member Jill Wynns observed, the food industry viewed children simply as future customers.[28]

Food service companies provided more than fast food to school lunchrooms. The National School Lunch Program budget had never adequately funded nutrition education. With the budget cuts of the 1980s, however, education became an even greater problem for school lunch operators. Private food-service companies happily stepped in with elaborate promotional materials that they offered to the schools for nutrition education. Neither the schools nor the Department of Agriculture's Food and Nutrition Service could compete with the marketing appeal of the private industry—or with the new products offered on trial in school lunchrooms. When it came to brand names, product advertising, and educational materials, school lunch professionals were complicit partners. The American School Food Service Association regularly consulted with food-service companies and advised them on how to bring their products into compliance with USDA nutrition guidelines. According to one report, the educational materials supplied by food companies ranged "from interactive classroom lesson plans and videos on exercise and nutrition to songs, games, quizzes, and cards filled with fun facts."[29] The Apricot Producers of California, for example, presented at the ASFSA 2001 Trade Show a new Advisory Panel ready to distribute "new activities and recipes" for school lunchrooms and professional development materials for school lunch administrators.[30] These products and services were particularly attractive in poor districts where supplies and equipment were difficult to obtain and where funds for professional development were in short supply.

Despite the special vitamin-enhanced products, fast food continued pose a problem for school lunch administrators. Often, the pizza, tacos, and hamburgers offered by private companies did not meet the Department of Agriculture's minimal nutrition requirements. During the 1990s, for example, the department guidelines required that children receive no more than 30 percent of their calories from fat. As late as the mid-1990s, however, one study found that overall 38 percent of the calories in school lunches came from fat, and 15 percent from saturated fat.[31] When parents, nutritionists, and even school officials worried that fast-food companies were not meeting nutritional standards, the USDA assured them that "the Government and private vendors are working together to bring more tasty, nutritious, healthy meals to our Nation's school children."[32] In truth, however, the fast-food school lunch often did not meet the test. Taco Bell, for example, tried to re-formulate its products for the school lunch market, but its chicken and bean enchiladas and "fiesta casseroles" were found to contain some 35 percent of their calories from fat. Chic-Fil-A similarly promised to deliver schools a reimbursable fried-chicken sandwich, but it turned out to contain 27 percent of calories from fat. Subway was the only company that did not need to modify its products to meet the USDA fat requirement. The USDA school lunch administrators were not hard to convince. By the 1990s any qualms about commercial products in school lunchrooms had all but vanished. Agriculture Department spokesman Phil Shanholtzer, for example, had no problem recommending pizza as "a healthy food." Nutrition guidelines, he pointed out, "are judged over a week's menu cycle rather than an individual meal," so schools could offer "a relatively high fat item one day and make up for it on other days."[33] In 2004, the Physicians Committee for Responsible Medicine warned of an impending obesity crisis among American children. School meals, the physicians feared, contributed to children's "over-consumption of calories, fat, cholesterol, salt, and sugar." Finding child obesity to be at "an all-time high," the committee ominously predicted that this generation "may be the first to have shorter lives than their parents."[34]

Department of Agriculture nutrition guidelines were not entirely without effect. To enter the school lunch market, companies did re-formulate many of their products. Thus, although children ate Domino's Pizza and Taco Bell tacos, these products were different in important respects from the pizza and tacos sold outside the school. Taco Bell, for example, offered schools an enhanced breakfast burrito that included an egg, cheese, and sausage that, it assured school lunch administrators, met the USDA nutritional requirements. The case of pizza was instructive. One of the most popular items on school lunch menus, pizza was also one of the most problematic when it came to nutrition. Under the school lunch nutrition standards, any pizza sold as part of the school lunch program had to meet the "2-ounce protein" requirement. That is, in order to qualify as a main dish offering, the pizza had to contain at least two ounces of protein. When Pizza Hut, a major national chain, sought entry into the school lunch market, a company report noted that "the greatest challenge" was trying to reduce the fat content of its pizza slices. Pizza sauce and pepperoni are high in salt, and cheese is a high fat food. After spending "enormous amounts of resources" on a complete nutrition analysis, the company was convinced its product could be presented to schools as part of a reimbursable (and presumably nutritional) meal. "We've always said pizza served with fruit, vegetables, whole grain products and low-fat milk meets the Dietary Guidelines for Americans," noted company spokesman Chris Romoser. The company finally presented its specially formulated pizza to schools, noting that "accompanied by fruit, milk, and maybe a vegetable," their product would constitute a reimbursable meal. Not wanting their product to become identified with poor children, however, Pizza Hut stipulated that in schools where there were "a lot of kids that qualify for reduced-price lunches," their pizzas be sold in the regular lunch line. When the Houston Independent School District adopted Pizza Hut products, for example, the cafeteria manager worked with the company to make sure the pizzas did not appear to be only for poor children.[35]

The extent to which school lunches became part of a national food-service industry network could be seen in the heavy competition for the school markets and the wide reach of food industry interests. Styrofoam plates and cups, plastic forks, and the myriad of containers and wrappings necessary for large-scale food service meant lucrative markets for companies, such as Sysco Systems, that supplied restaurants and schools alike. Dupont, for example, sold polyester packing film wrap to school food-service departments. Other companies supplied the component elements of school meals. Frozen sauces and chicken patties, for example, could be heated on-site. Rich Products, of Buffalo, New York, sold frozen pizza dough in pre-proportioned balls or par-baked crusts so schools could "develop their own brands."[36]

School lunch menus reflected American consumer trends not only in fast-food tastes but in the rise of the ethnic food market as well. Beginning during the 1970s, food markets embraced increasing kinds of ethnic foods and a willingness to expand the definition of "American" cuisine. Schools across the country began to offer tortillas and even sushi on their lunch menus. Casa Christina Foods, which began to sell tortillas to schools during the late 1980s, saw a major increase in demand over the next decade. When they first introduced their product in North Carolina, company president Chester Brunty noted that the tortilla was "a novel food." Within a short time, however, schools throughout the Southeast began to serve tortilla chips and burritos. Schools instituted "taco day" along with quesadillas and wraps. Happy to accommodate the school market, tortilla companies marketed their product as "low fat, flavored and organic." Companies like Casa Christina or La Tapatia Tortilleria, in Fresno, California, eagerly attended school food shows and workshops, sponsored by the USDA or by other food corporations, and were happy to assist school food-service directors in devising new menu items using their products. La Tapatia president Helen Chavez-Hansen said she felt "in tune" because most of them were women who shared a deep concern with children's nutrition and health. "We really are all working moms" she pointed out. Casa Christina's president got to the bottom line, however. "The kids in these schools are going to grow up with the tortilla," he observed. "They and their children will be good customers of our products. We're laying a foundation for our industry's future."[37]

Privatization, fast-food, and national brands dramatically altered the atmosphere in school lunchrooms. School lunch professionals were divided, however, when it came to evaluating the impact of the new trends on children's nutrition. Some believed that privatization vastly improved lunch programs and made the free lunch program more viable. During the 1990s, for example, Rhode Island adopted a corporate model in order to maintain its free lunch program. In a major budget crisis the state slashed school lunch appropriations, throwing several hundred workers onto the unemployment lines and threatening to eliminate free lunches. School lunch administrators contracted with the Marriott Corporation to take over the system. The company introduced brand-named foods, offered children choices in the lunch line, and invited students and parents to meet with the company's food-service directors to test products and plan menus. State school officials claimed that student school lunch participation "soared" and nutrition levels improved. Paying children returned to the lunchroom, and even the state's poorest districts generated a profit in their lunchrooms. According to one report, the project was so successful that the janitors who had previously found tons of wasted food now noticed that the children "cleaned their plates." Woonsocket principal John Caparco admitted that his fellow state school lunch administrators had been simply "out to lunch" when it came to making food appealing. In his district, over 77 percent of the children qualified for free and reduced price meals. Before privatization he had served 2,652 lunches a day, but after bringing in Marriott his numbers averaged 3,486. A student's comment proved most revealing. "The other stuff," this child observed, "was, you know, welfare food, and it tasted like it." The new menu, she said, is now "regular food."[38]

For critics of "big government," privatization of school lunchrooms signaled a triumph of local initiative over federal policy. In this view, individual school cafeterias or even district-wide food service was simply inefficient. Rhode Island Republicans, for example, favored "devolution" of nutrition programs and a federal block grant system that would send each district a set level of federal reimbursement. When critics argued that the block grants would not cover an unexpected—or even a predicted—increase in student enrollment, the state's legislators, Republican as well as Democratic, insisted that under the privatized scheme more children would buy their lunches, thus providing a sure subsidy for free meals. This was not a new idea. Indeed, states had long operated under the assumption that paying students would subsidize the poor. In truth, however, the contribution gleaned from student fees had never been sufficient to pay for free lunches for poor children. Rhode Island legislators believed that in privatization they found a way around the dilemma. In what one state representative called a "clever payment system," schools paid an annual fee to the food-service company to run their programs. The fee was supposed to cover capital improvements, salaries, and food. School districts kept student fees plus the per-meal federal subsidies. If revenues fell short, the contractor assumed the loss. "This way the district can't lose money and the contractor has an incentive to keep costs down while serving more meals."[39] Under this system, the Woonsocket district claimed to run a "self-sufficient" program that actually earned $24,000 in profit during its first year. The money went to buy a new dishwasher and a truck. Providence claimed a profit of over $100,000. This was fine until costs began to rise and the private companies began to raise their fees. Although the Department of Agriculture contracts prohibited food-service corporations from making a profit on school lunches, the companies were allowed to collect management fees."[40] In effect, as some critics pointed out, private food-service contracts provided public subsidies to for-profit corporations.

Some school lunch officials were less sanguine about the virtues of private contracts. USDA official Ellen Haas predicted that allowing private companies into the school lunchroom would lead to "short-term malnutrition and a lifetime of serious and costly health problems." Democratic representative Dick Gephardt, equated the process with "a dagger pointed at the hearts of our children."[41] Indeed, while the private corporations claimed to meet or exceed nutritional requirements, the fact was that they often fudged the numbers. In the Rhode Island case, Marriott measured the nutrition content of its menus over a ten-week period. Like Pizza Hut, Marriott justified high fat offerings by serving lower fat dishes on other days or on the side.[42] What they did not do, however, was keep any record of which offerings the children took. Thus a child might end up eating the high fat offering each day even though other foods were available.

The extent to which school lunches were embedded within the vast network of a private, commercial food industry was revealed when the Department of Agriculture set about to publicize new nutrition guidelines during the 1990s. The department formed "Team Nutrition" in which government personnel worked with private industry including the Walt Disney Company to shape public relations and develop motivational materials. Calling this a "groundbreaking partnership," the department looked to Disney to "develop healthy eating messages to be used on television." With the technical assistance and training from the Disney Company, the Department of Agriculture now depended on the private industry to help shape and modify children's food habits. The USDA also contracted with Scholastic to produce "age appropriate nutrition information" for children as well as for parents.[43]

The culture and the politics of food collided as schools attempted to make their lunchrooms financially viable, cover the costs of free meals, and at the same time provide children with nutritious food. Although no longer aimed at Americanizing an immigrant population, nutritionists' advice still was predicated on the assumption that children would bring good eating habits home to their mothers and families. Teachers, advertisers, and nutritionists alike still believed that education and reason would shape diets and influence people's eating habits. As Dr. Richard Carmona, U.S. Surgeon General, put it, the importance of "behavior modification" in food choices could not be stressed enough.[44] The Surgeon General was specifically addressing the problem of obesity in children, but he could as well have been talking about eating habits in general. Figuring out a way to finance free lunches for poor children was as difficult as figuring out how to change people's eating habits. Just as children continued to make "bad" food choices, school districts, state legislatures, and Congress itself continued to make political choices when it came to financing children's meals. Neither school officials nor lunchroom supervisors liked to turn children away from the lunch line. But determining which children deserved—that is, "qualified" for—a free lunch proved to be no easier in the twenty-first century than it had been earlier. Although schools expended extraordinary resources verifying free lunch eligibility applications, some legislators still feared that parents (if not the children themselves) were "cheating" and trying to illegally claim a right to free food.[45] The ASFSA, on the other hand, believed that the school lunch poverty levels were too low and that the "near poor," that is, children who technically qualified for reduced-price meals, could not in reality afford the price of lunch. Even the conservative Hoover Institute recognized the difficulties in trying to determine which children truly needed free meals. "Tighter income-verification procedures," a Hoover sponsored study concluded, would mean lower participation rates. No one wanted this outcome. In the end, most schools simply lacked the resources to track and document the often changing incomes of hundreds of families.[46]

At the turn of the twenty-first century, parents, educators, and health professionals began a new campaign to ban vending machines, candy, and soda from schools. Termed the "Junk Food Wars," by the American School Food Service Association, children's nutrition once again took center stage in the media as well as in the halls of Congress.[47] This time around, a new culprit threatened children's nutritional choices. The very measures that schools had introduced during the 1980s to solve the lunchroom financial crisis—fast food and vending machines—now loomed as major obstacles to nutrition education and good eating habits. Much of the impetus for local bans came from a report submitted to the House Appropriations Committee in January 2001 entitled, "Foods Sold in Competition with USDA School Meal Programs." This report revealed the extent to which the nation's public schools had become dependent on vending machines and private food-service companies to keep their meal programs going. The Oakland school system, for example, brought in an estimated $600,000 each year from vending machine sales and an additional amount from the sale of soda and candy bars in school cafeterias. A vending industry trade report estimated that school sales provided $750 million for school districts around the country.[48] While the report praised the lunch program for providing children with more nutrition than they might otherwise receive, it also documented the health risks associated with the so-called competitive foods, that is, candy, sodas, and snacks. Children participating in the program, the report emphasized, are "more likely than non-participants to consume vegetables, milk and milk products, and meat and other protein-rich foods." Children who participated in the School Breakfast Program had higher intakes of "food energy," including calcium, phosphorous, and vitamin C.[49] At the same time, however, the report warned that competitive foods, which are high in fat, added sugars, and calories, presented diet risks and "may affect the viability of school meal programs." The National School Lunch Program, the report stressed, was established "as a program for all children."[50]

Despite the fact that schools depended on private industry to supply everything from educational posters and athletic equipment to pre-package meals, some parents began a campaign to remove vending machines selling sugar-based snacks from school halls. In February 2003, all sales of soda and candy in Oakland schools was prohibited. The Los Angeles Unified School District Board of Education followed, with a ban on the sale of carbonated drinks during school hours beginning in January 2004. The Los Angeles ban was applauded by a new generation of nutrition reformers who had marched to the district's headquarters "wearing neon green shirts with signs mocking soda advertisements." School districts around the country followed suit. According to one report, twenty states introduced bills to limit the sale of junk food in schools. As if reinventing the wheel, Jennifer LeBarry, Oakland administrative supervisor, for food services, warned that "just yanking soda isn't enough. You've got to have nutrition education so students and their parents know why drinking a soda with every meal is the wrong choice." Indeed, in its own defense, National Soft Drink Association spokesman Sean McBride blamed the children for their own poor health, saying it was "really about the couch and not the can."[51]

Because only children with money could buy food from the vending machines, the "junk food war" revealed the persistent class divide in school lunchrooms. Although the school lunch program, in theory, was aimed at all children, the "Foods Sold in Competition" report rightly warned that "children may perceive that school meals are primarily for poor children rather than nutrition programs for all children."[52] It was a bit late in the game to begin re-claiming the school lunchroom from the "stigma" of poverty. While some school districts resisted vending machines and fast food, they could only do so if they could come up with local resources to supplement the state and federal education appropriations. The most well-publicized example of school lunch nutritional reform was the famed chef Alice Waters's natural foods project in the Berkeley, California, schools. During the summer of 2004 Waters initiated a nutrition curriculum designed to teach children the virtues of fresh vegetables and whole grains. Waters had earlier started school garden projects, which she now used to prepare school meals. "We have to go into the public-school system and educate children when they're very young," Waters said, echoing long-held goals of home economics and nutritionists.[53] The problem was, however, that her project was subsidized by a generous grant of $3.8 million from her own foundation. When school officials and others questioned whether her plan was viable in the long run, she responded, "We have to change the paradigm on how we spend money in this country."[54] While Waters's model inspired other foundations and wealthy individuals to fund school lunch projects in other parts of the country, the fact was that these efforts depended on special contributions.[55] Neither Waters nor other private donors addressed the public policy issues that produced school lunch difficulties in the first place.

School lunch politics for American children has turned out to be more complicated than parents or policy makers ever imagined. For one thing, as nutritionists and parents know all too well, it is difficult, if not impossible, to convince people—whether children or adults—to eat what is good for them, rather than what tastes good. For another, nutrition recommendations seem to change all too frequently. In 1968 one nutritionist wondered, "How do you condition the mind to want broccoli and tuna salad when it is used to greens and ham hocks?"[56] Today that same nutritionist might indeed recommend greens over tuna salad, with its fat-laden mayonnaise and mercury-tainted fish. Reformers may understand the science of nutrition, but they have yet to understand the culture of food. But beyond the issue of individual tastes and communal food cultures, school lunch politics in the twentieth century required instituting public policies that would address economic and racial inequalities. In crafting a National School Lunch Program, legislators convinced themselves that they could subsidize agricultural markets and at the same time ensure the nutritional well-being of the nation's children. It was a goal that was welcomed by teachers, doctors, welfare reformers, and parents alike. Centering a child nutrition program in the schools seemed the perfect way to teach children—and parents as well—how to choose "good" foods over "bad." While policy makers and legislators alike boasted that the National School Lunch Program was intended to protect the nutritional health of all children, no one was willing to appropriate the funds it would take to actually carry out that goal. The competing agendas that have shaped school lunchrooms over the past half-century reflect larger fissures and tensions within American public policy. Like American welfare programs more generally, school lunchrooms have suffered from conservative distrust of federal programs and reluctance to ask taxpayers to pay for public services and from a liberal reluctance to confront the structural causes of economic and racial inequalities. But the idea of feeding children in school has brought together unexpected alliances and coalitions that have not always fit with the usual political categories of liberal or conservative. When it comes to children, food, and welfare, school lunch politics challenges all players—agriculture, the food-service industry, nutritionists, children's welfare advocates, and elected officials alike—to serve up balanced meals that include substantive resources along with healthy diets.

Notes

INTRODUCTION. THE POLITICS OF LUNCH

1. See, e.g., Lisa Belkin, "The School Lunch Test," *New York Times Magazine*, August 20, 2006, and Burkhard Bilger, "The Lunch-Room Rebellion," *The New Yorker*, September 4, 2006. Belkin discusses lunchroom projects sponsored by the Agatston Research Foundation, and Bilger discusses a project funded by the Chez Panisse Foundation.

2. Alice O'Connor explicates this nicely in *Poverty Knowledge: Social Science, Social Policy, and the Poor in Twentieth-Century U.S. History* (Princeton: Princeton University Press, 2001), 9.

3. The WIC (Women, Infants, and Children) Program targets pregnant women, infants, and toddlers, and the Food Stamp Program is geared toward adults and families.

4. See Food Research Action Center, "Federal Food Programs"; data on public schools comes from school-system Web sites, including New York Public Schools; Atlanta Public Schools Comprehensive Assessment, January 2004; Texas Poverty, Hunger, and Program Participation; Chicago Public Schools, "Operations Food Services"; and USDA National School Lunch Program: Participation and Lunches Served as of August 24, 2006.

5. James Vernon has recently argued that "the seemingly mundane practicalities of identifying hungry children and feeding them at school were intricately connected to a broader history of the changing meanings of hunger and ideas about the responsibilities of government." See his, "The Ethnic of Hunger and the Assembly of Society: The Techno-Politics of the School Meal in Modern Britain," *American Historical Review*, 110, no. 3 (June 2005): 693–725, 695. In Britain, according to Vernon, school meals were, from the start, associated with the poor. In the United States, as this book argues, school lunches until the 1970s were more closely associated with agriculture than with welfare and had a broader class base both in terms of support and in terms of the children served.

6. Recent examples of food histories centered in the United States are Harvey M. Levenstein's *Revolution at the Table: The Transformation of the American Diet* (New York: Oxford University Press, 1988) and *Paradox of Plenty: A Social History of Eating in Modern America* (Berkeley: University of California Press, 2003); Carole M. Counihan, ed., *Food in the USA: A Reader* (London: Routledge, 2002); Donna A. Gabaccia, *We Are What We Eat: Ethnic Food and the Making of Americans* (Cambridge, Mass.: Harvard University Press, 1998); Hasia Diner, *Hungering for America: Italian, Irish, and Jewish Foodways in the Age of Migration* (Cambridge, Mass.: Harvard University Press, 2001). Warren Belasco and Phillip Scranton have edited a volume of essays about food cultures internationally, *Food Nation: Selling Taste in Consumer Societies* (London: Routledge, 2002).

CHAPTER 1. A DIET FOR AMERICANS

1. Rima D. Apple, "Constructing Mothers: Scientific Motherhood in the Nineteenth and Twentieth Centuries," in Rima D. Apple and Janet Golden, eds., *Mothers and Motherhood: Readings in American History* (Columbus: Ohio State University Press, 1997), and Nancy Tomes, *The Gospel of Germs: Men, Women and the Microbe in American Life* (Cambridge, Mass.: Harvard University Press, 1998). On scientific housework, see Susan Strasser, *Never Done: A History of American Housework* (New York: Pantheon, 1982); Ruth Schwartz Cohen, *More Work for Mother: The Ironies of Household Technology from the Open Hearth to the Microwave* (New York: Basic Books, 1983); Dolores Hayden, *The Grand Domestic Revolution: A History of Feminist Designs for American Homes, Neighborhoods, and Cities* (Cambridge: MIT Press, 1981); and Kathryn Kish Sklar, *Catharine Beecher: A Study in Domesticity* (New Haven: Yale University Press, 1973).

2. Many works discuss the history of nutrition. See Levenstein, *Revolution at the Table*; Richard Osborn Cummings, *The American and His Food: A History of Food Habits in the United States* (Chicago: University of Chicago Press, 1941); Laura Shapiro, *Perfection Salad: Women and Cooking at the Turn of the Century* (New York: Farrar, Straus, and Giroux, 1986); Rima Apple, *Vitamania: Vitamins in American Culture* (New Brunswick, N.J.: Rutgers University Press, 1996); Maurice Aymard, "Toward the History of Nutrition: Some Methodological Remarks," in Robert Forster and Orest Ranum, eds., *Food and Drink in Hisotry: Selections from the Annales Economies, Societes, Civilisations* (Baltimore: Johns Hopkins University Press, 1979); and E. V. McCollum, Elsa Orent-Keiles, and Harry G. Day, *The Newer Knowledge of Nutrition* (New York: Macmillan, 1947).

3. A considerable literature exists on women, reform, and welfare in the Progressive Era. See, e.g., Gwendolyn Mink, *The Wages of Motherhood: Inequality in the Welfare State, 1917–1942* (Ithaca, N.Y.: Cornell University Press, 1995); Linda Gordon, *Pitied but Not Entitled: Single Mothers and the History of Welfare: 1890–1935* (New York: Free Press, 1994); and Robyn Muncy, *Creating a Female Dominion in American Reform, 1890–1935* (New York: Oxford University Press, 1991). Also Sonya Michel, "The Limits of Maternalism: Policies Toward American Wage-Earning Mothers during the Progressive Era," in Seth Koven and Sonya Michel, eds., *Mothers of a New World: Maternalist Politics and the Origins of Welfare States* (New York: Routledge, 1993); Linda Gordon, ed., *Women the State, and Welfare* (Madison: University of Wisconsin Press, 1990); Ellen Fitzpatrick, *Endless Crusade: Women Social Scientists and Progressive Reform* (New York: Oxford University Press, 1990); Molly Ladd-Taylor, *Mother-Work: Women, Child Welfare, and the State, 1890–1930* (Urbana: University of Illinois Press, 1994); and Alice Kessler-Harris, *In Pursuit of Equity: Women, Men, and the Quest for Economic Citizenship in the Twentieth Century* (New York: Oxford University Press, 2001).

4. David Smith and Malcolm Nicholson, "Nutrition, Education, Ignorance, and Income: A Twentieth Century Debate," in Hamke Kamminga and Andrew Cunningham, eds., *The Science and Culture of Nutrition, 1840–1940* (Amster-

dam: Editions Rodope B.V., 1995), 310. A good selection on the symbolic meaning of food can be found in Carole Counihan and Penny Van Esterik, eds, *Food
and Culture: A Reader* (New York: Routledge, 1979), particularly the essays by
Mead, Barthes, Levi-Strauss, Douglas, Soler, Harris, and Anderson.

5. On food and housewives, see Ellen Ross, *Love and Toil: Motherhood in
Outcast London, 1870–1918* (New York: Oxford University Press, 1993).

6. Charles E. Rosenberg, *No Other Gods: On Science and American Social
Thought* (Baltimore: Johns Hopkins University Press, 1997), 187.

7. In 1888 Atwater became the first head of the Agriculture Department's Office of Experiment Stations, which later became the Agricultural Extension Service. In this capacity he was one of the first American chemists to identify vitamin
A. A number of studies discuss Atwater's work: Shapiro, *Perfection Salad*; Levenstein, *Revolution at the Table*; Cummings, *The American and His Food*; Rima
Apple, "Science Gendered: Nutrition in the United States, 1840–1940," in Kamminga and Cunningham, *Science and Culture of Nutrition*; and K. Y. Guggenheim, *Basic Issues of the History of Nutrition* (Jerusalem: Akademia University
Press, 1990). The discovery of vitamins allowed nutrition scientists to move beyond protein, carbohydrates, and fats to the isolation of particular foods as essential to health. See Apple, *Vitamania*, and Rosenberg, *No Other Gods*, esp. ch. 12.

8. Mikulas Teich, "Science and Food during the Great War: Britain and Germany," in Kamminga and Cunningham, *Science and Culture of Nutrition*, 223.
On Atwater and the food/fuel theory, see Rosenberg, *No Other Gods*. Also see
Dietrich Milles, "Working Capacity and Calorie Consumption: The History of
Rational Physical Economy," and Hamke Kamminga, "Nutrition for the People,
or, the Fate of Jacob Moleschott's Contest for a Humanist Science," both in Kamminga and Cunningham, *Science and Culture of Nutrition*; and Anson Rabin-
bach, "The European Science of Work: The Economy of the Body at the End of
the Nineteenth Century," in Steven Laurence Kaplan and Cynthia J. Koepp, eds.,
Work in France: Representations, Meanings, Organization, and Practice (Ithaca,
N.Y.: Cornell University Press, 1986).

9. See Rosenberg, *No Other God*, 140, and 186–87.

10. On the history of vitamins and the "new nutrition," see Apple, *Vitamania*;
Levenstein, *Revolution at the Table*; and E. V. McCollum, *The Newer Knowledge
of Nutrition: The Use of Food for the Preservation of Vitality and Health* (New
York: Macmillan, 1918).

11. Shapiro, *Perfection Salad*, 70. Shapiro notes that his recommendations
were much higher than present-day theories. Also see Nick Fiddes, *Meat: A Natural Symbol* (London: Routledge, 1991), and Michelle Stacey, *Consumed: Why
Americans Love, Hate, and Fear Food* (New York: Simon and Schuster, 1994).

12. Guggenheim, *Basic Issues*, 85.

13. Kamminga, "Nutrition for the People," 39. Also see Madeleine Mayhew,
"The 1930s Nutrition Controversy," *Journal of Contemporary History* 23
(1988): 445–64. Also see Ross, *Love and Toil*, and Catherine Giessler and
Derek F. Oddy, *Food, Diet and Economic Change Past and Present* (Leicester:
Leicester University Press, 1993), esp., E. Margaret Crawford, "The Irish Work-
house Diet, 1840–90," and Michael Nelson, "Social-Class Trends in British Diet,

1860–1980." Also John Walton, *Fish and Chips and the British Working Class, 1870–1940* (London: Leicester University Press, 1992).

14. Harold Francis Williamson, *Edward Atkinson: The Biography of an American Liberal, 1827–1905* (Boston: Old Corner Book Store, 1934), 231. Also see Edward Atkinson, *Addresses upon the Labor Question* (Boston: Franklin Press and Rand, Avery & Company, 1886) (thanks to Karen Sawislak for this reference).

15. Quoted in Levenstein, *Revolution at the Table*, 56. For a good discussion of working-class response to scientific discoveries—in this case, germs and sanitation—see Nancy Tomes, *The Gospel of Germs,* esp. ch. 9.

16. Williamson, *Edward Atkinson*, 234.

17. United States Bureau of Census, *Historical Statistics of the United States from Colonial Times to 1970*, Part 1, Earnings, Hours, and Working Conditions (Washington, D.C., 1976).

18. Williamson, *Edward Atkinson*, 233ff.

19. Atkinson, *Addresses*, 37; and Shapiro, *Perfection Salad*, 141–43.

20. Williamson, *Edward Atkinson*, 235: "Mr. Atkinson was especially disappointed at his failure to interest the poorer classes in the use of the Aladdin Cooker, for he had a genuine interest in improving the condition of these groups. During the latter years of his life he became convinced that he should have first tried to 'save the rich' with his cooking apparatus, because it seemed so much easier to get the poor to adopt something already in use by the wealthier classes than something designed for their own particular use."

21. See Susan Levine, *Degrees of Equality: The American Association of University Women and the Challenge of Twentieth Century Feminism* (Philadelphia: Temple University Press, 1995). On home economics as a women's profession, also see Shapiro, *Perfection Salad*, and Sarah Stage and Virginia B. Vincenti, eds., *Rethinking Home Economics: Women and the History of a Profession* (Ithaca, N.Y.: Cornell University Press, 1997), esp. Rima Apple's, "Science Gendered."

22. Historians have labeled this generation "maternalists" because, while affirming equality for women they also emphasized traditionally female roles in children's welfare and social policy. See Mink, *Wages of Motherhood*; Ladd-Taylor, *Mother-Work*; Muncy, *Creating a Female Dominion*; and Koven and Michel, *Mothers of a New World.*

23. Caroline L. Hunt, *The Life of Ellen H. Richards, 1842–1911* (1912; 8th printing, Washington, D.C.: American Home Economics Association, 1980), 37. Hunt suggests that MIT agreed to the "special" status so they could continue to say that they did not admit women students.

24. See Hunt, *Ellen Richards*. On Richards, also see Shapiro, *Perfection Salad*; Sara Stage, "Ellen Richards and the Social Significance of the Home Economics Movement," in Stage and Vincenti, eds., *Rethinking Home Economics*; Rima Apple, in her essay, "Science Gendered," says that nutrition science "enhanced women's position in the domestic sphere and gave women an arena in which to practice science" (p. 129).

25. Nancy K. Berlage, "The Establishment of an Applied Social Science: Home Economists, Science, and Reform at Cornell University, 1870–1930," in Helene Silverberg, ed., *Gender and American Social Science, the Formative Years* (Princeton: Princeton University Press, 1989). She argues that historians have put too

much emphasis on the dichotomy between "technocratic" (or male) versus advocacy (or female) interests and credits home economists with both a reform tradition and a commitment to objectivity and science (184–87, 198).

26. Ellen H. Richards, *The Cost of Food: A Study in Dietaries* (New York: John Wiley & Sons, 1917), 7.

27. See Shapiro, *Perfection Salad*, 127–31.

28. *Journal of Home Economics* (hereafter JHE), April 1932, editorial.

29. Quoted in Shapiro, *Perfection Salad*, 129. Also see Levenstein, *Revolution at the Table*.

30. Hunt, *Ellen Richards*, 103. Abel won the first prize ever offered in Home Economics for her essay. The prize money was donated by Henry Lomb, founder of the Bausch and Lomb Company.

31. Shapiro, *Perfection Salad*, 144–45. For a brief biography of Mary Hinman Abel, see her entry in *Feeding America: The Historic American Cookbook Project*, MSU Libraries, http://digital.lib.msu.edu/projects/cookbooks/html/authors/author_abel.html.

32. Hunt, *Ellen Richards*, 105–6. Also see Shapiro, *Perfection Salad*, and Apple, "Science Gendered." On the standardization of recipes, see Anne Mendelson, *Stand Facing the Stove: The Story of the Women Who Gave Us the Joy of Cooking* (New York: Henry Holt, 1996).

33. Hunt, *Ellen Richards*, 105; and Richards, *The Cost of Food*.

34. Hunt, *Ellen Richards*, 107–8. The model kitchen was named after Benjamin Thompson, Count Rumford of Bavaria, who was reputed to have coined the term "nutrition science." He pioneered in institutional feeding of the poor and was also credited with introducing the potato to the poverty diet in Europe. See C. M. McCay, "Four Pioneers in the Science of Nutrition—Lind, Rumford, Chadwick, and Graham," in Adelia M. Beeuwkes, E. Neige Todhunter, and Emma Seifrit Weigley, eds., *Essays on History of Nutrition and Dietetics* (Chicago: American Dietetics Association, 1967), 263–68.

35. Also see Hayden, *The Grand Domestic Revolution*.

36. Levinstein, *Revolution at the Table*, discusses this transition.

37. Richards, *The Cost of Food*, 2–3.

38. Hunt, *Ellen Richards*, 109.

39. Margaret Rossiter, *Women Scientists in America: Struggles and Strategies to 1940* (Baltimore: Johns Hopkins University Press, 1982), 66. A similar dynamic operated in England as reformers attempted to teach working-class housewives scientific nutrition. See, e.g., Ross, *Love and Toil*. She observes that reformers believed they could rescue children from their "slum tastes," 36; and see Walton, *Fish and Chips*.

40. Lucy H. Gillett, "How Can Our Work in Foods Be Made More Vital to the Health of the Child?" JHE, September 1920, p. 391. On religious teaching and food, also see John Burnett, "The Rise and Decline of School Meals in Britain," in John Burnett and Derek J. Oddy, eds., *The Origins and Development of Food Policy in Europe* (London: Leicester University Press, 1994). Little information is available on Lucy Gillett. She was probably a student of Mary Swartz Rose at Columbia.

41. Richards, *The Cost of Food*, 27; and Hunt, *Ellen Richards*. She calls Richards a "missionary of science" (103).

42. Hunt, *Ellen Richards*, 112.

43. Tomes, *The Gospel of Germs*, has a good discussion of the missionary zeal with which scientists and reformers (not to mention entrepreneurs) promoted theories of germs and disease. The nutrition advocates exhibited a similar zeal in their efforts to convince Americans to alter their eating habits.

44. The figure of 29% appears in many sources. See Bernadette M. Marriott and Judith Grumstrup-Scott, eds., *Body Composition and Physical Performance: Applications for the Military Service* (Washington, D.C.: National Academy Press, 1992), 39. Also, Howard Markel and Janet Golden, "Successes and Missed Opportunities in Protecting Our Children's Health: Critical Junctures in the History of Children's Health Policy in the United States," *Pediatrics* 115, no. 4 (April 2005); 1129–33. By most estimates, in addition, about one-quarter of all draftees were illiterate.

45. E. V. McCollum and Nina Simmonds, *Food, Nutrition, and Health* (Baltimore: the Authors, 1925), 30.

46. Gillett, "How Can Our Work in Foods Be Made More Vital?" 386.

47. For a discussion of modernization and attitudes toward health, see Lynne Curry, "Modernizing the Rural Mother: Gender, Class, and Health Reform in Illinois, 1910–1930," in Apple and Golden, eds., *Mothers and Motherhood*.

48. On food as a cultural, social, and psychological structure, see Maurice Aymard, "Toward the History of Nutrition: Some Methodological Remarks," Roland Barthes, "Toward a Psychosociology of Contemporary Food Consumption," and Jean Soler, "The Semiotics of Food in the Bible," all in Forster and Ranum, eds., *Food and Drink in History*. Also, Mary Douglas, "Deciphering a Meal," in Counihan and Van Esterik, *Food and Culture*; and Sidney Mintz, *Tasting Food, Tasting Freedom: Excursions into Eating, Culture, and the Past* (Boston: Beacon Press, 1996).

49. Mink, *Wages of Motherhood*, 89. The achievements and limits of maternalism are discussed in a number of works. See, e.g., Muncy, *Creating a Female Dominion*; Michel, "The Limits of Maternalism"; Gordon, ed., *Women the State, and Welfare*; Fitzpatrick, *Endless Crusade*; Ladd-Taylor, *Mother-Work*; and Kathryn Kish Sklar, *Florence Kelley and the Nation's Work* (New Haven: Yale University Press, 1995).

50. George Sanchez, "Go after the Women: Americanization and the Mexican Immigrant Woman, 1915–1929," Working Paper Series No. 6, June 1984, Stanford Center for Chicano Research, 17 and 1. Sanchez argues that, initially, Americanization represented social settlement and social gospel traditions, "These individuals felt that society had an obligation to assimilate the Mexican immigrant and hoped to improve societal treatment of immigrants in general." But with World War I, nativism took over and business took an interest in the Americanization movement as a method of combating radicalism among foreigners (p. 9). Settlement workers valued immigrant "gifts" to American culture while Americanizers did not. These efforts were also common in Europe. See Ross, *Love and Toil*; and Walton, *Fish and Chips*.

51. Levenstein, *Revolution at the Table*, 104.

52. Michael M. Davis, Jr., *Immigrant Health and the Community* (Montclair, N.J.: Patterson Smith, 1971), 71. Burnett, "The Rise and Decline of School Meals," discusses food imperialism in the Socialist Labor party.

53. Dorothy Dickins, "Negro Food Habits in the Yazoo Mississippi Delta," JHE, September 1926, p. 524.

54. Mary Swartz Rose and Gertrude Gates Mudge, "A Nutrition Class," JHE, February 1920, p. 49. During the first three decades of the twentieth century, social investigators undertook scores of surveys of immigrant and working-class households. These studies were often used to judge how close various groups came to achieving an "American standard of living." Trade unions used household budget studies to argue for a "living wage," while employers used similar studies to argue that workers' living standards were adequate and that they should learn to spend their money more wisely. See Susan Levine, "A Bit of Mellifluous Phraseology: The 1922 Railroad Shopcraft Strike and the Living Wage," in John Belchem and Neville Kirk, eds., *Languages of Labour* (Aldershot: Ashgate Publishing, 1997).

55. See Rossiter, *Women Scientists*, 66; and Shapiro, *Perfection Salad*. Rossiter suggests that they sought to "train, "Americanize," and generally "homogenize and upgrade these unwashed hordes into respectable middle-class citizens" (66).

56. Velma Phillips and Laura Howell, "Racial and Other Differences in Dietary Customs," JHE, September 1920, p. 396.

57. Grace A. Farrell, "Homemaking with the "Other Half" along Our International Border," JHE, June 1929, p. 413.

58. Sophonisba Breckinridge, *New Homes for Old* (1921; rpt., Montclair, N.J.: Patterson Smith, 1971).

59. Ibid., 132.

60. "Notes from the Field," JHE, October 1921, p. 527.

61. Gillett, "Factors Influencing Nutrition Work, among Italians," JHE, January 1922, p. 19. Also see Davis, *Immigrant Health*, 247. He says, "There is much that we may learn from these people. . . . if we study their ways and customs and acquaint ourselves with their foods we shall be able to help them to adjust." He claimed that during the 1918 flu epidemic, "gallons of American soups and broths were served to these people only to be thrown out untouched." He concluded that "our milk soups are nutritious but so are theirs" (248).

62. Lucy H. Gillett, "Factors Influencing Nutrition Work," p. 14. Emphasis in the original. Also see Gillett, "How Can Our Work in Foods Be Made More Vital?," 389, and her essay, "The Great Need for Information on Racial Dietary Customs," JHE, June 1922. Michael M. Davis, in *Immigrant Health and the Community*, states, "Knowledge of the foods of the foreign born and of their native dietaries is the foundation of all success in this endeavor" (275).

63. See discussion of Atwater's theory in chapter 1.

64. Gillett, "How Can Our Work in Foods Be Made More Vital?," 389.

65. Gillett, "Factors Influencing Nutrition Work," 19.

66. Gillett, "The Great Need for Information on Racial Dietary Customs," p. 258.

67. Breckinridge, *New Homes*, 132. The story was reproduced in William M. Liserson, *Adjusting Immigrant and Industry* (New York: Harper and Brothers,

1924), 69. He said the social worker discovered "that dampness in Polish houses and the tendency of paper to come off the walls were due to the continual flow of steam from the kitchen stove. The Poles boiled their food and boiled it for hours. The use of the oven was scarcely known. Cabbage soup, boiled meat, and pastry bought at the store were about all the food items they knew."

68. Breckinridge, *New Homes*, 122, 59. See also Michael M. Davis, Jr., and Bertha M. Wood, "The Food of the Immigrant in Relation to Health," JHE, January 1921, pp. 19–20.

69. Cummings, *The American and His Food*, 198.

70. Breckinridge, *New Homes*, 127–28. (For this reason, Breckinridge favored more standardized grocery stores.) On the other hand, she found that the Italian groceries regularly stocked an impressive array of greens.

71. See Donna R. Gabaccia, *We Are What We Eat: Ethnic Food and the Making of Americans* (Cambridge, Mass.: Harvard University Press, 1998; and Lizabeth Cohen, *Making a New Deal: Industrial Workers in Chicago, 1919–1939* (New York: Cambridge University Press, 1990).

72. Gillett, "Factors Influencing Nutrition Work," 16.

73. Breckinridge, *New Homes*, 124.

74. See Irving Bernstein, *Lean Years: A History of the American Worker, 1920–1933* (Baltimore: Penguin Press, 1966).

75. Breckinridge, *New Homes*, 129. Also see Phillips and Howell, "Racial and Other Differences in Dietary Customs," p. 399; Lucy Gillett, " A Minimum Food Allowance and a Basic Food Order," JHE, July 1920, p. 324; and Salome S. C. Bernstein, "Home Economics in a Family Case Agency," JHE, February 1926, p. 95.

76. Karen Graves, *Girls' Schooling during the Progressive Era: From Female Scholar to Domesticated Citizen* (New York: Garland Publishing, 1998), finds that African American girls were more likely than white girls to be targets of home economics classes in 1920s St. Louis.

77. See Cohen, *Making a New Deal*.

78. Paul E. Mertz, *The New Deal and Southern Poverty* (Baton Rouge: Louisiana State University Press, 1978), 12. Just because families lived on the land did not mean they had nutritious food to eat. Mertz points out that tenant farmers' diets often lacked fresh vegetables because they used every acre of land for the cash crop of cotton. Also see Phillips and Howell, "Racial and Other Differences in Dietary Customs," p. 396; and Davis, *Immigrant Health*, 246.

79. Gillett, "Our Work in Foods," 395. Gwendolyn Mink is less sanguine about the reformers' appreciation of immigrant culture. She finds the education project "culturally intrusive" even though reformers "warned against aggressive monoculturalism" (*Wages of Motherhood*, 84). See esp. ch. 4. Also see Ross, *Love and Toil*.

80. Michael Worboys, "The Discovery of Colonial Malnutrition between the Wars," in David Arnold, ed., *Imperial Medicine and Indigenous Societies* (Manchester: Manchester University Press, 1988). Worboys makes the argument that

the science of nutrition created the problem of malnutrition, particularly in the context of the development of colonial medicine.

81. Mary Swartz Rose, "Child Nutrition and Diet," JHE, March 1923, p. 130.

82. On the "discovery" of malnutrition, see Arnold, *Imperial Medicine*, esp. Worboys, "The Discovery of Colonial Malnutrition." Also James Vernon, "The Ethics of Hunger and the Assembly of Society: The Techno-Politics of the School Meal in Modern Britain," *American Historical Review* 110, no. 3 (2005). Vernon sees the movement to weigh and measure hungry children as a way to depoliticize hunger by offering a scientific and technocratic solution.

83. James Kerr, *Newsholme's School Hygiene: The Laws of Health in Relation to School Life* (New York: Macmillan, 1916), 195. On malnutrition historically, see Aymard, "Toward the History of Nutrition."

84. On weighing children, see Jeffrey P. Brosco, "Weight Charts and Well Child Care: When the Pediatrician Became the Expert in Child Health," in Alexandra Minna Stein and Howard Markel, eds., *Formative Years: Children's Health in the United States, 1880–2000* (Ann Arbor: University of Michigan Press, 2002). Also Vernon, "The Ethics of Hunger."

85. Rose, "Child Nutrition and Diet," 129.

86. "Preparing Child to Start School," editorial, JHE, September 24, 1929, p. 409. Levenstein, *Revolution at the Table*, describes the scale as using height, weight, eyesight, breathing, muscularity, mental alertness, and rosy complexion (115). On Baldwin Woods, also see Cummings, *The American and His Food*, 192. In 1921 the Child Health Organization of America called a conference of seven professional organizations to consider the possibility of adopting a uniform table of weight for height and age. There was substantial agreement among the various tables used. JHE, April 1921, p. 192.

87. "Height-Weight Tables for Children," note by Sybil Woodruff, JHE, July 1924, p. 391. Roberts, *Nutrition Work with Children* (Chicago: University of Chicago Press, 1935), 107. The Baldwin-Woods scale slightly modified the original Dunfermline measurements by allowing for greater zones for each age and weight. Except for a few modifications these scales remained in use well into the twentieth century. (A number of authors refer to it as the Dumferline scale. See, e.g., Levenstein, *Revolution at the Table*, 114–15.) Also see Julius Levy, "Child Hygiene in New Jersey," *Survey* 44, no. 7 (May 15, 1920), and Julia Roberts, "Weight as a Measure of Nutrition," JHE, August 1924.

88. See Levenstein, *Revolution at the Table*, 114–15.

89. "Standards of Child Nutrition," editorial, JHE, October, 1921, p. 517. Also see Brosco, "Weight Charts."

90. Gillett, "Factors Influencing Nutrition Work," 16–18. African American diets also came under scrutiny. See, e.g., Phillips and Howell, "Racial and Other Differences." They observe that, "while the Negroes had a much greater quantity of food and spend more for it than the foreign families, they received the least nourishment" from it. Their diets, the authors observed, lacked vital grains and were low in protein (406–7).

91. Woodruff, "Height-Weight Tables for Children," 391.

92. See Mink, *Wages of Motherhood*; and Ladd-Taylor, *Mother-Work*. Also Robert D. Johnston, "Contemporary Anti-Vaccination Movements in Historical Perspective," in Robert D. Johnston, ed., *The Politics of Healing: Histories of Twentieth-Century North American Alternative Medicine* (New York: Routledge, 2004).

93. Mary G. McCormick, "The Home Economics Teacher and the Community," JHE, January 1922, p. 4.

94. Amy Drinkwater Storer and Gertrude Gates Mudge, "The Red Cross Nutrition Program in New York City," JHE, November 1921, p. 539. Brosco, in "Weight Charts," argues that the malnutrition scare ended in the 1930s as monitoring children's weight became part of the physician's regular care.

95. Mary G. McCormick, "Nutrition Work in the Schools," *Survey*, 47, no. 2 (October 1921): 51.

96. Levenstein, *Revolution at the Table*, ch. 9.

97. Both studies quoted in Cummings, *The American and His Food*, 166.

98. "News from the Field," JHE, December 1922, p. 648. Levenstein calls this "the great malnutrition scare." On the push to measure children, see *Revolution at the Table*, 113.

99. See Bailey B. Burnett, "Attacking Defective Nutrition," *Survey* 44, no. 12 (June 19, 1920).

100. Caroline L. Hunt, "The Daily Meals of School Children," JHE, October 1909, p. 363.

101. McCormick, "The Home Economics Teacher," 3.

102. Lottie Milam, "The Rural School Lunch Today," JHE, March 1922, p. 129. On early school cafeterias, see Mary DeGambo Bryan, *The School Cafeteria* (New York: Crofts, 1943).

103. Miss E. W. Cross, "The Daily Meals of School Children," JHE, October 1929, p. 364.

104. Rose, "Child Nutrition and Diet," 131.

105. "News from the Field," JHE, December 1921, p. 625.

106. Katharine Curry Bartley and Nancy S. Wellman, "School Lunch: A Comparison of its Development in the United States and England," *School Food Service Research Review* 10, no. 1 (1986): 6.

107. For an early history of school lunches in the United States, see Gordon W. Gunderson, "The National School Lunch Program: Background and Development," Food and Nutrition Service, 63, U.S. Department of Agriculture, 1971.

108. Molly Ladd-Taylor, "When the Birds Have Flown the Nest, the Mother-Work May Still Go On: Sentimental Maternalism and the National Congress of Mothers," in Apple and Golden, *Mothers and Motherhood*.

109. United States Department of Agriculture, "School Lunch in Country and City," Bulletin No. 1899 (Washington, D.C., 1942). During the 1920s some Latin American states instituted school meal programs as well. See Bartley and Wellman, "School Lunch: A Comparison."

110. See Muncy, *Creating a Female Dominion*; and Mink, *The Wages of Motherhood*.

111. Paul V. Betters, *The Bureau of Home Economics: Its History, Activities, and Organization* (Washington, D.C.: Brookings Institution, 1930).

112. "Notes from the Field," JHE, July 1921, p. 335. The Columbia Teachers College Nutrition Program was established in 1909 as the Department of Nutrition and Food Economics in the School of Household Arts. Students of Ellen Richards found employment there through the 1920s. See also Juanita A. Eagles, Orrea F. Pye, and Clara M. Taylor, *Mary Swartz Rose, 1874–1941: Pioneer in Nutrition* (New York: Teachers College, 1979), 38. In 1921 the Carnegie Corporation funded the American Food Research Institute at Stanford, giving $700,000 over ten years for "an intensive study of problems connected with the production, distribution, and consumption of food." Home economics, according to Margaret Rossiter, underwent "rapid institutionalization as an academic field for women after 1910" (*Women Scientists*, 65). Also Rossiter, "The Origin of the Agricultural Sciences," and John Higham, "The Matrix of Specialization," both in Alexandra Oleson and John Voss, eds., *Knowledge in Modern America, 1860–1920* (Baltimore: Johns Hopkins University Press, 1979). Also see Walton C. John, "Land-Grant College Education, 1910–1920," Part V, Home Economics, United States Department of the Interior, Bureau of Education Bulletin 1925, No. 29, Washington, D.C., 1925, and Hamilton Craven, "Establishing the Science of Nutrition at the United States Department of Agriculture: Ellen Swallow Richards and Her Allies," *Agricultural History* 64 (1990): 122–33.

113. Elizabeth Sanders, *Roots of Reform: Farmers, Workers, and the American State, 1877–1917* (Chicago: University of Chicago Press, 1999), 391.

114. Rosenberg, *No Other Gods*, see, e.g., 140. Kenneth Finegold and Theda Skocpol, *State and Party in America's New Deal* (Madison: University of Wisconsin Press, 1995), characterize the Department of Agriculture as "an island of state strength" in an otherwise relatively weak institutional state structure.

115. Graves, *Girls' Schooling*, makes this argument. See p. 212.

116. Sanders, *Roots of Reform*, 390.

117. Adam D. Sheingate, *The Rise of the Agricultural Welfare State: Institutions and Interest Group Power in the United States, France, and Japan* (Princeton: Princeton University Press, 2001), 101.

118. See ibid., 193. Also David E. Hamilton, *From New Day to New Deal: American Farm Policy from Hoover to Roosevelt, 1928–1933* (Chapel Hill: University of North Carolina Press, 1991).

119. On Rose, see Eagles et al., *Mary Swartz Rose*, 6–9. According to the authors, "she became the first woman to have a professorial appointment in nutrition in the United States" when she took the position at Teachers College in 1909. Rose was the only woman among the eleven "founding fathers of the American Institute of Nutrition in 1928" and was its first woman president in 1937. In 1939 she was described as "the strongest living link between the laboratory and the consumer of food." Also see Alonzo E. Taylor, "After-the-War Economic Food Problems," JHE, January 1921, p. 1. On the popularization of vitamins during the war, see Apple, *Vitamania*, 217, 310, and Cummings, *The American and His Food*. On the World War I impact on food policy, see Levenstein, *Revolution at the Table*, 137–49, and Mark Weatherall, "Bread and Newspapers," in Kamminga and Cunningham, *The Science and Culture of Nutrition*, 180. Also see

Elmer Verner McCollum, "Our Present Knowledge of the Vitamins," in Louis B. Wilson, *Lectures on Nutrition: A Series of Lectures Given at the Mayo Foundation and the Universities of Wisconsin, Minnesota, Nebraska, Iowa, and Washington (St. Louis), 1924–1925* (Philadelphia: W. B. Saunders, 1925).

120. On vitamins and health, see Levenstein, *Revolution at the Table*, and Apple, *Vitamania*; also Nancy Tomes, "Spreading the Germ Theory: Sanitary Science and Home Economics, 1880–1930," and Lynn K. Nyhart, "Home Economists in the Hospital, 1900–1930," both in Stage and Vincenti, *Rethinking Home Economics*. Nyhart says that fears of scurvy and beriberi among the troops spurred a demand for nutrition research and dietetic advice. See p. 138.

121. See Susan Estabrook Kennedy, "Herbert Hoover and the Two Great Food Crusades of the 1940s," in Lee Nash, ed., *Understanding Herbert Hoover: Ten Perspectives* (Stanford, Calif.: Hoover Institute Press, 1987), and "Herbert Hoover: A Biographical Sketch," Herbert Hoover Presidential Museum, www.hoover.nara.gov/education/hooverbio.html. Also see Carolyn M. Goldstein, "Rationalizing Consumption at the Bureau of Home Economics, 1923–1940," paper presented at the Schlesinger Library, April 30, 1998. Goldstein argues that home economists' role in Hoover's food conservation campaigns was important for institutionalizing expertise and sought to define "a vocational role" in the public sphere.

122. See Levenstein, *Revolution at the Table*, 137–46.

123. See, e.g., Rowena Schmidt Carpenter, "Menus and Recipes for Lunches at School," USDA Miscellaneous Publication No. 246, 1928, Countway Library, 36.c. 1928.2–246. Also see Annual Reports, North Carolina Agricultural Extension Service, 1920–26, vols. 7–12, 44–45, and 82–85. Thanks to Lu Ann Jones for these references.

124. Mabel Hyde Kitterdge, "School Lunches in Large Cities of the United States," JHE, September 1926.

125. C. Rowena Schmidt, "The Psychology of Child Nutrition," JHE, May 1925, p. 264.

126. Irene C. Harrington, "The High School Lunch: Its Financial, Administrative, and Educational Policies." JHE, November 1924, p. 625.

127. Anna L. Steckelberg, "Planning for the Hot Lunch in Rural Schools," JHE, November 1923, pp. 643–44.

128. Mabel Hyde Kitridge, "School Lunches in Large Cities," 510.

129. McCormick, "The Home Economics Teacher," 3.

130. Rose, "Child Nutrition and Diet," 138.

CHAPTER 2. WELFARE FOR FARMERS AND CHILDREN

1. For a discussion of food relief policy, see Janet Poppendieck, *Breadlines Knee Deep in Wheat: Food Assistance in the Great Depression* (New Brunswick, N.J.: Rutgers University Press, 1986).

2. See Madeleine Mayhew, "The 1930s Nutrition Controversy," *Journal of Contemporary History* 23 (1988): 445–64.

3. "20% of City Pupils Are Found Underfed," *New York Times* (hereafter, NYT), October 29, 1932.

4. United States Congress, House Committee on Agriculture, *Hearings on the School Lunch Program*, 79th Cong., 1st Sess., March 23–May 24, 1945 (hereafter House Hearings, 1945). Reported by Dr. W. H. Sebrrell, Medical Director, United States Public Health Service, 25–26.

5. "For Child Health: A National Call," NYT, October 1, 1933. Also see "Food in Crisis," NYT, May 1, 1936.

6. See 1932 study of 400 Philadelphia families, Evan Clague, "When Relief Stops, What Do They Eat?" *Survey*, 67, no. 16 (November 16, 1932).

7. "Parents Warned on Economy Diets," NYT, April 20, 1936.

8. House Hearings, 1945, p. 26.

9. "Finds Nervous Ills in Homes of Idle," NYT, January 16, 1932.

10. House Hearings, 1945, pp. 54–56.

11. United States Congress, Senate Subcommittee on Agriculture and Forestry, *Hearings on Bills to Assist the States to Establish and Maintain School-Lunch Programs*, May 2–5, 1944, 78th Cong., 2nd Sess. (hereafter Senate Hearings, 1944), 46–48.

12. The states were California, Colorado, Connecticut, Indiana, Massachusetts, Michigan, Missouri, New Jersey, New York, North Carolina, Ohio, Pennsylvania, Vermont, Washington, and Wisconsin. See H. M. Southworth and M. I. Klayman, "The School Lunch Program and Agricultural Surplus Disposal" (Washington, D.C.: Bureau of Agricultural Economics, USDA, 1941), 14ff.

13. See ibid., 14.

14. Edward Berkowitz and Kim McQuaid, *Creating the Welfare State: The Political Economy of Twentieth-Century Reform*, 2nd ed. (New York: Praeger, 1988), 138.

15. Adam D. Sheingate, *The Rise of the Agricultural Welfare State: Institutions and Interest Group Power in the United States, France, and Japan* (Princeton: Princeton University Press, 2001). Also see Kenneth Finegold and Theda Skocpol, *State and Party in America's New Deal* (Madison: University of Wisconsin Press, 1995).

16. See, e.g., Alice Kessler-Harris, *In Pursuit of Equity: Women, Men, and the Quest for Economic Citizenship in 20th Century America* (Oxford: Oxford University Press, 2001), Linda Gordon, *Pitied but Not Entitled: Single Mothers and the History of Welfare: 1890–1935* (New York: Free Press, 1994); and Joanne L. Goodwin, " 'Employable Mothers' and 'Suitable Work': A Reevaluation of Welfare and Wage Earning for Women in the Twentieth-Century United States," in Rima D. Apple and Janet Golden, eds., *Mothers and Motherhood: Readings in American History* (Columbus: Ohio State University Press, 1997.

17. M. L. Wilson, "Nutritional Science and Agricultural Policy," *Journal of Farm Economics* 24:1, Proceedings Number (February 1942): 188–205. Quote on 199.

18. Southworth and Klayman, "The School Lunch Program," 15.

19. Ellen S. Woodward, "The Works Progress Administration School Lunch Project," *Journal of Home Economics* (hereafter JHE), November 1936, p. 592.

Woodward estimated that 592 of the 5,000 women were "economic heads of families" (36).

20. See Gordon W. Gunderson, "The National School Lunch Program: Background and Development," Food and Nutrition Service, 63, U.S. Department of Agriculture, 1971, p. 9 and Southworth and Klayman, "The School Lunch Program," 36.

21. On gender and race in the WPA, see Linda Faye Williams, *The Constraint of Race: Legacies of White Skin Privilege in America* (University Park: Penn State University Press, 2003).

22. Southworth and Klayman, "The School Lunch Program," 38.

23. Anita K. Hynes, "W.P.A. School Lunch Project in Jefferson City," JHE, November 1936, p. 608.

24. Ellen S. Woodward, "The Works Projects Administration School Lunch Project," 593.

25. Southworth and Klayman, "The School Lunch Program," 36; and "The Fate of School Feeding," JHE editorial, June 1943, p. 360.

26. Milburn Lincoln ("M. L.") Wilson, who became Assistant Secretary of Agriculture in 1934, is best known as the major architect of the "domestic allotment" policy under which the government adjusted farm income by guaranteeing (purchasing) a portion of the crop at protected prices. This policy became the backbone of New Deal agricultural policy. Wilson was also an advocate of nutrition, believing that better nutrition would strengthen not only American workers but also consumer food markets. See Rebecca L. Spang, "The Cultural Habits of a Food Committee," *Food and Foodways* 2 (1988): 359–91. Also see Sheingate, *The Rise of the Agricultural Welfare State*, 112–14. Sidney Baldwin, *Poverty and Politics: The Rise and Decline of the Farm Security Administration* (Chapel Hill: University of North Carolina Press, 1968), argues that the conflict was less a question of liberal versus conservative than between "*different* bodies of fact and information which led naturally to competing conclusions and conflicting behaviors" (83). Wilson was raised on a farm in Iowa and became the first county state extension agent for Montana. After World War I he studied agricultural economics and returned to Montana to become an agricultural economist at Montana State. Howard Ross Tolley worked at the Bureau of Agricultural Economics in the mid 1920s where he and Wilson met. See also David E. Hamilton, *From New Day to New Deal: American Farm Policy from Hoover to Roosevelt, 1928–1933* (Chapel Hill: University of North Carolina Press, 1991), 180–81.

27. On the differences in agricultural policy, see Paul E. Mertz, *New Deal Policy and Southern Rural Poverty* (Baton Rouge: Louisiana State University Press, 1978), 256–57; William D. Rowley, *M. L. Wilson and the Campaign for the Domestic Allotment* (Lincoln: University of Nebraska Press, 1970); and Edward L. Schapsmeier and Frederick H. Schapsmeier, "Farm Policy from FDR to Eisenhower: Southern Democrats and the Politics of Agriculture," *Agricultural History* 53, no. 1 (January 1979): 352–71. The latter authors argue that the AAA, passed in 1933, aimed to "raise farm income by restricting total output" (359). Also see Willard W. Cochrane and Mary E. Ryan, *American Farm Policy, 1948–1978* (Minneapolis: University of Minnesota Press, 1976), and John Mark Hansen, *Gaining Access, Congress and the Farm Lobby, 1919–1981* (Chicago: University of Chicago Press, 1991).

28. Sheingate, *The Rise of the Agricultural Welfare State*. This author argues that "small changes in production can produce large swings in (farm commodity) price" (24).

29. Some surplus food was also used for the first, short-lived food stamp program. This program was disbanded during World War II. Maurice MacDonald, *Food Stamps and Income Maintenance* (New York: Academic Press, 1977). Janet Poppendieck argues that the move of surplus policy into the Agriculture Department "marked the beginning of a process by which food assistance was increasingly divorced from federal relief and integrated with the Agriculture Department's price support programs" (*Breadlines*, 175).

30. Gunderson, "The National School Lunch Program," 7. P.L. 320, August 1935, authorized the Secretary of Agriculture to make available money from customs duties to "encourage the domestic consumption of certain agricultural commodities . . . by diverting them from the normal channels of trade and commerce." This was not the first time the USDA had ventured into the realm of markets. As early as the Progressive Era, the USDA had created an Office of Markets, which became the Bureau of Markets in 1919 and, finally, the Office of Farm Management and Bureau of Crop Estimates, part of the Bureau of Agricultural Economics. See Elizabeth Sanders, *Roots of Reform: Farmers, Workers, and the American State, 1877–1917* (Chicago: University of Chicago Press, 1999), 393. Also see MacDonald, *Food Stamps and Income Maintenance*, 2. On Milo Perkins, also see Richard Osborn Cummings, *The American and His Food: A History of Food Habits in the United States* (Chicago: University of Chicago Press, 1941), 218. Also see Milo Perkins, "Our Population is Commodity Rich and Consumption Poor," address, n.d. (probably October 1940), Martha May Eliot Papers, Box 17, folder 236, Schlesinger Library. On Tolley, see Richard S. Kirkendall, "Howard Tolley and Agricultural Planning in the 1930s," *Agricultural History* 33 (January 1965); 25–33, and Rowley, *M. L. Wilson*. Tolley and Wilson worked together during the 1920s. Rowley suggests that Tolley, like Wilson, saw three factors as key to the development of American farming: large-scale tractors and power machinery, increasing the size of family farms, and reducing costs to farmers. See pp. 50–51. On Milo Perkins, see Baldwin, *Poverty and Politics*, 243. Perkins came from Texas and left a successful burlap bag business to work with Secretary of Agriculture Wallace. He went to work for the Farm Security Administration in 1937.

31. This first food stamp program was disbanded during World War II.

32. House Hearings, 1945, pp. 3–4.

33. "The Fate of School Feeding," JHE editorial, June 1943, p. 360. Dora S. Lewis and Phyllis Sprague, "A Survey of School Lunchrooms," JHE, November 1936, p. 602.

34. See *Statistical Abstract of the United States*, 91st ed. (Washington, D.C.: Bureau of the Census, 1970), Table 146, "School Enrollment by Type of School, 1930–1968," 104, and *Statistical Abstract of the United States, 1980*, 101st ed., Table 218, "Public and Private School Number by Level, 1940–1979," 138.

35. Gunderson, "The National School Lunch Program," 8. According to one study, 25% of the schools and 60% of the children served by the new surplus disposal program were in rural communities in the South and mountain states,

and most were in elementary schools. "School Lunch in Country and City," USDA Farmers' Bulletin No. 1899 (Washington, D.C. 1942), 8.

36. Southworth and Klayman, "The School Lunch Program," 42–44.

37. Don Paarlberg, *Farm and Food Policy: Issues of the 1980s* (Lincoln: University of Nebraska Press 1980), 104. Paarlberg says that the significance of government purchases on prices for specialty crops like prunes and pears was measurable, but for most other commodities, including meat, there was little impact. The program, he claims, "was a charade, and all the principals knew it." He argues that government programs meant to alleviate the surplus actually aggravated it by boosting prices and stimulating production (103–4).

38. Poppendieck, *Breadlines*, 225. Also see Harvey Levenstein, *Paradox of Plenty: A Social History of Eating in Modern America* (Berkeley: University of California Press, 2003), 78.

39. House Hearings, 1945, p. 3. Testimony of Marvin Jones.

40. Senate Hearings, 1944, p. 14.

41. Senate Hearings, 1944, p. 84.

42. House Hearings, 1945, pp. 109–10.

43. Southworth and Klayman, "The School Lunch Program," 19.

44. *Report of the Chief of the Bureau of Home Economics*, Annual Reports of the Department of Agriculture, 1941 (Washington, D.C., 1941), 5. Thanks to Carolyn Goldstein for this reference.

45. Southworth and Klayman, "The School Lunch Program," 16. Also see Richard Osborn Cummings, *The American and His Food*, 202. Surplus food also went to parochial schools.

46. See Robyn Muncy, *Creating a Female Dominion in American Reform, 1890–1935* (New York: Oxford University Press, 1991), also Cummings, *The American and His Food*, 201, 216. He points out that dietetics emerged out of nutrition and home economics and became a special organization within the American Home Economics Association specializing in food, nutrition, and institutional management. According to one source, the BHE research on diets and consumption provided FDR with the source of his often quoted observation that "one-third of our nation is ill-fed, ill-housed and ill-clothed." See Jacqueline L. Dupont, "Reflections: Hazel Katherine Stiebeling (1896–1989)," *Nutrition Reviews*, October 2002.

47. Gunderson, "The National School Lunch Program," 9, and Southworth and Klayman, "The School Lunch Program," 16, 36–38. Also see Cummings, *The American and His Food*, 202. This figure is probably exaggerated. Baldwin, *Poverty and Politics*, estimates that in 1939, 82% of the department's total employees worked outside Washington. This included the Farm Security Administration and the Soil Conservation Service in addition to the Extension Service (239).

48. Press release, October 19, 1943, USDA History Collection, Series 1, Subseries 2, Documentary Files, Section iv, Distribution of Products, Box 1.2/9, and Nutrition Standards and Civilian Food Supply, 1943–46, Office of War Information, Department of Agriculture, National Agricultural Library.

49. "Public's Aid Asked on School Lunches," NYT, April 17, 1944.

50. House Hearings, 1945, p. 53.

51. Senate Hearings, 1944, p. 150. Also see testimony of Mrs. Grace Gosselin, United Neighborhood Houses of New York; "The need is more obvious today

because such large numbers of women are at war work and, therefore, must find another way to provide an adequate and good midday meal for their children" (156).

52. Senate Hearings, 1944, p. 187.

53. Richard Russell to President Roosevelt, July 22, 1942; Franklin Roosevelt to Richard Russell, August 18, 1943, and October 1, 1942; Richard Russell Collection, Series IX B, Box 44, Richard B. Russell Library for Political Research and Studies, University of Georgia Libraries, Athens.

54. Groups endorsing the National School Lunch Program included the General Federation of Women's Clubs, American Association of University Women, League of Women Voters, League of Women Shoppers, National Consumers League, National Parent Teacher Association, National Council of Jewish Women, National Council of Negro Women, the United Auto Workers Union Women's Auxiliary, and the Congress of Industrial Organizations Women's Auxiliary.

55. "Has Your Child Half a Hog's Chance?" *Ladies' Home Journal*, October 1944.

56. House Hearings, 1945, p. 53. Also see Senate Hearings 1944, p. 110, for PTA statement.

57. "Public's Aid Asked on School Lunches," NYT, April 17, 1944.

58. *Congressional Record*, 79th Cong., 2nd Sess., 92:2, February 19, 1946, p. 1460.

59. Ibid., 1453.

60. See, e.g., Sheingate, *The Rise of the Agricultural Welfare State*, 118–19.

61. Virgil W. Dean, *An Opportunity Lost: The Truman Administration and the Farm Policy Debate* (Columbia: University of Missouri Press, 2006). Dean says that within eighteen months of the war's end "the USDA was completely reconstituted" and had regained authority over food programs including school lunches (23).

62. Senate Hearings, 1944, pp. 7 and 25.

CHAPTER 3. NUTRITION STANDARDS AND STANDARD DIETS

1. M. L. Wilson, "Nutritional Science and Agricultural Policy," *Journal of Farm Economics* 24:1, no. 1, Proceedings Number (February 1942): 188–205, 189.

2. British social planners also adopted the school lunch. In 1944 parliament passed an Education Act that included lunch as "a full part of the school program." Meals were free to all children. Unlike in the United States, however, British school meals were part of state welfare policy and were not tied to agricultural policy. James Vernon, "The Ethics of Hunger and the Assembly of Society: The Techno-Politics of the School Meal in Modern Britain," *American Historical Review* 110, no. 3 (June 2005): 693–725; and Katharine Curry Bartley and Nancy S. Wellman, "School Lunch: A Comparison of Its Development in the United States and England," *School Food Service Research Review* 10, no. 1 (1986): 8.

3. United States Congress, Senate Subcommittee on Agriculture and Forestry, *Hearings on Bills to Assist the States to Establish and Maintain School-Lunch Programs*, May 2–5, 1944, 78th Cong., 2nd Sess. (hereafter Senate Hearings, 1944), 62.

4. Ibid., p. 84.

5. George Chatfield to Allen J. Ellender, May 2, 1944, in ibid., p. 86.

6. United States Congress, House Committee on Agriculture, *Hearings on the School Lunch Program*, 79th Cong., 1st Sess., March 23–May 24, 1945 (hereafter House Hearings, 1945), 19. Andresen also had an interesting exchange with Joseph Meegan. When Meegan suggested that one reason families in his neighborhood could not afford to pay for lunch even though both mother and father were working was the large size of families, Andresen commented, "That is a penalty, I suppose, for having big families." Meegan replied, "Not a penalty sir: it is a blessing" (161).

7. Press release, October 19, 1943, USDA History, Series 1.2/20, Documentary Files, Section iv, Distribution of Products, Box 1.2/9, Nutrition Standards and Civilian Food Supply, 1943–46, Office of War Information, Department of Agriculture, Special Collections, National Agricultural Library.

8. Federal Security Agency, "Proceedings of the National Nutrition Conference for Defense," May 26–28, 1941 (Washington, D.C.: United States Government Printing Office, 1942), 230.

9. Ibid., viii.

10. Ibid., 231–32.

11. Senate Hearings, 1944, p. 60.

12. Federal Security Agency, "Proceedings of the National Nutrition Conference," 34–37. Also see Hershey's statement, House Hearings, 1945, p. 48.

13. Senate Hearings, 1944, p. 60.

14. *Congressional Record*, 79th Cong., 2nd Sess., 92:2, February 19, 1946, p. 1465.

15. Ibid., 1454.

16. Susan M. Hartmann, *The Home Front and Beyond: American Women in the 1940s* (Boston: Twayne, 1982), 77–78.

17. House Hearings, 1945, p. 53.

18. One might imagine that working mothers would be a central factor in public debates about the school lunch program. This was never the case. Proponents usually mentioned the value of school lunches to women in defense industries in passing or as an added benefit. Their main arguments centered around combatting malnutrition and aiding farmers. Opponents occasionally suggested that lunch was rightfully the responsibility of mothers in the home, but they too focused on other issues, most notably, the pitfalls of creating a new federal program.

19. Senate Hearings, 1945, p. 51.

20. Ibid., 190–92. A UAW survey indicated that 90% of the women in one war plant "signified their desire to remain on their jobs after the war" (192).

21. U.S. Department of Labor, Children's Bureau, "Nutrition in the National Defense Program," September 15, 1940, in Martha May Eliot Papers, Box 17, Folder 236, Schlesinger Library. Also, "Suggestions Regarding the Organization

of Personnel in the Government to Prepare Outlines of Alternative Plans for Nutri-tion Activities in the National Advisory Defense Commission," n.d., in Martha May Eliot Papers, Box 17, Folder 237, Schlesinger Library. On "security" and naitonal social policy, see Jennifer Klein, *For All These Rights: Business Labor, and the Shaping of America's Public-Private Welfare State* (Princeton: Princeton University Press 2003).

22. See Memo to Miss Lenroot from Dr. Eliot, June 6, 1940, Martha May Eliot Papers, Box 17, Folder 237. Eliot comments that Louise Stanley, head of the Bu-reau of Home Economics, "is planning to develop the school lunch program" (4).

23. "Material for Dr. Eliot's Committee (School Lunch Phase)," n.d., Martha May Eliot Papers, Box 17, Folder 237.

24. Gordon W. Gunderson, "The National School Lunch Program: Back-ground and Development," Food and Nutrition Service, 63, U.S. Department of Agriculture, 1971, p. 8.

25. House Hearings, 1945, p. 180.

26. Lydia J. Roberts, *Nutrition Work with Children* (Chicago: University of Chicago Press, 1935).

27. See Alfred E. Harper, "Contributions of Women Scientists in the U.S. to the Development of Recommended Dietary Allowances," *Journal of Nutrition* (2003): 3698–702. Also Jacqueline L. Dupont, "Reflections: Hazel Katherine Stiebeling (1896–1989)," *Nutrition Reviews*, October 2003.

28. Harper, "Contributions of Women Scientists."

29. Ibid., 3699. Stiebeling's papers on "A Dietary Goal for Agriculture" (1937) and "Better Nutrition as a National Goal" (1939) were particularly influential. See Dupont, "Reflections."

30. See Bette Caan and Sheldon Mayrgen, "What Is the Future of the Recom-mended Dietary Allowances?"; Alfred E. Harper, "Recommended Dietary Allow-ances: Are They What We Think They Are?"; and Ross Hume Hall, "The RDAs and Public Policy," all in Joan Dye Gussow and Paul R. Thomas, *The Nutrition Debate: Sorting Out Some Answers* (Palo Alto, Calif.: Bull Publishing, 1986).

31. See Richard Osborn Cummings, *The American and His Food: A History of Food Habits in the United States* (Chicago: University of Chicago Press, 1941); and Lydia Roberts, "Beginnings of the Recommended Dietary Allow-ances," in Adelia M. Beeuwkes, E. Neige Todhunter, and Emma Seifrit Weigley, eds., *Essays on History of Nutrition and Dietitics* (Chicago: American Dietetics Association, 1967).

32. Rebecca L. Spang, "The Cultural Habits of a Food Committee," *Food and Foodways* 2 (1988): 359–91, 396.

33. Cummings, *The American and His Food*, 204–5. He recounts the objec-tions of meat packers to nutritionists' advice to eat less meat in warm weather. He also notes that the millers' association resisted efforts to promote whole grains instead of white flour. Also see Dupont, "Reflections," 3.

34. U.S. Department of Agriculture, "Principles of Nutrition and Nutritive Value of Food," Miscellaneous Publication no. 546, Washington, D.C. (1944), 6–7. The RDAs also recommended 85–100 grams of protein for teenaged boys and 75–80 for girls "regardless of the degree of activity." The protein RDAs for men

were 100 and for women 60, but for pregnant women 85 and for lactating women 100 (12).

35. Roberts, "Beginnings," 107. Also see Harold G. Halcrow, *Food Policy for America* (New York: McGraw-Hill, 1977), 519. Hazel Steibeling is largely credited with guiding the discussion, but there is, apparently, no written record of her contribution. See Harper, "Contributions"; Dupont, "Reflections" and Susan Welsh, "A Brief History of Food Guides in the United States," *Nutrition Today*, December 1992.

36. Cummings, *The American and His Food*, 233. Also see Michael Worboys, "The Discovery of Colonial Malnutrition between the Wars," in David Arnold, *Imperial Medicine and Indigenous Societies* (Manchester: Manchester University Press, 1988).

37. Marion Nestle and Donna V. Porter, "Evolution of Federal Dietary Guidance Policy: From Food Adequacy to Chronic Disease Prevention," *Caduceus* (Summer 1990): 47.

38. "Experts Map Plan of Diet Education for Our Defense," *New York Times*, January 22, 1941.

39. Nestle and Porter, "Evolution," 43.

40. Senate Hearings, 1944, p. 91.

41. Office of War Information, Department of Agriculture, Press Release, April 1, 1943, USDA History Collection, 1.2/20, Types of Diets 1942–46, IV A 2a(2), Special Collections, National Agricultural Library.

42. Roberts maintained that the RDAs were meant to be "goals," not absolute amounts of nutrients required by each individual. They were meant to be estimates of what was needed for good health, not minimums. The fact that the RDAs were taken as requirements rather than goals reflects the problem with popularizing scientific research. The subtleties are lost. See ch. 7 on Mollie Orshansky.

43. M.F.K. Fisher, *How to Cook a Wolf* (San Francisco: North Point Press, 1988), 4–6; and Susan Ware, ed., *Notable American Women: A Biographical Dictionary, Completing the Twentieth Century* (Cambridge, Mass.: Belknap Press of Harvard University Press, 2004), 41–43.

44. For the shift to the WFA, see "Child Nutrition Programs: Issues for the 101st Congress," *School Food Service Research Review* 13, no. 1 (1989): 28. On the Type A, B, and C meals, see Gunderson, "The National School Lunch Program."

45. House Hearings, 1945, p. 216. In all cases, the only milk subsidized was whole milk.

46. See Rima Apple, *Vitamania: Vitamins in American Culture* (New Brunswick, N.J.: Rutgers University Press, 1996), and L. S. Sims, *The Politics of Fat: Food and Nutrition Policy in America* (Amonk, N.Y.: M. E. Sharpe, 1998).

47. On Mead, see Dolores Janiewski and Lois W. Banner, *Reading Benedict/ Reading Mead: Feminism, Race, and Imperial Vision* (Baltimore: Johns Hopkins University Press, 2004); Phyllis Gosskurth, *Margaret Mead* (London: Penguin Press, 1988); and Mary Catherine Bateson, *With a Daughter's Eye: A Memoir of Margaret Mead and Gregory Bateson* (New York: W. Morrow, 1984).

48. Margaret Mead, "The Relationship between Food Habits and Problems of Wartime Emergency Feeding," May 1942, typescript, Martha May Eliot Papers, Box 17, Folder 236."

49. Druzilla C. Kent, "Nutrition Education in the School Program," *School Life* 26 (1941); 14. Reprint by Federal Security Agency. Also see United States Department of Agriculture, " School Lunches in Country and City," Farmers' Bulletin No. 1899, 1942, p. 21.

50. Amy Bentley, *Eating for Victory: Food Rationing and the Politics of Domesticity* (Urbana: University of Illinois Press, 1998), 25.

51. Mead, "The Relationship between Food Habits."

52. Ibid. Emphasis in the original.

53. "The School Lunch—A Symposium," JHE, November 1937, p. 613.

54. House Hearings, 1945, p. 68.

55. *CIO News*, June 11, 1945.

56. "The School Lunch—A Symposium," 614.

57. Mead, "The Relationship between Food Habits."

58. House Hearings, 1945, p. 139.

59. Public as well as private and parochial schools were eligible. Local non-profit organizations could also sponsor lunch programs.

60. "The War Food Administration will help your community start a School Lunch Program," leaflet/ad reprinted in *Ladies Home Journal*, October 1944.

CHAPTER 4. A NATIONAL SCHOOL LUNCH PROGRAM

1. "Has Your Child Half a Hog's Chance?" *Ladies Home Journal*, October 1944.

2. P.L. 396 passed June 4, 1946. Gordon W. Gunderson, "The National School Lunch Program: Background and Development," Food and Nutrition Service, 63, U.S. Department of Agriculture, 1971, pp. 14–15.

3. "Truman Approves School Lunch Bill," *New York Times* (hereafter, NYT), June 5, 1946.

4. Richard E. Neustadt, "Extending the Horizons of Democratic Liberalism," in J. Joseph Huthmacher, *The Truman Years: The Reconstruction of Postwar America* (Hinsdale, Ill.: Dryden Press, 1972), 81.

5. Alan Brinkley, *The End of Reform: New Deal Liberalism in Recession and War* (New York: Alfred A. Knopf, 1995), 168.

6. Barton J. Bernstein, "The Limitations of the Liberal Vision," in ibid., 108–9.

7. Martha May Eliot, speech, October 1940, Martha May Eliot Papers, Box 17, Folder 236, Schlessinger Library.

8. "Material for Dr. Eliot's Committee, "School Lunch Phase," n.d. (1940), Martha May Eliot Papers, Box 17, Folder 237.

9. Faith Williams to H. L. Wilson, December 18, 1940, Martha May Eliot Papers, Box 17, Folder 237.

10. Federal Security Agency, "Proceedings of the National Nutrition Conference for Defense," May 26–28, 1941 (Washington, D.C.: United States Government Printing Office, 1942), 98.

11. H. M. Southworth and M. I. Klayman, "The School Lunch Program and Agricultural Surplus Disposal" (Washington, D.C.: Bureau of Agricultural Economics, USDA, 1941), iii.

12. See Robyn Muncy, *Creating a Female Dominion in American Reform, 1890–1935* (New York: Oxford University Press, 1991).

13. United States Congress, Senate Subcommittee on Agriculture and Forestry, *Hearings on Bills to Assist the States to Establish and Maintain School-Lunch Programs*, May 2–5, 1944, 78th Cong. 2nd Sess. (hereafter Senate Hearings, 1944), 52.

14. Ibid., 93.

15. United States Congress, House Committee on Agriculture, *Hearings on the School Lunch Program*, 79th Cong., 1st Sess., March 23–May 24, 1945 (hereafter, House Hearings, 1945), 88.

16. Senate Hearings, 1944, p. 49.

17. Pete Alcock, Howard Glennerster, Ann Oakley, and Adrian Sinfield, eds., *Welfare and Wellbeing: Richard Titmuss's Contribution to Social Policy* (Bristol: Policy Press, 2001), 83–84; and James Vernon, "The Ethnics of Hunger and the Assembly of Society: The Techno-Politics of the School Meal in Modern Britain," *American Historical Review* 110, no. 3 (June 2005): 693–725.

18. Sidney Baldwin, *Poverty and Politics: The Rise and Decline of the Farm Security Administration* (Chapel Hill: University of North Carolina Press, 1968), 236; and Walter W. Wilcox, *The Farmer in the Second World War* (Ames: Iowa State College Press, 1947), 364–67. The largest growth was 1933–39, when the number of employees went from 21,023 to 59,113.

19. *Congressional Record: 79th Cong., 2d Sess.*, 92:2, February 19, 1946–March 28, 1946 (hereafter *Congressional Record*), February 26, 1946, p. 1610.

20. Senate Hearings, 1944, p. 36.

21. Ibid., 23. Also see Harvey Levenstein, *Paradox of Plenty: A Social History of Eating in Modern America* (Berkley: University of California Press, 2003), esp. 78.

22. Alonzo L. Hamby, *Liberalism and Its Challengers: From F.D.R. to Bush*, 2nd ed. (New York: Oxford University Press, 1992), 246.

23. Gilbert C. Fite, *Richard B. Russell, Jr., Senator from Georgia* (Chapel Hill: University of North Carolina Press, 1991), 496.

24. Hamby, *Liberalism and its Challengers*, 245.

25. Fite, *Richard Russell*, 187.

26. Thomas A. Becnel, *Senator Allen Ellender of Louisiana: A Biography* (Baton Rouge: Louisiana State University Press, 1996), 142.

27. Allen Ellender to Mr. R. O. Moncla (secretary of the Lafourche Parish school board), March 1, 1947, Allen J. Ellender Archives, Folder 39, Box 624, School Lunch, Ellender Memorial Library, Thibodaux, La.

28. Jerry Voorhis, *Confessions of a Congressman* (Garden City, N.Y.: Doubleday, 1947), 144.

29. Ibid., 339.

30. See Ira Katznelson, "Limiting Liberalism: The Southern Veto in Congress, 1933–1950," *Political Science Quarterly* 108, no. 2 (Summer 1993): 283–306. 286.

31. Paul E. Mertz, *New Deal Policy and Southern Rural Poverty* (Baton Rouge: Louisiana State University Press, 1978), 105.

32. Robert C. Lieberman, *Shifting the Color Line: Race and the American Welfare State* (Cambridge, Mass.: Harvard University Press, 1998), argues that Southern support for the New Deal was "of two minds." Southerners were "wary of expanding federal power, especially in social policy," but at the same time they "desperately needed New Deal largesse" (37).

33. *Congressional Record*, February 26, 1946, p. 1626.

34. *Congressional Record*, February 19, 1946, p. 1465.

35. Ibid., p. 1460.

36. *Congressional Record*, February 26, 1946, p. 1610.

37. Senate Hearings, 1944, p. 29.

38. House Hearings, 1945, p. 29. Cooley was in the Senate from 1934 to 1967. He chaired the Agriculture Committee in the 81st, 82nd, and 84th to 89th Congresses.

39. *Congressional Record*, February 19, 1946, p. 1451.

40. Ibid., p. 1467. Gwynne served in the House from 1935 to 1949.

41. Ibid.

42. Ibid., p. 1460.

43. House Hearings, 1945, p. 252; "School Luncheons Restored by House," NYT, June 2, 1944; "School Lunch Cost Assailed in House," NYT, February 20, 1946; and "House Votes Fund for School Meals," NYT, February 22, 1946.

44. "School Lunch Cost Assailed in House," NYT, February 20, 1941.

45. *Congressional Record*, February 26, 1946, p. 1611.

46. *Congressional Record*, February 19, 1946, p. 1454.

47. This strategy, later dubbed "the Powell Amendment," attracted considerable controversy both among liberals generally and within the civil rights movement. Charles V. Hamilton, *Adam Clayton Powell, Jr.: The Political Biography of an American Dilemma* (New York: Atheneum, 1991), 225–27. Three years after the school lunch debate, the NAACP adopted an official policy of opposing federal financial support for segregated facilities. This strategy was opposed by groups, including the National Council of Negro Women, particularly when it came to public housing legislation. According to Hamilton, some groups "knew that if an anti-segregation amendment were attached . . . this would lose the political support of Southerners who wanted the money but not the desegregation, as well as conservatives who hated any federal support for social programs." They feared an anti-segregation amendment would thus kill the legislation entirely. Hamilton suggests that Powell first introduced his amendment in 1950 to a federal aid to education bill. He says Powell's amendment simply stipulated that federal funds "should be distributed without discrimination" and argues that this "did not satisfy the NAACP at all." The problem was that Powell's language "could be entirely compatible *with segregated* facilities." Hamilton concludes that Powell was initially careless in the language he used to draft the amendment, not realizing the extent to which southern legislators claimed that segregation did not consti-

tute discrimination. The NAACP sent Powell a letter noting that the amendment, as written, "did not cover racial segregation" and offered more effective language. Hamilton says, "Clearly, Powell was caught short in his attentiveness to the distinction between segregation and discrimination." After that, Powell and the NAACP worked together. It is clear from the school lunch debate that Powell had begun to experiment with his amendment before 1950.

48. *Congressional Record*, February 20, 1946, p. 1493.

49. Ibid., 1494.

50. Ibid., 1496.

51. Ibid., 1506.

52. Ibid., 1496.

53. Ibid., 1495. The case Poage cited was one involving the Dallas *News*.

54. Ibid.

55. Ibid. 1503. Rankin was also notoriously anti-Semitic. To end his speech opposing Powell's amendment he read a statement by the Jewish War Veterans who advocated an anti-discrimination clause in the GI Bill. "This group of Jews," Rankin said, "would deny the benefits of the GI Bill to every white veteran south of the Ohio River. I wonder what would have happened if those brave men from the Southern States had failed to do their duty in this war, and we had depended upon these Jews to do all the fighting."

56. Ibid., 1498.

57. Leiberman, *Shifting the Color Line*, 24.

58. House Hearings 1945, p. 89.

59. Senate Hearings 1944, p. 235.

60. *Congressional Record*, February 19, 1946, p. 1453.

CHAPTER 5. IDEALS AND REALITIES IN THE LUNCHROOM

1. "Food for Thought," *New York Times* (hereafter, NYT), November 19, 1961.

2. The number of schools increased from 54,157 in 1950 to 64,000 in 1962. U.S. Department of Agriculture Production and Marketing Administration, Food Distribution Branch, "Supplement to School Lunch and Food Distribution Programs, Selected Statistics, Fiscal Years 1939–1951," Washington, D.C. March 1952.

3. Estimates based on: "Child Nutrition Programs: Issues for the 101st Congress," *School Food Service Research Review* 13, no 1 (1989): 38. (In 1962 total school enrollment including public and parochial in the U.S. and territories was 43.4 million; United States Congress, Senate Subcommittee on Agriculture and Forestry, *Hearings, National School Lunch Act*, 87th Cong., 2nd Sess., June 19, 1962 (hereafter, Senate Agriculture Subcommittee, 1962), 18. USDA, "Supplement to School Lunch and Food Distribution Programs." United States Congress, House Committee on Education and Labor, *Hearings*, 91st Cong., 1st Sess., March 6, 1969 (hereafter, House Committee on Education and Labor, 1969), 39.

4. On post-war consumer society, see Lizabeth Cohen, *The Consumer's Republic: The Politics of Mass Consumption in Postwar America* (New York: Alfred A. Knopf, 2003).

5. Virgil W. Dean, *An Opportunity Lost: The Truman Administration and the Farm Policy Debate* (Columbia: University of Missouri Press, 2006), 26.

6. "Truman Approves School Lunch Bill," NYT, June 5, 1946.

7. Richard E. Neustadt, "Extending the Horizons of Democratic Liberalism," in J. Joseph Huthmacher, *The Truman Years: The Reconstruction of Postwar America* (Hinsdale, Ill.: Dryden Press, 1972), 81.

8. On the limitations of the Truman years see Barton J. Bernstein, "The Limitations of the Liberal Vision," in ibid., 108–9.

9. See Edward D. Berkowitz and Kim McQuaid, *Creating the Welfare State: The Political Economy of Twentieth Century Reform* (New York: Praeger, 1980), 159; Linda Faye Williams, *The Constraint of Race: Legacies of White Skin Privilege in America* (University Park: Penn. State University Press, 2003), 101; and Ira Katznelson, "Limiting Liberalism: The Southern Veto in Congress, 1933–1950," *Political Science Quarterly* 108, no. 2 (Summer 1993): 283–306.

10. Robert C. Lieberman, *The Color Line: Race and the American Welfare State* (Cambridge, Mass.: Harvard University Press, 1998), 122.

11. Democratic platform text in NYT, July 24, 1952. The school lunch program was part of the party's platform that year.

12. Richard B. Russell to Walter J. Shaffer, April 20, 1949, Richard B. Russell Collection, Series IX B, Box 41, Richard B. Russell Library for Political Research and Studies, University of Georgia Libraries, Athens.

13. "Cut Called Danger to School Lunches," NYT, May 8, 1953; and "Benson Is Opposed on Cut in Subsidy," NYT, April 14, 1953.

14. Carl M. Brauer, "Kennedy, Johnson, and the War on Poverty," *Journal of American History*, 69, no. 1 (June 1982): 98–119, 101. Also, "Child Nutrition Programs: Issues for the 101st Congress," *School Food Service Research Review* (Spring 1989), 51.

15. "Child Nutrition Programs: Issues for the 101st Congress," 27; Senate Agriculture Subcommittee, 1962, p. 18.

16. " U.S. Lunch Plan Scored in Study," NYT, June 19, 1969.

17. "Truman Approves School Lunch Bill," NYT, June 5, 1946.

18. Karl A. Fox, Vernon W. Ruttan, Lawrence W. Witt, eds. *Farming, Farmers, and Markets for Farm Goods: Essays on the Problems and Potentials of American Agriculture*, Supplementary Paper No. 15, Committee for Economic Development, New York, November 1962, p. 130.

19. United States Congress, Senate, Select Committee on Nutrition and Human Needs, 90th Cong., 2nd. Sess. (hereafter Senate Select Committee), Part 11, February 18–20, 1969, p. 3510.

20. USDA, Production and Marketing Administration, Food Distribution Branch, "Supplement to School Lunch and Food Distribution, Selected Fiscal Years, 1939–1951," Wsahington D.C., March 1952.

21. United States Congress, House Committee on Education and Labor, *Hearings on Malnutrition and Federal Food Service Programs*, 90th Cong., 2nd. Sess.,

Part I, May 21–June 3, 1968, (hereafter, House Committe on Education and Labor, 1968) 151.

22. United States Congress, Senate Committee on Agriculture and Forestry, *Hearings, School Lunch and Child Nutrition Programs*, 91st Cong., 2nd Sess., September 29–October 1, 1969 (hereafter, Senate Agritculture Committee, 1969), 185.

23. Senate Agriculture Subcommittee, 1962, p. 11.

24. "Pupils Get Food in 60,000 Schools," NYT, August 9, 1959.

25. See, e.g., memo from Orville Freeman to President Johnson, December 27, 1966, WHCF EX AG7, Box 10, Folder AG7 11/13 66-. LBJ Library. In this case, the growers asked that the government "buy heavily for the School Lunch Program." Freeman considered this "a proper request" within his mission under Section 32.

26. William L. Lanier to Richard B. Russell, March 10, 1966, and Howard B. Davis to Richard B. Russell, March 28, 1966, Richard Russell Collection, Series IX B, Box 10, Richard B. Russell Library for Political Research and Studies, University of Georgia Libraries, Athens.

27. J. D. Ratcliff, "They're Playing Politics with Our Children's Health," *McCalls Magazine*, September 1950. (From National Agricultural Library, USDA History Collection, Box 1.3/15, "Free Distribution to Low Income Groups (SLP)," 1949–53.)

28. Senate Select Committee, Part 11, 3504–5.

29. Ibid., Part 11, 3600. Also see Committee on School Lunch Participation, *Their Daily Bread* (Atlanta, Ga.: McNelley-Rudd, 1968), 79.

30. See Robyn Muncy, *Creating a Female Dominion in American Reform, 1890–1935* (New York: Oxford University Press, 1991).

31. James T. Bonnen, "The Crisis in the Traditional Roles of Agricultural Institutions," in Fox et al., eds., *Farming, Farmers, and Markets*.

32. Senate Select Committee, Part 1, 154–55.

33. See Muncy, *Creating a Female Dominion*, 155. Also, Barbara Miller Solomon, *In the Company of Educated Women: A History of Women and Higher Education in America* (New Haven: Yale University Press: 1985).

34. Senate Select Committee, Part 1, p. 21.

35. Ibid., Part 1, p. 176. Mead's example was the fact that no public objections were raised when an orange juice substitute with no nutritional value was introduced on the market.

36. Patricia L. Fitzgerald, "Decades of Dedication: The Formative Fifties," *School Foodservice and Nutrition*, December 1995, p. 36.

37. Ibid., 40.

38. Ibid.; and Don Paarlberg, *American Farm Policy: A Case Study of Centralized Decision Making* (New York: John Wiley, 1964), 277.

39. Fox et al., eds., *Farming, Farmers, and Markets*, 130.

40. United States Congress, Senate Committee on Agriculture and Forestry, *Hearings, School Milk and Breakfast Programs*, 89th Cong., 2nd Sess., June 21, 1966, (hereafter, Senate Agriculture Committee, 1966), 16.

41. Jean Mayer, Final Report, White House Conference on Food, Nutrition, and Health, 1969, p. 236; and Peter H. Rossi, *Feeding the Poor: Assessing Federal Food Aid* (Washington, D.C.: AEI Press, 1998), 79.

42. Senate Select Committee, Part 5A, 1770.

43. Ibid., Part 5A, 1771.

44. United States Congress, House Subcommittee on the District of Columbia, *Hearings, to amend the District of Columbia Public School Food Services Act*, 90th Cong., 2nd Sess., July 19, 1968 (hereafter, House Subcommittee on D.C.), 8.

45. Ibid., 30.

46. House Committee on Education and Labor, 1968, p. 352.

47. Senate Agriculture Committee, 1969, p. 185.

48. Senate Agriculture Subcommittee, 1962, p. 18. Senate, Agriculture Committee, 1969, p. 78–79; United States Congress, House Select Committee on Education, Committee on Education and Labor, *Hearings, National School Lunch Act*, 89th Cong., 2nd Sess., July 21, 1966 (hereafter, House Select Committee, 1966), 6. Where, for example, in 1949 the federal contribution to the program totaled about 30% of the food expenses, by 1960 only 22% of the program expenses came from federal sources.

49. Committee on School Lunch Participation, *Their Daily Bread*, chart on pages 38–39.

50. "Fall in Surpluses Hits Pupil Lunches," NYT, May 16, 1952. Also Senate Agriculture Committee, 1969, p. 223. Also see testimony of Howard Davis, Senate Agriculture Subcommittee, 1962, p. 11–12; and Senate Agriculture Committee, 1966, 14–16. As late as 1980 children's fees accounted for 32% of the total NSLP budget, while state and local contributions only accounted for 20%. Paarlberg, *Farm and Food Policy*, 104.

51. Between 1947 and 1960 the number of children served increased from 7 to 14 million, and the number of schools participating increased from 34,000 to 64,000. Accurate statistics on the National School Lunch Program are difficult to compile. Districts and states had widely differing measures of participation rates and different financial structures, so the reported numbers often are not comparable. I have used a variety of sources to estimate trends and approximate rates of participation and funding. Paarlberg, *American Farm Policy*, 278; Senate Agriculture Subcommittee, 1962, 18; Senate Agriculture Committee, 1966, p. 12; House Select Committee, 1966, 6; and Mayer, Final Report, White House Conference, 260–63.

52. The Georgia Attorney General ruled in 1932 that state funds could not be used to support school lunches. See Josephine Martin to William F. Griffeth, March 1, 1967, Richard Russell Collection, Series IX B Box 10, Richard B. Russell Library for Political Research and Studies, University of Georgia Libraries, Athens. Also see Committee on School Lunch Participation, *Their Daily Bread*, 38–39.

53. Senate Agriculture Committee, 1966, pp. 13–14.

54. Senate Agriculture Subcommittee, 1962, p. 25. The report noted that some areas ran lunch programs outside the federal program. Cleveland, for example, ran its own lunch program in 34 out of its 130 elementary schools.

55. Gilbert Y. Steiner, *The Children's Cause* (Washington, D.C.: Brookings Institution, 1976), 181.

56. Committee on School Lunch Participation, *Their Daily Bread*, 42, also 79.

57. Senate Select Committee, Part 11, p. 3512.

58. "School Lunches Aid 14 Million Children," NYT, December 27, 1961.

59. House Select Committee, 1966, p. 6. The report estimated that at least nine million children nationwide attended schools with no food service at all.

60. Ibid.

61. Committee on School Lunch Participation, *Their Daily Bread*, 114.

62. *Ibid.*, 117.

CHAPTER 6. NO FREE LUNCH

1. Department of Agriculture Administrative History, ch. 4, "Growing Nations and a World without Hunger," p. 3, LBJ Library. Most notable were school lunch programs in Japan.

2. United States Congress, Senate Select Committee on Nutrition and Human Needs, 90th Cong., 1st and 2nd Sess., 1968–69 (hereafter Senate Select Committee), Part 1, "Problems and Prospects," December 17–19, 1968, p. 161.

3. Carl Brauer, "Kennedy, Johnson, and the War on Poverty," *Journal of American History* 69, no. 1 (January 1982): 98–119, 101; and Nicholas Leamann, *The Promised Land: The Great Black Migration and How It Changed America* (New York: Vintage Books, 1991).

4. See, e.g., Peter K. Eisinger, *Toward an End to Hunger in America* (Washington, D.C.: Brookings Institution Press, 1998), 12.

5. Orville Freeman, "Malthus, Marx, and the North American Bread Basket," in Vernon W. Ruttan, Arlen D. Waldo, and James P. Houck, eds., *Agricultural Policy in an Affluent Society: An Introduction to a Current Issue of Public Policy* (New York: Norton, 1969), 282. The article originally appeared in the July 1967 issue of *Foreign Affairs*.

6. See, e.g., Earl O. Heady, "Consumer Gains and Nutrition under Agriculture Policy of the United States," in Donald S. McLaren, ed., *Nutrition in the Community: A Critical Look at Nutrition Policy, Planning, and Programmes*, 2nd ed. (Chichester, U.K.: John Wiley and Sons, 1983), 208.

7. Orville L. Freeman, "Malthus, Marx, and the North American Breadbasket," 291.

8. Memorandum for the President from Richard W. Reuter, July 27, 1965, EX HE 1–1, HE2, Food and Nutrition, White House Central Files, Box 13, LBJ Library.

9. United States Congress, House Committee on Education and Labor, *Hearings on Malnutrition and Federal Food Service Programs*, 90th Cong., 2nd Sess., May 21–June 3, 1968 (hereafter, House Committee on Education and Labor, 1968), 212.

10. "Severe Hunger Found in Mississippi," *New York Times* (hereafter, NYT), June 17, 1967.

11. "Physician Tells of Malnutrition among Carolina Negro Children," NYT, November 10, 1967.

12. United States Congress, Senate Subcommittee on Employment, Manpower, and Poverty, Committee on Labor and Public Welfare, *Hearings, to Establish a Select Committee on Nutrition and Human Needs*, 90th Cong., 2nd Sess., May 23–June 13, 1968 (hereafter, Senate Employment Subcommittee), 109.

13. Senate Select Committee, Part 11, July 9–11, 1969, p. 3571.

14. Alvin L. Schorr, note to Mr. Califano and attachment, "Effects of Malnutrition on Physical and Mental Growth," November 30, 1967, p. 3, 1968 Interagency Task Force on Nutrition and Adequate Diets, LBJ Library.

15. Michael Harrington, *The Other America: Poverty in the United States* (New York: Macmillan, 1962), and Dwight MacDonald, "Our Invisible Poor," *The New Yorker* 38/48 (January 19, 1963), 82–132.

16. On the War on Poverty, see James T. Patterson, *Grand Expectations: The United States, 1945–1974* (New York: Oxford University Press, 1996); John Morton Blum, *Years of Discord: American Politics and Society, 1961–1974* (New York: W. W. Norton, 1991); and William H. Chafe, *The Unfinished Journey: America since World War II* (New York: Oxford University Press, 1986).

17. Dan Olson, "Remembering Orville Freeman," National Public Radio, February 21, 2003, http://news.minnesota.publicradio.org/features/2003/02/01.

18. See James N. Giglio, "New Frontier Agricultural Policy: The Commodity Side, 1961–1963," *Agricultural History* 61 no. 3 (Summer 1987): 53–70.

19. United States Congress, Senate Committee on Agriculture and Forestry, *Hearings, School Milk and Breakfast Programs*, 89th Cong., 2nd Sess., June 21, 1966 (hereafter, Senate Agriculture Committee, 1966), 17.

20. "Legislation with Civil Rights Implications," 11; Legislative Proposals, December 8, 1965, Office Files of Harry McPherson, Civil Rights—1965, Box 21, LBJ Library.

21. Senate Hearings, Agriculture Committee, 1966, p. 17.

22. "Legislation with Civil Rights Implications," 11, Legislative Proposals, December 8, 1965, Office Files of Harry McPherson. This report admitted, "There appears to exist an unfortunate correlation between the presence of large numbers of abysmally low income families and grossly inadequate statewide welfare services. Thus, in the States of the South in which Negro poverty is most concentrated, the kinds of programs available for assistance are much more restricted than in other States" (10).

23. Memorandum for Orville Freedman from Harry C. McPherson, Jr., September 28, 1965, Box 21, Office Files of Harry McPherson.

24. House Committee on Education and Labor, 1968, p. 311.

25. The school lunch funds came from Title 1 of the 1965 Elementary and Secondary School Act.

26. Memorandum, Phillip Hughes to Mr. Califano, December 10, 1965, WHCF EX LE/HE, 1–1, Box 59, LBJ Library.

27. Legislative Proposals, December 8, 1965, V. Legislation with Civil Rights Implications, Box 21, Office Files of Harry McPherson.

28. Senate Select Committee, Part 1, December 17–19, 1968, p. 48. Also see "Legislation with Civil Rights Implications," Legislative Proposals, December 8, 1965, p. 10, Office Files of Harry McPherson. This memo proposed that the school lunch and school milk programs "be removed to the Welfare Administration."

29. Maurice MacDonald, *Food Stamps and Income Maintenance* (New York: Academic Press, 1977); Leamann, *Promised Land*; and Brauer, "Kennedy, Johnson and the War on Poverty."

30. Committee on School Lunch Participation, *Their Daily Bread* (Atlanta, Ga.: McNelley-Rudd, 1968), 89–91.

31. Senate Agriculture Committee, 1966, p. 23.

32. Ibid., 1966, p. 10.

33. John A. Schnittker to Joseph Califano, Jr., November 19, 1965, LBJ Library, WHCF EX LE/HE 1–1, Box 59. Also see memo from Phillip Hughes to Califano, "Child Feeding Programs," December 10, 1965. Hughes recommends leaving school lunches in the Department of Agriculture.

34. Senate Agriculture Committee, 1966, p. 11.

35. United States Congress, Senate Subcommittee on Agriculture and Forestry, *Hearings, National School Lunch Act*, 87th Cong., 2nd Sess., June 19, 1962 (hereafter, Senate Agriculture Committee, 1962), 12. While the program amendments directly addressed domestic poverty, much of the senators' attention went to a provision that would extend the program to American Samoa. Puerto Rico, Guam, and the Virgin Islands were already covered, but American Samoa had been left out of the original legislation. Some senators opposed sending food aid to Puerto Rico. North Carolina's Everett Jordan said that "they cannot even speak English." He thought that "if they are going to receive aid from the United States, they ought to be able to speak English and say, 'I would like to have a little bread,' instead of calling it something other than bread" (31).

36. Senate Agriculture Committee, 1966, p. 17.

37. Ibid., 1966, p. 18–19.

38. Administrative History, Department of Agriculture, vol. 1, ch. 8, p. 61, LBJ Library.

39. Memo from John A. Schnittker to Harry McPherson, November 16, 1966, Papers of Harry McPherson, Box 50, Folder: Joe Califano, LBJ Library.

40. Senate Agriculture Subcommittee, 1962, p. 23; memorandum to the President from Orville Freeman, November 5, 1965. Freeman admits that "many schools, especially older ones in many urban centers cannot meet the needs for free lunches, when up to 50 percent of the pupils may be unable to pay their share." White House Central Files, EX AG 7, AG 7–2, School Lunch Program, Box 10, LBJ Library.

41. "Position of the American School Food Service Association on the Proposed Repeal of Existing Child Nutrition Legislation," n.d. (probably October 4, 1975), Washington, D.C., Office, Box 285, Children—Nutrition, 1975–76, National Council of Jewish Women Papers, Library of Congress.

42. House Subcommittee on D.C., p. 8. Washington, D.C., school cafeteria wages were below the national norm and below minimum wage (31).

43. Committee on School Lunch Participation, *Their Daily Bread*, 49.

44. Ibid., 449–50.

45. Ibid.

46. See, e.g., Robert C. Lieberman, *Shifting the Color Line: Race and the American Welfare State* (Cambridge, Mass.: Havard University Press, 1998), 161 and 167–68; and Sheldon Danziger, "Welfare Reform Policy From Nixon to Clinton: What Role for Social Science?" paper prepared for conference, "The Social Sciences and Policy Making," Institute for Social Research, University of Michigan, March 13–14, 1998.

47. See Gordon W. Gunderson, "The National School Lunch Program Background and Development," Food and Nutrition Service, 63, U.S. Department of Agriculture, 1971.

48. Senate Employment Subcommittee, 1968, p. 70.

49. See Brauer, "Kennedy, Johnson"; Lieberman, *Shifting the Color Line*; Alex Waddan, *The Politics of Social Welfare: The Collapse of the Centre and the Rise of the Right* (Cheltenham, U.K.: Edward Elgar, 1977). He argues that the War on Poverty was not, in fact, a war on inequality (55).

50. Senate Select Committee, Part 4, February 18–20, 1969, p. 1246.

51. Senate Employment Subcommittee, 1968, p. 213.

52. United States Congress, House Select Subcommittee on Education, Committee on Education and Labor, *Hearings to Amend the National School Lunch Act*, 89th Cong., 2nd Sess., July 28, 1968 (hereafter, House Subcommittee on Education, 1968), 8.

53. Senate Employment Subcommittee, 1968, p. 213.

54. United States Congress, House Subcommittee on the District of Columbia, *Hearings to Amend the District of Columbia Public School Food Service Act*, 90th Cong., 2nd Sess., July 19, 1968 (hereafter, House Subcommittee on D.C.), 8.

55. Senate Select Committee, Part 11, July 9–11, 1969, p. 3413. See also Lee G. Burchinal and Hilda Schiff, "Rural Poverty," in Louis A. Ferman, Joyce L. Kornbluh, Alan Harber, eds., *Poverty in America: A Book of Readings* (Ann Arbor: University of Michigan Press, 1965), 104. "To some extent, poverty is a relative concept, reflecting societal standards of living. Shades of gray obscure any fine line between being 'really poor,' being 'deprived,' or simply being less well off than most. Still, there are absolute limits below which it is difficult or impossible to maintain or foster human health, growth, and dignity."

56. Senate Select Committee, Part 5A, March 10, 11, 1969, pp. 1538–39.

57. United States Congess, Senate Committee on Agriculture and Forestry, *Hearings, School Lunch and Child Nutrition Programs*, 90th Cong., 2nd Sess., September 29–October 1, 1969 (hereafter, Senate Agriculture Committee, 1969), 51–55.

58. Richard Russell to A. J. Shaw (Deputy Office of the County Council, Modesto, Calif.) November 3, 1969, Richard Russell Papers, Series IX:B, Box 7, Folder: School Lunch Program January 1969–November 1969, Richard Russell Library, Athens, Georgia.

59. Senate Select Committee, Part 5A, March 10, 11, 1969, pp. 1538–39.

60. Ibid., Part 5B, March 11, 1969, p. 2011.

61. United States Congress, Senate Committee on Agriculture and Forestry, *Hearings on the School Lunch Program*, 92nd Cong., 1st Sess., September 16, 1971 (hereafter, Senate Agriculture Committee, 1971), 2.

62. Committee on School Lunch Participation, *Their Daily Bread*, 24. Also see United States Congress, House Committee on Education and Labor, *Hearings*, 91st Cong., 1st Sess. March 6, 1969 (hereafter, House Committee on Education and Labor, 1969), 100; and Senate Select Committee, Part 11, July 9–11, 1969, p. 3431. Some principals took into consideration whether the child could go home for lunch or could bring "a suitable lunch from home." Ibid., 3413.

63. See Brauer, "Kennedy, Johnson"; Leamann, *Promised Land*; and Wadden, *Politics of Social Welfare*.

64. "Many in Appalachia Hungry Despite U.S. Aid," NYT, June 18, 1971.

65. Senate Select Committee, Part 11, July 9–11, 1969, p. 3463.

66. United States Congress House Select Committee on Education, Committee on Education and Labor, *Hearings, National School Lunch Act*, 89th Cong., 2nd Sess., July 21, 1966 (hereafter, House Select Committee, 1966), 28.

67. See Meg Jacobs, *Pocketbook Politics: Economic Citizenship in Twentieth Century America* (Princeton: Princeton University Press, 2005).

68. Sanford F. Schram, *Words of Welfare: The Poverty of Social Science and the Social Science of Poverty* (Minneapolis: University of Minnesota Press, 1995). The 1955 Agriculture Department study found that families at every income level spent about one-third of their incomes on food. According to one account, Orshansky intended to measure family need, but her figures came to be used to measure destitution instead. Still, her figures linked poverty to income and the cost of food. The later switch to the consumer-price index unlinked poverty from food and established a line that no longer referred to income and nutrition at all. See ibid. Also see Gordon F. Bloom, "Distribution of Food," in Jean Mayer, ed., *U.S. Nutrition Policies in the Seventies* (San Francisco: W. H. Freeman, 1973), 128; Michael Morris and John B. Williamson, *Poverty and Public Policy: An Analysis of Federal Intervention Efforts* (New York: Greenwood Press, 1984), 14; S. M. Miller and Pamela Roby, "Poverty: Changing Social Stratification," in Daniel Patrick Moynihan, ed., *On Understanding Poverty: Perspectives from the Social Sciences* (New York: Basic Books, 1969), 77; and John Cassidy, "Relatively Deprived: How Poor Is Poor?," *The New Yorker*, April 3, 2006.

69. Mollie Orshansky, "Counting the Poor: Another Look at the Poverty Profile," in Ferman et al., eds., *Poverty in America*, 45. Also see Orshansky, "The Shape of Poverty in 1966," Social Science Research, March 1968. She told the Senate Select Committee that her formula was "a far from generous measure . . . it is a minimum for a household." Senate Select Committee, Part 2, January 8–10, 1969, p. 639. Thanks to Jan Rosenberg for first introducing me to Mollie Orshansky.

70. Harrington, *The Other America*, 183. The government began to use the Consumer Price Index rather than the actual cost of food. This, according to Schram, meant that "the food-income relation which was the basis for the original poverty measure was no longer the current rationale." Schram, *Words of Welfare*, 207, nn. 22 and 81.

71. Shram, *Words of Welfare*, 78–81 and 208, n. 35. According to Shram, Orshansky intended her formula to be an "overall research tool, not as a means for determining eligibility for anti-poverty programs." See 206, n. 19. Arnold E.

Schaefer, Chief Nutrition Program, Health Services and Mental Health Administration, Public Health Service, testified in 1969 that the "O'Shanky Index" was adopted "primarily . . . due to our urgent need to make a quick screen." See House Hearings, Education Committee, 26.

72. Wadden argues that liberals aimed to cure poverty by integrating the poor into the economic mainstream and that they preferred services over income transfers. Thus, they needed some way to figure out who needed the services. Hence, a poverty line. *The Politics of Social Welfare*, 57–60.

73. Interagency Task Force on Nutrition and Adequate Diets, 1968, LBJ Library. This report noted, "Many local communities have been unwilling or financially unable to accept the local costs associated with the operation of a food stamp program." The task force recommended that the law be amended to allow federal funding of local costs "where extraordinary actions are necessary to start or to continue a program," 2.

74. Committee on School Lunch Participation, *Their Daily Bread*, 35.

75. Ibid., 33.

76. House Committee on Education and Labor, 1969, p. 100.

77. Senate Select Committee, Part 11, July 9–11, 1969, p. 3413.

78. House Subcommittee on D.C., p. 33.

79. Senate Select Committee, Part 1, December 17–19, 1968, p. 157.

80. John Perryman, "School Lunch Programs," in Mayer, *U.S. Nutrition Policies in the Seventies*, 217–18.

81. Daniel Patrick Moynihan, "Professors and the Poor," in Moynihan, ed, *On Understanding Poverty*, 22; David Zarefsky, *President Johnson's War on Poverty: Rhetoric and History* (n.p.: University of Alabama Press, 1986), 41; and Waddan, *Politics of Social Welfare*.

82. Senate Select Committee, Part 1, December 17–19, 1968, p. 25.

83. House Subcommittee on Education, 1968, p. 186.

84. Historian Richard J. Jensen observed that while the Democrats tried to extend New Deal type social measures, they were unable to do so because of "the strength of the conservative coalition consisting of the great majority of Republican congressmen in alliance with most of the Southern Democrats. . . . this coalition depended upon modern, middle-class families, who were opposed to taxes, and hence spending, except for national defense expenditures." See his *Grass Roots Politics: Parties, Issues, and Voters, 1854–1938* (Westport, Conn.: Greenwood Press, 1983), 14.

85. (Mrs.) Helen A. Davis to the President, March 25, 1966, WHCF Gen AG 7–2, Box 11, LBJ Library (emphasis in the original).

86. Vella (Mrs. Olin) Bellinger to the President, WHCF Gen AG 7–2, Box 11, LBJ Library.

87. Senate Select Committee, Part 11, p. 3413.

88. C. L. Mooney to the President, WHCF Gen AG 7–2, Box 11, LBJ Library.

89. Committee on School Lunch Participation, *Their Daily Bread*, 46.

90. Ibid. Also see Senate Employment Subcommittee, p. 112. In one Texas district, children had to carry the trays, wipe tables, and wash dishes.

91. (Miss) Genevieve Olkiewicz to the President, March 14, 1966, WHCF Gen AG 7–2, Box 11, LBJ Library.

92. "Child Nutrition Programs: Issues for the 101st Congress," *School Food Service Research Review*, Spring 1989, p. 34.

93. House Select Committee, 1966, p. 23. The American Parents Committee resurfaced during this debate. See (Mrs.) Barbara D. McGarry to the President, January 18, 1966, WHCF, Gen AG 7–2, Box 11, LBJ Library.

94. House Select Education Committee, 1966, p. 14.

95. Ibid., p. 15.

96. Ibid., p. 14.

97. See John Burnett, "The Rise and Decline of School Meals in Britain, 1860–1900," in John Burnett and Derek J. Oddy, eds., *The Origins and Development of Food Policy* in Europe (London: Leicester University Press, 1994). Burnett suggests that "the issue of whether certain children attending school should be fed at public expense has a strong moral and political overtone and has been hotly, even passionately debated . . . because it raises fundamental questions about the responsibility of the state as against that of parents" (56).

98. C. L. Mooney to the President (signed by five board members), WHCF Gen AG 7–2, Box 11, LBJ Library.

99. Memo, Thomas R. Hughes to Henry Wilson, February 17, 1966, WHCF EX LE/HE 1–1, Box 59, LBJ Library.

CHAPTER 7. A RIGHT TO LUNCH

1. Kenneth Schlossberg, "Nutrition and Government Policy in the United States," in Beverley Winikoff, ed., *Nutrition and National Policy* (Cambridge: MIT Press, 1978), 329.

2. United States Congress, Senate Subcommittee on Employment, Manpower, and Poverty, Committee on Labor and Public Welfare, *Hunger in America: Chronology and Selected Background Materials*, 90th Cong., 2nd Sess., October 1968 (hereafter, Senate Subcommittee on Employment).

3. United States Congress, Senate Select Committee on Nutrition and Human Needs, Senate, 90th and 91st Cong., 1968, (hereafter, Senate Select Committee), Part 9, p. 1069.

4. White House Conference on Food, Nutrition, and Health: Final Report (Washington, D.C. 1969), p. 260–62. According to a Department of Agriculture 1968 survey, total enrollment in public and private schools was 50.7 million. About 36.8 million, or 73%, were enrolled in schools participating in the lunch program. Actual participation rate was only 18.9 million, or 37%. Free and reduced price meals were provided for about 12% of the participating children. See Gordon W. Gunderson, "The National School Lunch Program: Background and Development," Food and Nutrition Service, 63, U.S. Department of Agriculture, 1971, p. 26.

5. Committee on School Lunch Participation, *Their Daily Bread: A Study of the National School Lunch Program* (Atlanta: McNelley-Rudd, 1968), 15.

6. Ibid., 16.

7. Ibid., 16.

8. See Judith Segal, *Food for the Hungry: The Reluctant Society* (Baltimore: Johns Hopkins University Press, 1970), 11.

9. The Citizens' Crusade represented a coalition of religious, trade union, and other liberal activist groups. It was supported by the Chicago-based Field Foundation and led by Leslie Dunbar.

10. "Sever Hunger Found in Mississippi," *New York Times* (hereafter, NYT), June 17, 1967.

11. Senate Select Committee, Part 1, December 17–19, 1968, v.

12. Ibid., p. 6.

13. For an overview, see Lawrence M. Friedman, "The Social and Political Context of the War on Poverty: An Overview," and discussions by Nick Kotz and Robert Lapman in Robert H. Haveman, ed., *A Decade of Federal Antipoverty Programs: Achievements, Failures, and Lessons* (New York: Academic Press, 1977).

14. United States Congress, Senate Subcommittee on Employment, Manpower, and Poverty of the Committee on Labor and Public Welfare, *Hearings to Establish a Select Committee on Nutrition and Human Needs*, 90th Cong., 2nd Sess., May 23–June 13, 1968, Senate Hearings, Employment Subcommittee, 1968, p. 12.

15. Ibid. Congressional focus on hunger culminated in George McGovern's formation of a Senate Select Committee at the end of 1968. This committee met in venues across the country for almost ten years. While the Committee reported no legislation to the Senate floor, it nonetheless drew national attention to the problem of hunger and poverty. In 1977 the Committee terminated its hearings after national legislation eliminating the purchase price of food stamps. See Peter K. Eisinger, *Toward an End to Hunger in America* (Washington, D.C.: Brookings Institution Press, 1998), 78–83.

16. See Susan Lynn, "Gender and Progressive Politics: A Bridge to Social Activism of the 1960s," and Harriet Hyman Alonso, "Mayhem and Madness: Women's Peace Advocates during the McCarthy Era," both in Joanne Myerowitz, *Not June Cleaver: Women and Gender in Postwar America, 1945–1960* (Philadelphia: Temple University Press, 1994).

17. On the women's movement in the post–World War II period, see Susan Levine, *Degrees of Equality: The American Association of University Women and the Challenge of Twentieth Century Feminism* (Philadelphia: Temple University Press, 1995). Also, Leila J. Rupp and Verta Taylor, *Survival in the Doldrums: The American Women's Rights Movement 1945 to the 1960s* (Columbus: Ohio State University Press, 1991); Meyerowitz, *Not June Cleaver*; Dorothy Sue Cobble, *The Other Women's Movement: Workplace Justice and Social Rights in Modern America* (Princeton: Princeton University Press, 2004); and Daniel Horowitz, *Betty Friedan and the Making of the Feminine Mystique: The American Left, the Cold War, and Modern Feminism* (Amherst: University of Massachusetts Press, 1998).

18. Committee on School Lunch Participation, *Their Daily Bread*, 3.

19. These organizations worked together in a number of arenas. The NCJW, NCNW, NCCW, and Church Women United, for example, also formed Women in Community Service (WICS), a group that recruited for the Job Corps and

worked on employment training. Michael L. Billett, *Launching the War on Poverty: An Oral History* (New York: Twayne Publishers, 1996), 305.

20. Olya Margolin to Helen Raebeck, April 18, 1966; Jean Fairfax to Mrs. Joseph Willen, July 5, 1966; Jean Fairfax to Mrs. Adele Trobe, March 22, 1967, National Council of Jewish Women (NCJW), Washington, D.C., Office, Box 191, School Lunch Program Correspondence, 1966–67, Library of Congress. Ultimately, the CSLP interviewers also included staff members from the American Friends Service Committee and the Georgia Council on Human Relations as well as volunteers from the member organizations.

21. Jean Fairfax to Howard Davis, March 24, 1966, NCJW Washington, D.C., Office, Box 191, School Lunch Program Correspondence, 1966–67.

22. Committee on School Lunch Participation, *Their Daily Bread* 24.

23. Ibid., 13, 2, 4.

24. Ibid., 38–40.

25. Ibid.. 38–39

26. Ibid., 13–19.

27. Ibid., 26–28, 49–50.

28. Ibid., 53.

29. Ibid., 124.

30. Olya Margolin to Jean Fairfax, April 5, 1968, NCJW Washington, D.C., Office, Box 191, School Lunch Program Correspondence, January–April 1968.

31. Telegram from the Committee on School Lunch Participation to Orville Freeman, April 16, 1968 (signed by all five participating organizations). NCJW, Washington, D.C., Office, Box 191, School Lunch Program Correspondence, January–April, 1968. Also see William H. Chafe, *Civilities and Civil Rights: Greensboro, North Carolina and the Black Struggle for Freedom* (New York: Oxford University Press, 1980).

32. See Ruth Rosen, *The World Split Open: How the Modern Women's Movement Changed America* (New York: Penguin Books, 2000). In ch. 3, Rosen emphasizes the social rifts of the late 1960s.

33. Confidential letter, Jean Fairfax to "Friends" (Olya), April 17, 1968, NCJW, Washington, D.C., Office, Box 191, School Lunch Program Correspondence, January–April 1968. Fairfax later founded Women and Philanthropy and the Association of Black Foundation Executives. During the 1980s, Jean, along with her sister Betty Fairfax, took up philanthropy, concentrating their resources on education for black youth.

34. Senate Employment Subcommittee, 1968, p. 68.

35. Memorandum to Members of the Committee on School Lunch Participation from Jean Fairfax, April 22, 1968, NCJW, Washington, D.C., Office, Box 191, School Lunch Correspondence, January–April 1968; and Jeffrey M. Berry, *Feeding the Hungry: Rulemaking in the Foodstamp Program* (New Brunswick, N.J.: Rutgers University Press, 1984), 48.

36. United States Congress, House Committee on Education and Labor, *Hearings, Malnutrition and Federal Food Service Programs*, 90th Cong., 2nd Sess., May 21–June 3, 1968 (hereafter, House Committee on Education and Labor, 1968) 6.

37. Department of Agriculture Administrative History, vol. 1, ch. 8, p. 110, LBJ Library.

38. Senate Select Committee, Part 11, July 9–11, 1969. Vermont, New Jersey, Pennsylvania, Maine, Illinois, Minnesota, Iowa, and California all undertook tax reviews.

39. Ibid., 3478.

40. Senate Select Committee, Part 10, May 14, June 27, 1969, p. 3283.

41. Legal historian Hendrik Hartog discusses the idea of "rights" and collective claims for a redress of grievances. See his "The Constitution of Aspiration and 'The Rights that Belong to Us All,' " *Journal of American History*, 74, no. 3 (December 1987); 1013–34.

42. Department of Agriculture Administrative History, vol. 1, ch. 3., p. 120. LBJ Library.

43. Press release, United States Department of Agriculture, Washington, D.C., April 16, 1968. NCJW—Washington, D.C. Office, Box 191, School Lunch Program Correspondence, January–April 1968; Memorandum to Josepha A. Califano, Jr., from Orville L. Freeman, February 1, 1968, White House Central Files, EX AG 7, AG7–2, Box 10, LBJ Library.

44. Department of Agriculture Administrative History, vol. 1, ch. 3, p. 104, LBJ Library.

45. "More Physicians Sought in Nation," NYT, March 6, 1968, and "Senate Approves Pilot Lunch Plan," NYT, April 18, 1968.

46. For 1967–68, national enrollment in public and private schools was 50.7 million. An estimated 36.8 million, or 73%, were enrolled in participating schools. "Actual" average participation in the National School Lunch Program was 18.9 million, or 37%, of national enrollment. Gunderson, "The National School Lunch Program," 21.

47. Henry M. Levin, "A Decade of Policy Developments in Improving Education and Training for Low-Income Populations," in Robert H. Haveman, ed., *A Decade of Federal Antipoverty Programs: Achievements, Failures, and Lessons* (New York: Academic Press, 1977), 131.

48. Laurence E. Lynn, Jr., "A Decade of Policy Developments in the Income-Maintenance System," in Haveman, ed., *A Decade of Federal Antipoverty Programs*; and Berry, *Feeding the Hungry*.

49. "Administration Making Significant Gains in Anti-Hunger Drive," NYT, February 5, 1971.

50. Senate Select Committee, Part 11, July 9–11, 1969, p. 3408.

51. United States Congress, Senate Committee on Agriculture and Forestry, *Hearings, School Lunch and Child Nutrition Programs*, 91st Cong., 2nd Sess., September 29–October 1, 1969 (hereafter, Senate Agriculture Committee, 1969), 156.

52. "McGovern Scores Lunch Program," NYT, November 26, 1970.

53. Henry M. Levin, "A Decade of Policy Developments in Improving Education and Training for Low-Income Populations," in Haveman, ed., *A Decade of Federal Antipoverty Programs*.

54. See Robert C. Lieberman, *Shifting the Color Line: Race and the American Welfare State* (Cambridge, Mass.: Harvard University Press, 1998). He argues that the policy conflict of the period centered between "contending institutional visions of welfare. On one side, an administration committed to an expansive vision of racial equality in social citizenship sought to nationalize welfare and

reduce local discretion. . . . On the other side, the parochial forces . . . pulling authority out of Washington and into the racially explosive politics of cities and states" (170).

55. Senate Agriculture Committee, 1969, p. 217. Also, "Action Report," The National Council on Hunger and Malnutrition in the United States. This was a coalition of groups including Ralph Abernathy, Leslie Dunbar, Walter Reuther, and Marian Wright Edleman. NCJW, Washington, D.C., Office, Box 369, National Council on Hunger and Malnutrtion in the United States, 1970.

56. Senate Agriculture Committee, 1969, p. 218.

57. Ibid.

58. See Feliia Kornluh, "A Human Right to Welfare?: Social Protest among Welfare Recipients after World War II," in Linda K. Kerber and Jane Sherron DeHart, eds., *Women's America: Refocusing the Past* (New York: Oxford University Press, 2000).

59. The New School Lunch Program Bill of Rights, pamphlet, Box 395, Folder: School Lunch Program Background Material, undated, NCJW, Washington, D.C. Office, Library of Congress.

60. Senate Select Committee, Part 11, July 9–11, 1969, p. 3410.

61. United States Congress, House Committee on Education and Labor, *Hearings*, 91st Cong., 1st Sess., March 6, 1969, p. 45. Also see Senate Agriculture Committee, 1969, p. 218. Private groups continued to contribute to the programs as well. In Georgia, for example, in 1970, the General Federation of Women's Clubs conducted a fund-raising campaign that brought in over $20,000 "to help Georgia schools provide lunches to the needy." *Food and Nutrition News*, Food and Nutrition Service, U.S. Department of Agriculture, April 1970. In NCJW Washington D.C. Office, Box 385, School Lunch Program Correspondence, July 1970.

62. Perryman, "School Lunch Programs," in Mayer, *U.S. Nutrition Policies*, 219.

63. All from Senate Agriculture Committee, 1969, p. 218.

64. T. W. Marz to Richard B. Russell, October 23, 1969, and Richard B. Russell to A. J. Shaw, November 3, 1969, Richard B. Russell Collection, Series IX B, Box 7, Richard B. Russell Library for Political Research and Studies, University of Georgia Libraries, Athens.

65. Clipping from the Riverside County, Calif., *Press Enterprise*, April 12, 1969, in Senate Select Committee, Part 11, July 9–11, 1969, p. 3615.

66. Ibid., 3409–10.

67. Ibid., 3534–35.

68. "Impact Reports: Everyman's Guide to Federal Programs," vol. 1, no. 1, p. 10, in Senate Select Committee, Part 11, Appendix.

69. Ibid., Part 10, May 14, June 27, 1969, pp. 3159–60.

70. Ibid., Part 11, July 9–11, 1969, pp. 3534–38.

71. Ibid., 3451.

72. Ibid., 3464.

73. House Committee on Education and Labor, 1968, p. 242.

74. The Agriculture Department was slow to force states to comply either with free lunch requirements or food stamp outreach. In the case of food stamps, it took a series of court actions to force the department to hire state coordinators

monitor local programs. See Maurice MacDonald, *Food, Stamps, and Income Maintenance* (New York: Academic Press, 1977), 17.

75. "Panel Finds Half of Poor Still Hungry," NYT, October 7, 1971.

76. Mrs. Norma Goff to President Johnson, March 16, 1966, White House Central Files, GEN AG 7–2, Box 11, 4/1/66–4/4/66, LBJ Library.

77. John Gehn to President Johnson, March 8, 1966, White House Central Files, GEN AG 7–2, Boc 11, 3/23/66–3/21/66, LBJ Library.

78. Jerry Peterson to President Johnson, February 18, 1966, White House Central Files, GEN AG 7–2, Box 11, 3/18/66–3/22/66, LBJ Library. Box 11 contains numerous files filled with letters from school administrators across the country.

79. Richard Russell to A. J. Shaw (Deputy Office of the County Council, Modesto, Calif.) November 3, 1969, Richard Russell Papers, Series IX:B, Box 7, Folder: The School Lunch Program, January 1969–November 1969, Richard B. Russell Collection, Richard B. Russell Library for Political Research and Studies, University of Georgia Libraries, Athens.

80. Senate Subcommittee on Employment, 153.

81. United States Congress, House Subcommittee on Education, Committee on Education and Labor, *Hearings on Bill to Establish Program of Nutrition Education*, 93rd Cong., 1st Sess., March 8 and July 11, 1973, p. 22. .

82. Ibid., 30.

83. Quoted in Gilbert Y. Steiner, *The Children's Cause* (Washington, D.C.: Brookings Institution, 1976), 176, 189.

84. See ibid., 193. Steiner says the ASFSA "marshaled an army of "little old ladies in tennis shoes" to oppose the program's redirection (193).

85. Patricia L. Fitzgerald, "Grassroots and Growing Pains," *School Foodservice and Nutrition*, May 1996.

86. Steiner, *The Children's Cause*, 178. In 1969 the National School Lunch Program as well as the Food Stamp Programs were put under the authority of the newly created Food and Nutrition Service.

87. Committee on School Lunch Participation, *Their Daily Bread*, 126.

88. United States Congress, Senate Committee on Agriculture and Forestry, *Hearings on the School Lunch Program*, 92nd Cong., 1st Sess., September 16, 1971, p. 21.

89. Ibid., 21.

90. On compromises in public policy, see Alice Kessler-Harris, *In Pursuit of Equity: Women, Men, and the Quest for Economic Citizenship in the 20th Century* (Oxford: Oxford University Press, 2001), and Kathryn Kish Sklar, *Florence Kelley and the Nation's Work* (New Haven: Yale University Press, 1995).

CHAPTER 8. LET THEM EAT KETCHUP

1. Patricia L. Fitzgerald, "Decades of Dedication: The Early Years," *School Foodservice and Nutrition* 2 no. 96 (October 1995): 55–60. On the public-private relationship in American social policy, see Jennifer Klein, *For All These Rights: Business, Labor, and the Shaping of America's Public-Private Welfare State* (Princeton: Princeton University Press, 2003).

2. Jean Mayer, "National and International Issues in Food Policy," Lowell Lecture, Harvard University, May 15, 1979, www.dcc.harvard.edu/pubs/lowell/jmayer.html, 3.

3. See Jean Mayer, "White House Conference on Food, Nutrition, and Health," *Journal of the American Dietetic Association* 55 no. 6 (December 1969): 553–56.

4. White House Conference on Food, Nutrition, and Health: Final Report (Washington, D.C., 1969), 237.

5. Ibid., 216.

6. See Robert D. McFadden, "Jean Mayer, 72, Nutritionist Who Led Tufts, Dies," *New York Times* (hereafter, NYT), January 2, 1993.

7. United States Congress, Senate Select Committee on Nutrition and Human Needs, 90th Cong., 2nd Sess., 1968 (hereafter, Senate Select Committee) Part 1, p. 14.

8. Kenneth Schlossberg, "Nutrition and Government Policy in the United States," in Beverley Winikoff, ed., *Nutrition and National Policy* (Cambridge: MIT Press, 1978), 331.

9. "U.S. Increases Pupil Lunch Aid," NYT, October 7, 1971.

10. David Orden, Robert Paarlberg, and Terry Roe, *Policy Reform in American Agriculture: Analysis and Prognosis* (Chicago: University of Chicago Press, 1999), 71. The authors argue that this shift reflected a decline in political clout of rural districts, whose representation fell from 83% of the House of Representatives in 1966 to 60% in 1973. (80).

11. Adam Sheingate, *The Rise of the Agricultural Welfare State: Institutions and Interest Groups in the United States, France, and Japan* (Princeton, N.J.: Princeton University Press, 2001), 148.

12. White House Conference: Final Report, 247. According to one estimate, during the 1970s the USDA increased its expenditures on nutrition from 11% of the budget in 1970 to 40% in 1980. This happened as the department decreased its expenditures on farm subsidies. Adam D. Sheingate, *The Rise of the Agricultural Welfare State*, 148.

13. In 1969 the Department of Agriculture created a new Food and Nutrition Service to oversee these key programs.

14. "President, at Food Parley, Pledges Fight on Hunger," NYT, December 3, 1969.

15. "Food Aid Officials Hampered by Law," NYT, December 26, 1970; "House Orders Nixon Aides Not to Cut Pupil Lunches," NYT, October 19, 1971; and "Pupil Lunch Bill Is Sent to Nixon," NYT, October 21, 1971.

16. See Maurice MacDonald, *Food Stamps, and Income Maintenance* (New York: Academic Press, 1977), 7–12.

17. Sheldon Danziger, "Welfare Reform Policy from Nixon to Clinton: What Role for Social Science?" paper prepared for Conference, "The Social Sciences and Policy Making," Institute for Social Research, University of Michigan, March 13–14, 1998.

18. "Position of the American School Food Service Association on the Proposed Repeal of Existing Child Nutrition Legislation," n.d. (October 4, 1975), Washington, D.C., Office, Box 285, Children—Nutrition, 1975–76, National

Council of Jewish Women (NCJW) Papers, Library of Congress. The NAFSA also feared the cuts would eliminate 120,000 of the 350,000 school food-service jobs in the country.

19. "History of NSLP." Http://USDA.gov; and United States Congress, House General Subcommittee on Education and Labor, *Hearings to Establish a Program of Nutrition Education*, 93rd Cong., 1st Sess., March and July 1973, (hereafter, House Subcommittee on Education, 1973), p. 143.

20. See Gilbert Y. Steiner, *The Children's Cause* (Washington, D.C.: Brookings Institution, 1976), 176.

21. Committee on School Lunch Participation, *Their Daily Bread: A Study of the National School Lunch Program* (Atlanta: McNelley-Rudd, 1968), 120.

22. T. W. Martz to Richard Russell, October 23, 1969, Richard Russell Papers, Series IX:B, Box 7, Folder, School Lunch Program, January 1969–November 1969, Athens, Georgia.

23. Steiner, *The Children's Cause*, 198; Ardith Maney, *Still Hungry after All These Years: Food Assistance Policy from Kennedy to Reagan* (New York: Greenwood Press, 1989), 124; Schlossberg, "Nutrition and Government Policy," 343, and "Child Nutrition Programs: Issues for the 101th Congress," *School Food Service Research Review*, (Spring, 1989) 7.

24. The School Breakfast program began on a small scale in 1966 but served 1.75 million children by 1974. See Steiner, *The Children's Cause*, 204. Also, Center on Budget and Policy Analysis, "Falling Behind: A Report on How Blacks Have Fared under Reagan," *Journal of Black Studies* 17, no. 2 (December 1986): 148–72.

25. Robert C. Leiberman, *Shifting the Color Line: Race and the American Welfare State* (Cambridge, Mass.: Harvard University Press, 1998), 174.

26. House Subcommittee on Education, 1973, 119.

27. "Many Students Decide Not to Buy More Costly School Lunches," NYT, October 21, 1981.

28. "Child Food Funds Backed in Hearing," NYT, September 27, 1982.

29. "Few States Seek to Ease Effects of Cuts for Poor," NYT, January 12, 1982.

30. "Many Students Decide Not to Buy More Costly School Lunches."

31. White House Conference: Final Report, 242, 249.

32. Senate Select Committee, Part 1, p. 114–15.

33. Ibid. The school lunch program's author, Richard B. Russell, believed that "it was not the intention of Congress to exclude items such as soft drinks," which he described as "a food product." Russell saw no problem with schools selling soft drinks "so long as they did not conflict with the school lunch." These products, he believed, "provided important supplemental revenue for the schools." Richard B. Russell to W. F. Barron, December 20, 1966, Richard Russell Collection, Series IX B, Box 10, Richard B. Russell Library for Political Research and Studies, University of Georgia Libraries, Athens. Barron was an executive with the Rome, Georgia, Coca-Cola Bottling Company.

34. See John Perryman, "School Lunch Programs," in Jean Mayer, ed., *U.S. Nutrition Policies in the Seventies* (San Francisco: W. H. Freeman, 1973).

35. "Trends in School," *School Management*, August 1961, p. 47.

36. Alfreda Jacobsen to President Johnson, May 17, 1967, WHCF Gen AG 7–2, Box 11, LBJ Library (emphasis in the original).

37. Alfreda Jacobsen to President Johnson, May 17, 1967.

38. United States Congress, House Subcommittee on Education, Committee on Education and Labor, *Hearings on Bill to Establish a Program of Nutrition Education for Children*, 93rd Cong., 1st Sess., March 8 and July 11, 1973 (hereafter, House Committee on Education, 1973), 23.

39. Senate Select Committee, Part 11, pp. 3485–86.

40. Ibid., 3416.

41. United States Congress, Senate Committee on Agriculture and Forestry, *Hearings, School Lunch and Child Nutrition Programs*, 91st Cong., 2nd Sess., September 29–October 1, 1969 (hereafter, Senate Agriculture Committee, 1969) 225–26.

42. Senate Select Committee, Part 1, p. 117.

43. Senate Select Committee, Part 2, p. 238.

44. United States Congress, House Committee on Education and Labor, *Hearings*, 91st Cong., 1st Sess., March 6, 1969, p. 60; and Senate Select Committee, Part 2, p. 231.

45. Senate Select Committee, Part 2, January 8–10, 1969, p. 232.

46. House Committee on Education and Labor, 1973, p. 20.

47. Ibid., 18–22.

48. Ibid.

49. United States Congress, Senate Subcommittee on Agriculture Research and General Legislation, Committee on Agriculture and Forestry, *Hearings to Amend National School Lunch Act*, September 13, 1973 (hereafter, Senate Agriculture Committee, 1973), 128.

50. Brody, "Personal Health," NYT, September 24, 2002. In 1997, for example, Colorado Springs signed "an 8 million, 10 year agreement with Coca-Cola that included cash bonuses for extra sales and incentives like a new car for a senior with high grades and a perfect attendance record."

51. Senate Agriculture Committee, 1973, p. 128.

52. Sharon Palmer, "Making the Grade with School-Lunch Programs," *Food Product Design*, November 2002; and Centers for Disease Control and Prevention, "Fact Sheet: Foods and Beverages Sold Outside of the School Meal Programs," CDC School Health Policies and Programs Study, 2000.

53. Palmer, "Making the Grade."

54. Ibid.

55. White House Conference: Final Report, 247.

56. "Child Nutrition Programs: Issues for the 101st Congress, *School Food Service Research Review* 13, no. 1 (1989): 35.

57. See, e.g., Steiner, *The Children's Cause*, 177.

58. " 'Junk Food' Plan Widely Criticized," NYT, July 13, 1979.

59. Food historian Warren Belasco argues that the corporate response to the 1970s ethnic revival "was to see new marketing opportunities." See his "Ethnic Fast Foods: The Corporate Melting Pot," *Food and Foodways*, 2 (1987): 1–30, 3.

60. Ronald J. Rhodes and Carol M. D'Arrezo, "How Two Lunch Programs Save Money," *Food and Nutrition* 6, no. 1 (February 1976): 6.

61. See Avner Offer, "Body Weight and Self-Control in the United States and Britain since the 1950s," *Social History of Medicine*, 14, no. 1 (2001): 79–106, 83 (emphasis in the original). (Thanks to Ina Zweiniger-Bargielowska for this reference.) He says "eating outside the home claimed less than 10 percent of food outlays" in 1955, but by 1995, eating out accounted for about 15% of all meals in Britain and 45% in the U.S. (86–87).

62. Senate Agriculture Committee, 1969, p. 234; "Lunch Becomes Big Business," NYT, May 29, 1978. Prisons spent about $1.85 per day for food service, an estimated one-third of the correctional institution's budgets. Also see Mary T. Goodwin, "Improving Your School Lunch Program," in Catherine Lerza and Michael Jacobson, eds., *Food for People, Not for Profit: A Sourcebook on the Food Crisis* (New York: Ballantine Books, 1975), 319–22.

63. Jim Hightower, *Eat Your Heart Out: Food Profiteering in America* (New York: Crown, 1997), 81. Also see Letitia Brewster and Michael F. Jacobson, *The Changing American Diet* (Washington, D.C.: Center for Science in the Public Interest, 1983). They estimate that McDonald's sales grew 30 times between 1964 and 1977 (3).

64. Senate Agriculture Committee, 1969, p. 181.

65. "A Deft (Some Say Heavy) Hand in the Kitchen," NYT, April 27, 2003.

66. Goodwin, "Improving Your School Lunch Program."

67. "Lunch Becomes Big Business."

68. Ross Hume Hall, *Food for Naught: The Decline in Nutrition* (New York: Harper and Row, 1994), preface.

69. Brewster and Jacobson, *The Changing American Diet*, 3.

70. See Offer, "Body Weight," 86.

71. "Trends in School," *School Management*, August 1961, p. 47.

72. "Lunch Becomes Big Business."

73. Ibid.

74. Belasco, "Ethnic Fast Goods," and Donna R. Gabaccia, *We Are What We Eat: Ethnic Food and the Making of Americans* (Cambridge, Mass.: Harvard University Press, 1998).

75. "Bagels for the Bicentennial," *Food and Nutrition*, February 1976. In National Council of Jewish Women (NCJW) Papers, Washington, D.C. Office, Box 285, Children–Nutrition, 1975–76, Library of Congress.

76. Senate Agriculture Committee, 1969, p. 181.

77. Senate Select Committee, Part 7, p. 2357.

78. Offer, "Body Weight," 87–88.

79. "Fast Foods Sell School Lunches in Las Vegas," NYT, January 19, 1978.

80. Ibid.

81. "John Dewey Pupils Rave over Fast Food School Lunches," NYT, April 6, 1978; and "Fast Food Lunches Planned to Lure New York's Pupils," NYT, November 23, 1977.

82. "John Dewey Pupils Rave."

83. Melissa Alexander, "Tortillas Become Staple Fare in Nation's Public Schools," *Milling and Baking News*, June 24, 1997, http://www.bakingbusiness.com.

84. Rhodes and Arrezo, "How Two Lunch Programs Save Money," 7.

85. Senate Agriculture Committee, 1969, p. 157.

86. Melissa Alexander, "Pizza in the School Lunch Program," *Milling and Baking News*, June 18, 1996, http://www.bakingbusiness.com.

87. Hightower, *Eat Your Heart Out*, 75.

88. "Fast Foods Sell School Lunches in Las Vegas"; " 'Junk Food' Plan Widely Criticized."

89. House Subcommittee on Education and Labor, 1973, p. 121.

90. Ibid.; Marion Nestle, *Food Politics: How the Food Industry Influences Nutrition and Health* (Berkeley: University of California Press, 2002); Eric Schlosser, *Fast Food Nation: The Dark Side of the All American Meal* (New York: Perennial Press, 2002); and Michael Pollan, *Omnivor's Dilemma: A Natural History of Four Meals* (New York: Penguin, 2006).

91. House Committee on Education and Labor, 1973, p. 121.

92. Ron Haskins, "The School Lunch Lobby," Education Next, The Hoover Institution, http://www.educationnext.org

93. House Committee on Education and Labor, 1973, p. 120.

94. Haskins, "The School Lunch Lobby."

95. See Laura S. Sims, *The Politics of Fat: Food and Nutrition Policy in America* (Amonk, N.Y.: M. E. Sharpe, 1998), 75.

96. Offer, "Body Weight," 83. Offer suggests that "average body weights rose about two BMI units and may have already reached their 1980 levels in Britain in the 1930s" and in the United States during the 1940s (81). By the 1990s, however, BMI figures were significantly higher.

97. Winifred M. Mayers, "Changing Attitudes Toward Overweight and Reducing," in *Lydia J. Roberts Award Essays* (Chicago: American Dietetic Association, 1968), 49.

98. Harvey Levenstein, *Paradox of Plenty: A Social History of Eating in Modern America* (Berkeley: University of California Press, 2003), 158.

99. Senate Select Committee, Part 1, pp. 38–39.

100. Sims, *The Politics of Fat*, 68ff (emphasis in the original).

101. "History of the National School Lunch Program," www.usda.gov/cgi-bin/waisga.

102. Senate Select Committee, Part 1, pp. 38–39.

103. The others were food stamps, subsidized housing, Medicaid, and Medicare. See "Half of Black Households Used School Lunch Program in 1980," NYT, November 26, 1982.

104. Center on Budget Policy and Analysis, "Falling Behind," 165.

105. Reagan proposed an overall cut of $4.2 billion in the Department of Agriculture budget. His proposed measures would also have eliminated the free milk program and shifted the costs of grading, inspection, and licensing fees onto farmers, reduced the number of farm loans available, and increased interest rates for others. See "Congress Cutting Food Programs," NYT, July 8, 1981. Also see Haskins, "The School Lunch Lobby."

106. "Many Students Decide Not to Buy More Costly School Lunches."

107. Robert G. St. Pierre and Michael J. Puma, "Controlling Federal Expenditures in the National School Lunch Program: The Relationship between Changes in Household Eligibility and Federal Policy," *Journal of Policy Analysis and Management* 11 no. 1 (1992): 42–57, 43.

108. Ibid., 44.

109. Ibid., 47. The authors concluded that the rate of misreporting was 4.8% in the school lunch program and 4.9% for food stamps (53).

110. Center on Budget and Policy Analysis, "Falling Behind," 166.

111. Physicians Task Force on Hunger in America, *Hunger in America: The Growing Epidemic* (Middletown, Conn.: Wesleyan University Press, 1985), 149.

112. Ibid., 148. Also see Janet Poppendieck, *Sweet Charity?: Emergency Food and the End of Entitlement* (New York: Penguin, 1998).

113. "Child Nutrition Programs: Issues for the 101st Congress," *School Food Service Research Review*, Spring 1989, p. 35.

114. Ibid.

115. "House Republicans Oppose Further Cuts for School Lunches," NYT, October 23, 1981.

116. "Child Nutrition Programs: Issues for the 101st Congress," 26–27. Similar cuts in school lunches were undertaken by Margaret Thatcher's administration in Britain. According to one report, after 1980 the percentage of children eating school lunches in Britain dropped to only 43 in 1988. "The welfare concept of a universal meal service had been abandoned." School meals were now a matter of family responsibility and consumer choice. John Burnett, "The Rise and Decline of School Meals in Britain," in John Burnett and Derek J. Oddy, eds., *The Origins and Development of Food Policy in Europe* (London: Leicester University Press, 1994), 66–67.

117. In 1995 the USDA still required school lunches to provide one-third of a child's RDA for protein, vitamins A and C, iron, calcium, and calories over the course of a week. For the first time, however, the standards specified that no more than 30% of calories come from fat and no more than 10% from saturated fat. Schools had until the 1996–97 school year to alter their menus, but waivers of this requirement could be granted. See Charlene Price and Betsey Kuhn, "Public and Private Efforts for the National School Lunch Program," *Food Review*, May–August 1996, p. 52.

118. Ibid., 53–54.

119. See Ward Sinclair, "School Lunches Flunk GAO Nutrition Test," and Richard Cohen, "Reagan's Life Style Contradicts Policies," both in *Washington Post*, September 15, 1981; Mary Thornton and Martin Schram, "U.S. Holds the Ketchup in Schools: Hold the Pickles, Hold the Relish, Hold the New School Lunch Regs," *Washington Post*, September 26, 1981; "Ketchup Set to Pour Again in School Lunch Rules," *Washington Post*, October 30, 1981.

120. Ibid.

121. "Notes on People," NYT, September 36, 1981.

122. Don Paarlberg, *Farm and Food Policy: Issues of the 1980s* (Lincoln: University of Nebraska Press, 1980), p. 105. Also see "History of NSLP." Http://USDA.gov.

123. "U.S. Acts to Shrink School Lunch Size in Economy Move," NYT, September 5, 1981.

124. "School Food: New Intent," NYT, September 14, 1981.

EPILOGUE. FAST FOOD AND POOR CHILDREN

1. See ASFSA "Your Child Nutrition eSource," www.asfsa.org/newsroom/sfsnews/legupdate0603.asp.

2. Peter H. Rossi, *Feeding the Poor: Assessing Federal Food Aid* (Washington, D.C.: AEI Press, 1998), 7. The lunch program cost in 1947 was $70 million; 1950, $119.7 million; 1960, $225.8 million; 1970, $565.5 million; 1975, $1.7 billion; 1980, $3.2 billion; 1973, $3.4 billion; and 1990, $3.7 billion. See USDA "Nutrition Program Facts," Food and Nutrition Service, National School Lunch Program.

3. Masao Matsumoto, "The National School Lunch Program Serves 24 Million Daily," *Food Review*, October–December 1992.

4. School lunch participation was 7.1 million in 1946; 1970, 22 million; 1980, 27 million; 1990, 24 million (reflecting Reagan era cuts); and 2003, 28.4 million (last data available). USDA "Nutrition Program Facts," Food and Nutrition Service, National School Lunch Program.

5. "Child Nutrition Programs: Issues for the 101st Congress," *School Food Service Research Review* 13, no. 1 (1989): 35–39.

6. "Half of Black Households Used School Lunch Program in 1980," *New York Times* (hereafter, NYT), November 26, 1981. The article also notes that the number of black households getting food stamps rose 11%, to 2.4 million, while recipients among white households rose by 12%, to 4.2 million. The number of Hispanic households was 700,000, or an increase of 17%. Overall, 6.8 million households got stamps, or about 8% of all households.

7. Constance Newman and Katherine Ralston, "Profiles of Participants in the National School Lunch Program: Data from Two National Surveys," United States Department of Agriculture, Economic Research Service, Economic Information Bulletin No. 17, August 2006 (Electronic Report), iii, 5, 9.

8. Saba Sultana Brelvi, "Current Policy Trends in the National School Lunch Program," Honors Thesis, Health and Society Department, Brown University, May 1, 1995 p. 15. Thanks to Ellen Messer for this reference. Also see Steven M. Lutz and Jay Hirschman, "School Lunch Reform: Minimal Market Impacts from Providing Healthier Meals," *Food Review*, January–April, 1998, p. 31.

9. Matsumoto, "The National School Lunch Program."

10. Ibid.

11. Barry Yeoman, "Unhappy Meals," *Mother Jones* (January/February 2003) http://www.motherjones.com. The proposed 2007 farm bill for the first time guaranteed USDA purchase not only of "surplus" commodities but of "specialty crops" as well. These new crops included fruits and vegetables that would satisfy "new concerns about nutrition in the federally funded school meals program." "To Subsidize Actual Food," *Chicago Tribune*, March 16, 2007.

12. http://www.asfsa.org/who/history.html. Also see Ron Haskins, "The School Lunch Lobby," Education Next, The Hoover Institution, http://www.educationnext.org.

13. The federal school lunch financing system remained arcane and complex. Schools received federal cash reimbursements at different levels for free, reduced-price, and full-price meals. In addition, schools could purchase USDA surplus commodities called "entitlement foods." These were distributed according to the number of meals served.

14. See, e.g., example, http://www.oseda.missouri.edu/kidcnt/pctfrln.html. This Web site of the Missouri education department stipulated that the percentage of students enrolled for free or reduced-price lunch is a measure to be used "to approximate the percent of children living in poverty, a census measure that is only available every ten years. Students whose families have incomes below 130% of the poverty line are eligible for free lunches through the National School Lunch Program." In 1994 over one-third of Missouri students were enrolled in the school lunch program.

15. "Schools Find New Route to Diversity," *Chicago Tribune*, January 28, 2002.

16. Melissa Alexander, "Tortillas Become Staple Fare in Nation's Public schools," *Milling and Baking News*, June 24, 1997, http://www.bakingbusiness.com.

17. Charlene Price and Betsy Kuhn, "Public and Private Efforts for the National School Lunch Program," *Children's Diets* (May–August 1996): 54.

18. Http://www.asfsa.org/who/history.htm.

19. Sharon Palmer, "Making the Grade with School-Lunch Programs," *Food Product Design: Foodservice Annual*, November 2002.

20. Price and Kuhn, "Public and Private Efforts," 55.

21. "Is Your Kid Failing Lunch?" *Consumer Reports*, September 1998, p. 50.

22. Ibid., 52. The report found that fast-food brands were offered in 13% of the nation's schools.

23. A few schools had already contracted with McDonald's during the 1970s, but it was not until the 1990s that fast-food franchises became commonplace in school cafeterias.

24. Centers for Disease Control and Prevention, "Fact Sheet: Food Service," CDC School Health Policies and Programs Study, 2000; and Alexander, "Tortillas Become Staple Fare."

25. Price and Kuhn, "Public and Private Efforts," 56.

26. Melissa Alexander, "Pizza in the School Lunch Program," *Milling and Baking News*, June 18, 1996, http://bakingbusiness.com.

27. Ibid.

28. Jane E. Brody, "Personal Health; Schools Teach 3 C's: Candy, Cookies, and Chips," NYT, September 24, 2002; and Yeoman, "Unhappy Meals."

29. Price and Kuhn, "Public and Private Efforts," 55.

30. "Apricot Archive," Apricot Producers of California, vol. 1, December 2004, http://www.apricotproducers.come/apricotArchive1.htm.

31. Saba Brelvi, "Current Policy Trends," 19.

32. Price and Kuhn, "Public and Private Efforts," 57.

33. Alexander, "Pizza in the School Lunch Program."

34. Physicians Committee for Responsible Medicine, "School Lunch Report Card," August 2004, pp. 1–2 www.prcm.org.

35. Alexander, "Pizza in the School Lunch Program." Chicken nuggets come in second in popularity.

36. Ibid.

37. Alexander, "Tortillas Become Staple Fare."

38. Stephen Glass, "Happy Meals: When Lunch Subsidies Are Chopped, Kids Eat Better," *Policy Review*, Summer 1995, http://www.policyreview.org.

39. Ibid.

40. For Kramer's criticism, see United States Congress, Senate Committee on Agriculture and Forestry, *Hearings, School Lunch and Child Nutrition Programs*, 91st Cong., 1st. Sess., September 29–October 1, 1969, p. 226.

41. Glass, "Happy Meals."

42. Ibid.

43. "History of the National School Lunch Program," http://USDA.gov; and Price and Kuhn, "Public and Private Effects," 54.

44. "First CN Reauthorization Hearing Held in House," ASFSA, Your Child Nutrition eSource, July 19, 2003, www.asfsa.org/newsroom/sfnews/hrgonereauth.asp.

45. Robert G. St. Pierre and Michael J. Puma, "Controlling Federal Expenditures in the National School Lunch Program: The Relationship between Changes in Household Eligibility and Federal Policy," *Journal of Policy Analysis and Management* 11, no. 1 (Winter 1992); 42–57.

46. See, e.g., "Sen. Dole Introduces Legislation to Increase Access to School Meals," Your Child Nutrition eSource, August 1, 2003, http://www.asfsa.org/newsroom/sfnews/doleleg.asp, and Haskins, "The School Lunch Lobby."

47. Susan Davis Gryder, "Junk Food Wars," *School Foodservice Nutrition*, Your Child Nutrition eSource, August 2003, http://member.asfsa.org/sfnarchives/0308/junkfood.asp.

48. See Kim Severson, "L.A. Schools to Stop Soda Sales," *San Francisco Chronicle*, August 28, 2002, and "Food in the News: Oakland Schools Ban Vending Machine Junk Food," *San Francisco Chronicle*, January 16, 2002. This reported estimated that vending machines yielded about $39,000 for each high school and $14,000 for middle schools.

49. USDA, "Foods Sold in Competition with USDA School Meal Programs: A Report to Congress," January 12, 2001, www.fns.usda.gov/cnd/Lunch/CompetitiveFoods.

50. The notion that the lunch program had been conceived of for all children was part of its lore. See, e.g., "Child Nutrition Programs: Issues for the 101st Congress"; "The school lunch program had been conceived in 1946 as a broad-based nutrition program for all children, and over the years this goal had been consistently reaffirmed by congress. Additionally, there was philosophical objection to what was viewed as turning child nutrition programs into welfare (income-tested) programs" (27).

51. See Severson, "L.A. Schools to Stop Soda Sales" and "Food in the News," and Chris Kenning, "Board to Vote on Limiting School Snacks," *Louisville Cou-*

rier-Journal, August 26, 2002; "Give Soda Machines the Can," *USA Today*, August 5, 2002.

52. USDA, "Foods Sold in Competition with USDA School Meal Programs."

53. Amanda Bower, "Retooling School Lunch," *Time*, June 11, 2006. Also see "Food Joins Academic Menu in Berkeley School District," *San Francisco Chronicle*, August 29, 2004, and " 'Delicious Revolution' Honored," *San Francisco Chronicle*, August 4, 1998.

54. "Food Joins Academic Menu in Berkeley School District."

55. See, e.g., "Lisa Belkin, "The School-Lunch Test," *New York Times Magazine*, August 20, 2006. Belkin describes project HOPS (Healthier Options for Public Schoolchildren) funded by the Agatston Research Foundation (created by Dr. Arthur Agatston, of South Beach Diet fame). The foundation donated money to schools to transform their lunch menus. Funds from Agatston made up the difference between government reimbursements and the cost of fresh and organic ingredients.

56. United States Congress, Senate Select Committee on Nutrition and Human Needs, 90th Cong., 2nd Sess., and 91st Cong., 1st Sess., 1968–69, Part 10, p. 3218. Quote is from Cook County, Illinois, public aid nutritionist.

Index